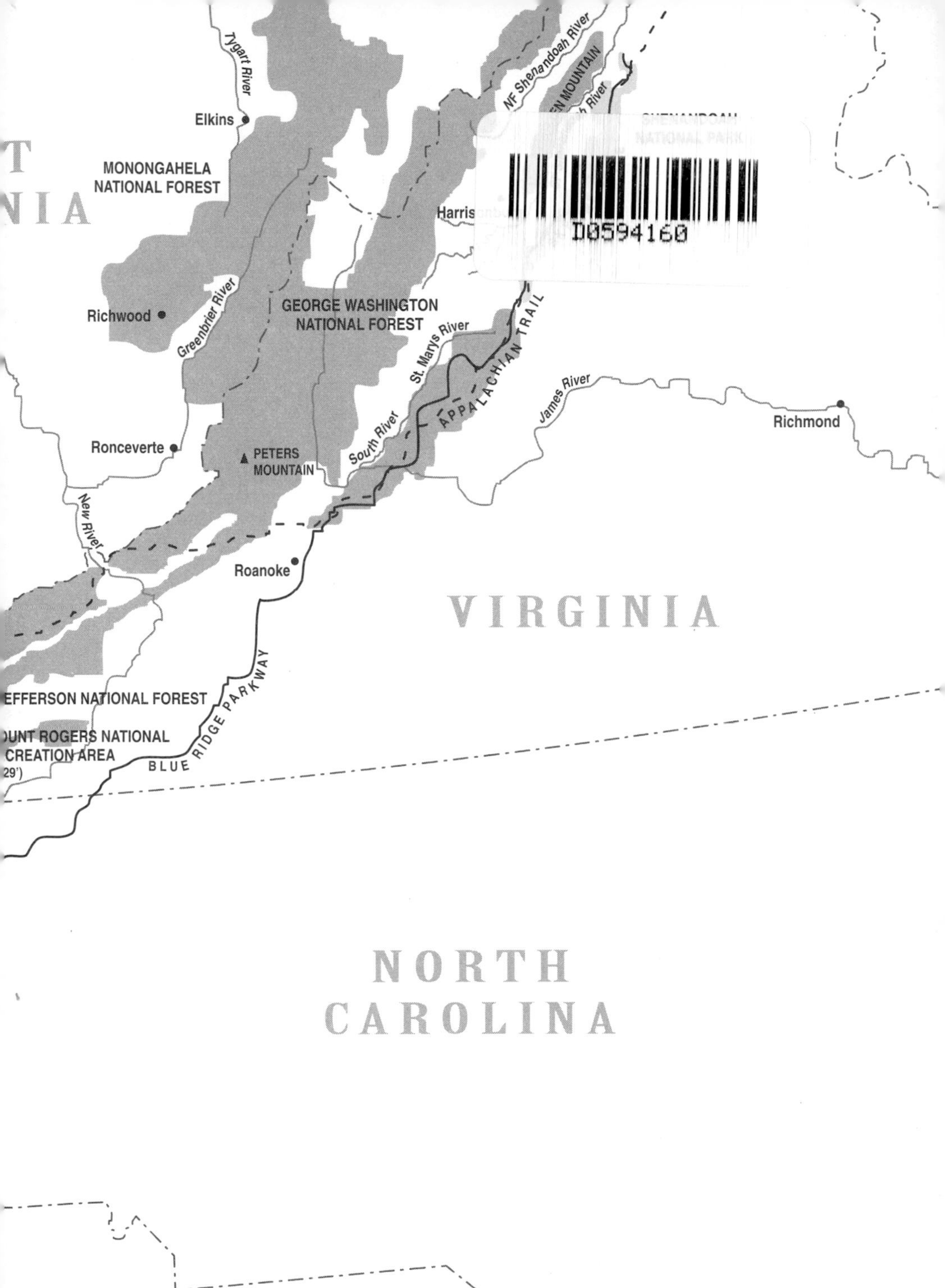
Tygart River
Elkins
MONONGAHELA
NATIONAL FOREST
NF Shenandoah River
Greenbrier River
Richwood
GEORGE WASHINGTON
NATIONAL FOREST
St. Marys River
APPALACHIAN TRAIL
James River
Richmond
South River
Ronceverte
PETERS
MOUNTAIN
New River
Roanoke
VIRGINIA
BLUE RIDGE PARKWAY
NORTH
CAROLINA
SOUTH
CAROLINA

THE APPALACHIAN FOREST

A Search for Roots and Renewal

May the forest be with you,

Chris Bolgiano

Chris Bolgiano

STACKPOLE
BOOKS

For Ralph

Also by Chris Bolgiano

MOUNTAIN LION: AN UNNATURAL HISTORY OF PUMAS AND PEOPLE
(Stackpole, 1995)

Published by
STACKPOLE BOOKS
5067 Ritter Road
Mechanicsburg, PA 17055
www.stackpolebooks.com

Printed in the United States of America

10 9 8 7 6 5 4 3

FIRST EDITION

Jacket photo by Paul Rezendes
Author photo by Tim Wright
Jacket design by Wendy A. Reynolds

Library of Congress Cataloging-in-Publication Data

Bolgiano, Chris.
The Appalachian forest: a search for roots and renewal / Chris Bolgiano.—1st ed.
p. cm.
Includes bibliographical references and index.
ISBN 0-8117-0126-3
1. Appalachian Region—History. 2. Forests and forestry—Appalachian Region—History. I. Title.
F106.B673 1998
974'.00943—dc21 98-17747
CIP

Contents

ACKNOWLEDGMENTS

THANKS ARE DUE TO MANY PEOPLE FOR HELPING TO MAKE THIS BOOK possible. Academic scholars provided essential points and counterpoints to balance my personal experience. Ronald Eller, director of the University of Kentucky's Appalachian Center, steered me to various sources including the center's forest historian, Tim Collins, who spent an afternoon discussing Appalachian attitudes toward land. Kate Black, Appalachian librarian at the university, not only devoted hours of her expertise to my quest but also directed me to free parking. Nancy Sorrells of the Museum of Frontier History in Staunton, Virginia, researched my questions on Scots-Irish land use practices. At West Virginia University, professor of plant pathology William MacDonald was generous with his knowledge about forest health, as was Ron Lewis, professor of history, about logging. William H. Martin, on leave from Eastern Kentucky University as director of the state's Division of Natural Areas, provided information on E. Lucy Braun and about the responses of various tree species to fire and logging. At James Madison University in Virginia, W. Cullen Sherwood and Lynn S. Fichter guided me through eras of geological upheaval, and William Boyer and Carole Nash interpreted archaeological data on Native American history. Staff at JMU's Carrier Library were tireless in filling my requests for obscure publications and unceasingly supportive in their cheerful manner. Conversations about Appalachian culture with librarian Lynn Cameron, noted environmentalist and native West Virginian, were particularly stimulating. Carol Singer of the National Agricultural Library provided extensive bibliographic searching.

Chris Haney, wildlife biologist for the Wilderness Society, supplied much information about current research in old-growth forests. Peter Kirby, southeastern regional director for the Wilderness Society, is a walking encyclopedia about Appalachian ecology and history whom I have often consulted. Robert Zahner, retired from Clemson University, and his wife, Glenda, have over several years devoted many hours to educating me about the biological intricacies of old growth. Jane Holt, ornithologist at the University of North Carolina at Asheville, shared not only her research on Neotropical migrant songbirds but her home as well. Michael Pelton, professor of wildlife biology at the University of Tennessee and an expert on black bears, also hosted my stay and personally guided me through Knoxville's snarled highway system. Joseph Mitchell, Virginia's leading herpetologist, has been my salamander mentor for many years. Fred Hebard of the American Chestnut Foundation patiently explained the genetic complexities of breeding blight resistance into American chestnut trees.

Karin Heiman has taken pains to keep in touch regarding the old growth at Big Ivy in the Pisgah National Forest throughout her wide-ranging travels as a consulting biologist. Susan Andrew, Taylor Barnhill, and Hugh Irwin of the Southern Appalachian Forest Coalition took time from their busy schedules to speak with me. Paul Kalisz, of the University of Kentucky's Forestry Department, showed me what eco-forestry meant on the ground and invited me to Appalachia-Science in the Public Interest at Livingston. There, director Al Fritsch provided not only hospitality but also much inspiration for living simply on the earth.

Amy South of West Virginia graciously allowed me to intrude on Peters Mountain and see why it meant so much to her. Buzz Williams and Nicole Hayler of the Chattooga River Watershed Coalition in Georgia opened their hearts to share their hopes and dreams. Than Hitt of the Ohio-based Appalachian Restoration Campaign reminded me of what youthful idealism can accomplish. Ernest Dickerman, the grand old man of eastern wilderness, showed me that wisdom and serenity can follow from good work well done. Robert Leverett, the dbh (diameter at breast height—a standard forestry measurement) guru in Massachusetts, has been unfailingly supportive with information about big trees and enthusiasm for learning more. Sue Morse, a fourth-generation forester in Vermont, taught me much about forest predators. Michael Milosch, director of the Cradle of Forestry Historic Site in Pisgah National Forest, kindly reviewed my presentation of Forest Service history.

Many Forest Service staffers helped to answer what I thought were basic questions about the Appalachian national forests but proved to involve a lot of digging. Dave Olson of the National Forests of Virginia was a model of prompt, thorough response to several rounds of questions. Mike Barber, archaeologist, brought Fenwick Mines in Jefferson National Forest to my attention. John Coleman, former Lee District ranger in the George Washington National Forest, has for many years been a font of information about local forest history and a leading force for preserving it. Steve Parsons and Dave Benavitch of the GWNF have also helped me greatly. I am grateful to wildlife biologist Bob Glasgow, formerly of the GWNF and now with the National Forests of Mississippi, for his concern and appreciation for the Cow Knob salamander and other unglamorous species. Steve Chandler, Kate Goodrich, and Gary Bustamente, of Monongahela National Forest, and Harry Mahoney, formerly of the Mon, delved into files and memory to answer my questions about clear-cutting controversies. Ruth Berner, Julie Trzeciak, Ken Alford, Pat Momich, and Rodney Snedeker of the National Forests of North Carolina; Karen Braddy of the Chattahoochee National Forest; Marie Walker of the Daniel Boone National Forest; Stephanie Neal of the Sumter National Forest; and Karen Green, Quentin Bass, and Laura Mitchell of the Cherokee National Forest all worked hard to provide the data I requested.

Bob Miller, public relations officer for the Great Smoky Mountains National Park, has always been a highly dependable source of information. Ron Wilson and Brenda Coleman of the Big South Fork National River and Recreation Area and Bambi Teague of the Blue Ridge Parkway were also very helpful.

Greg Cook of the West Virginia Department of Tourism provided information on mountain biking. Gil and Mary Willis of Elk River Touring Center in West Virginia spoke freely about their experiences in setting up a cross-country skiing and bike touring facility.

Mary Arpante of Virginia trusted me, a stranger, enough to introduce me to her friends Rita and Dewey Owle of the Cherokee tribe in North Carolina, who in turn trusted my intentions by offering me hospitality and introducing me to Freeman Owle and others on Qualla Boundary. Larry Blythe, Cherokee Reservation forester, was also generous with his time, knowledge, and friendship. Sarah Hill, guest curator at the Atlanta History Center in Georgia, shared her extensive research on Cherokee basketry.

Hoyte Dillingham of North Carolina and Jesse Bridge of Virginia, bear hunters, each kindly gave me an opportunity to explore their ideas and practices. Jennifer Hensley of Virginia made available to me her hard-won knowledge of bear hunting and hunters, and the philosophy to which her experience led her.

I am indebted to the Sierra Club, publisher, and to Charles Little, editor, for supporting my investigation of air pollution for a contribution to *An Appalachian Tragedy* and for permitting me to use some of it here. Hugh Morton of Grandfather Mountain graciously made himself available for interviews and his work against air pollution accessible for study. Larry Mohn of the Virginia Department of Game and Inland Fisheries took me to St. Mary's River and also made his work on the impacts of acid deposition there accessible.

Without the many different kinds of support I have received over the years from my mother, Elizabeth Walder, the dream that my husband, Ralph, and I had of living in the forest would have been much more difficult to realize. Parker and Addie Simmons of West Virginia, both now deceased, extended years ago what I now understand was a friendship full of risks to them.

I am much obliged to the other members of the Botanical Bike and Binge Club ("We brake for wildflowers") for the constant inspiration of their love and knowledge of flora both wild and domestic.

I owe much to my former editor Sally Atwater for prodding me into writing this book, and to my current editor Jane Devlin for her generous encouragement. My long-suffering friend Janet Wright read my entire draft and made many valuable suggestions; Barbara McIntyre did the same for parts of it. To my great relief, Vicki Gadberry and Ralph Bolgiano took on the task of indexing.

And of course, without Ralph I never would have gotten here.

ROOTS

TOSSING ROCKS FROM NORTH CREEK TO A LOW PLACE IN THE ROAD, I catch myself in midthrow. Lying heavy in my hands is a rectangular block of shale. One smooth, flat side is scored in small circles by shells of lives lived three hundred million years ago. I am stunned by this evidence of unquenchable time. Only the air I'm breathing and the water seeping into my sneakers are older.

Faint signals from an atrophied survival instinct move my feet out of the chilling water, while I stare and stare at the rock. Everything has a history. My hundred acres of woods in the central Appalachians are full of chronicles, and the rock reminds me that they are among earth's most venerable stories. The evolutionary heritage of life in the Appalachians is profoundly ancient, yet most of the signs I see are fleeting. A cluster of windthrows in Mushroom Flat testifies to a storm a decade ago, if my measure of moss on the root mass is accurate. Half a millennium, and the pits will be mostly filled in, the roots well rotted. Charred stumps in Finite Hollow are pages of billowing smoke, blistering fire. Inscribed maybe eighty years ago, in three hundred they'll be illegible.

A muddy streamside is a blackboard, scribbled by passing feet and erased by every rain. When snow falls, the forest is a white sheet embossed with animal tracks. I follow them, burying my mind in a vision of their creator, remembering myself only when I turn and face my own footprints.

I have a history, too. Like the pioneers, I am not native here. Like them, I came from an old, used world to a new one, and homesteaded a tract of land where no one had ever lived before. Let the romance stop right there; from the start, this is a postmodern Walden. For a while we lived in an aluminum trailer, for crissake. And if, in my earliest fantasies of self-sufficiency, I ever thought to live without electricity, that notion died with blessed speed. Reading light, washing machine, freezer for garden produce, and, eventually, computer came to rank among my basic requirements. Setting up a lifestyle to support them, in a modest but blatantly middle-class house in woods near a pond, was as close to pioneering as I ever want to get. As for frontiers, those of the mind are enough.

Coming from the suburbs of Washington, D.C., my husband, Ralph, and I had looked for land through our twenties and into our thirties in West Virginia, North Carolina, and Tennessee. For nearly a decade we owned a small farm in Virginia's Shenandoah Valley, where we found the jobs that allowed us to save money to buy a bigger piece of land. On the farm we learned to make hay, got serious about gardening, and tallied the economic and emotional investments of raising livestock. Most importantly, we discovered that what we were looking for lived not in the fields but in the fencerows. Those weedy, overgrown borders between pastures were home to wild things.

A real-estate agent called us one day about this place. It lay beyond the western edge of the Great Valley, on the other side of Little North Mountain. It was still within driving distance of jobs and amenities, yet crossing that mountain took us out of the tame lowlands and into wild Appalachia, into that mysterious forest world at which the fencerows could only hint. And this piece of land had something we had literally dreamed of but had never found before: a border along a national forest.

The George Washington National Forest covers more than a million acres along the Virginia–West Virginia state line. West of it is Monogahela National Forest. South of it, the Jefferson National Forest runs into the Cherokee and Pisgah National Forests, which are linked to Nantahala National Forest by the Great Smoky Mountains National Park. Along their southern borders are the Sumter and Chattahoochee National Forests. To the east are Shenandoah National Park and the Blue Ridge Parkway. Over the centuries, there have been many different definitions of Appalachia. Mine is based on these public lands. Altogether, they total some seven million acres of more or less contiguous, federally owned mountain lands (note the "more or less"; it becomes important later).

Adirondack State Park, which is not considered to be geologically Appalachian, encompasses six million acres, and only three million are permanently protected by state ownership. The rest are vulnerable to crazing, like an old porcelain dish, from encroaching roads and various development pressures. Our property, on the eastern edge of Appalachia, is on the threshold of the largest complex of public lands this side of the Mississippi River. Searching for wilderness, we stumbled through the doorway of its last, best hope in the East.

We didn't know that at first, of course, much less understand its implications. One of the earliest clues was the fossil rock. I found it as we filled potholes in the old logging roads that give such convenient access to our property. The mollusks pressed into the rock lived in a shallow salt ocean that existed for maybe seventy million years. The ocean had poured in, geologically speaking, during a time when the continental plates were moving apart. That was around four hundred million to three hundred million years ago, in the interval between the second and third of the three geologic upheavals that formed the Appalachian Mountains.

Earth's bulk of dry land may always have floated across a world of water, the land masses coalescing, then coming apart, like heavy-footed partners in a slow dance. What is now the Atlantic Ocean has opened and closed and opened again. Each time the far-flung edges of land plates pressed toward each other, they thrust up parallel mountain ranges along what became, after they had rifted apart again, the eastern coast of North America. The first episode of Appalachian mountain building occurred from 480 million to 440 million years ago; the second reached its peak from 400 million to 350 million years ago. These two prolonged events raised mountains from Pennsylvania to Newfoundland. In what would prove to be one of the great ironies of geologic time, the reach of the Appalachians extended across Greenland to Ireland and northern Great Britain before finally ending in Norway.

During the era of the shallow inland sea, the substance was formed that would later figure so largely in Appalachian life. Coal is what's left of the first forests. There were no trees yet, but club mosses and horsetails grew a hundred feet tall, with trunks six feet through. They were dense and prolific enough to die in vast mats, which were slowly compacted into thick seams of carbon. By then, insects were abundant, and amphibians had successfully ventured out of the water. By 250 million years ago, palmlike cycads were dominating the plant world, giving rise to magnolias 150 million years later. Ginkgoes grew from Alaska eastward all the way around to Siberia. Conifers—pines, cedars, firs, larches, and their relatives—developed around the same time, followed by flowering plants. Seeds dispersed widely as the continents drifted slowly apart after the third geologic collision. A circumpolar forest draped a green mantle around the northern half of the globe.

The third epoch of upthrust, which has been called the Appalachian Revolution, began about 290 million years ago. Over some 50 million years, mountains erupted from Pennsylvania to Alabama. There were repeated sporadic convulsions that crumpled and confused the landscape slowly, but at times violently. Rocks were folded, stacked in layers, cracked and twisted and turned sideways. Like most revolutions, it wasn't nearly as neat and decisive as you'd like.

Although the peaks of the Appalachians today are all below seven thousand feet, they may originally have reached fourteen thousand like the Rockies or even twenty thousand feet like the Himalayas. In a sense, there is only one history in the world, and my fossil rock bears witness to it. The creek whispers past me now, but I've heard it roar. Both voices sing the same old song of wearing down, carrying away. Here, time has had time enough to grind rocks into a filigreed foundation of soil and stability enough to raise an elaborate structure of biodiversity.

About a million and a half years ago, glaciers began to push southward in pulses of climate. They scoured the forests of the northern Appalachians but stopped about twelve thousand years ago, in central Pennsylvania. To the south, forests moved up and down the mountains in response to flows of cold from the north. Southern plant life was able to evolve fairly steadily, without catastrophic setback, for more than two hundred million years.

Since time began, the highest and best use of the Appalachian Mountains has been to grow trees. In Appalachia lives the richest temperate forest on the planet, rivaled only by its close relatives in a few sections of Asia, all of them remnants of the mother forest. In the coves of southern Appalachia are fifteen hundred species of flowering plants, including more kinds of trees than in all of northern Europe. Here are bewildering nuances of biodiversity, with mosses, fungi, spiders, salamanders, mussels, fish, birds, and peoples like none other on earth. Searching for home, we moved into one of the grand old mansions of the planet.

If "frontier" is defined as the outermost region of human reach, where ties to civilization are too tenuous to be life-supporting, then Appalachia was America's first frontier. Permanent settlements along the coast surged inland through the 1600s, supplied by shipments from the Old World, but for generations the Appalachians stalled the outreach of an otherwise vigorously expanding society. From Pennsylvania north, gaps into the valleys were easier to find, and a mix of peoples, mostly from northern Europe, moved in. But the central Appalachians stood in long, unbroken ridges like blue walls. West and south of them the ranges became chaotic and even steeper. All were covered with forests. Not until a people came along willing and able to cut the links to civilization and tackle Indians, wild beasts, and a killing kind of labor did the southern half of Appalachia become settled.

That people was the Scots-Irish, who were, properly speaking, neither Scottish nor Irish. Smaller numbers of other ethnic groups came with them, especially German, and including English, Welsh, Swiss, Dutch, Swedish, Finn, and the occasional French Huguenot. But it is the Scots-Irish, the people nobody wanted, who formed the backbone of Appalachian mountain culture. They defined the archetypal image of frontiersman and built the cultural hearth of American rural life.

The Scots-Irish originated on both sides of the Scottish border with England. The Borderers, they were called. They were ethnically diverse—descendants of Celts, Britons, Romans, Angles, Saxons, Norse, and other tribes that had traipsed over the island before and after the time of Christ. Over millennia, they synthesized a common culture. English was their language, and few of them sported the kilts, tartans, or bagpipes of the more Gaelic Highland Scots to the north. By the early 1600s, the Borderers had removed whatever forest cover existed in prehistoric times. Their lands were described as treeless and bare, except for marshes. These were still common, because neither technology nor the necessary social cooperation was available to drain them.

For more than five hundred years, as the Highland Scots and the English fought each other, the Borderers were trampled underhoof. Perhaps this was the genesis of their abiding hatred of authority. Insecurity surely contributed to their reliance on livestock instead of crops that couldn't trot out of the way of armies. The Borderers were further oppressed by feudal lords among their own kind, men who built castles and raided the countryside for cattle and women.

There were craftsmen and traders among the Borderers, as well as many peasants of miserable means. They lived in houses made of loose stones piled up without benefit of mortar, covered by thatched roofs, or in houses made simply of mud. It was an architecture of pragmatic despair that could be easily rebuilt after being pillaged. In moments of leisure they played haunting dirges of unbearable melancholy on stringed instruments.

When King James VI of Scotland became King James I of England upon Queen Elizabeth's death in 1603, the war over the border lost its point. While in Scotland, James had grown weary of the marauding of his lowland compatriots. As it happened, he inherited an Ireland whose last, northernmost province had just been defeated and needed to be kept subdued. It seemed like a good idea at the time: the Plantation of Ulster, established by the migration of the troublesome Borderers to a location where their energies could serve the interests of Great Britain. Throughout the 1600s, thousands of Borderers took ship, voluntarily and involuntarily, to the north of Ireland.

There they found a wooded land occupied by primitive people adept at guerrilla warfare. Within a century, the Ulster Scots, as they were called, had cleared and subdued it. The English did much the same throughout the rest of the island. "The greatest part of the kingdom," wrote Arthur Young in 1778, after a tour across Ireland, "exhibits a naked, bleak, dreary view for want of wood, which has been destroyed for a century past with the most thoughtless prodigality, and still continues to be cut and wasted as if it was not worth the preservation." In the examination of the land occasioned by the Ordnance Survey of the 1830s, the parish of Dungiven in Ulster was described as "entirely stript of tree or shrub . . . this was the ancient Glenconkein . . . formerly celebrated for its extensive forests."

The Ulster Scots built farms based on cattle and sheep and became expert weavers. Mostly Presbyterians themselves, they married few of the native Catholic Irish. They were shrewd, tough, and hardworking, passionately devoted to a principle of personal freedom, yet slavishly loyal to clan chiefs and kin. They proved altogether too successful for the English, who enacted trade barriers against exports from Ireland and persecuted Presbyterians. The Ulster Scots looked to North America. It would be their third frontier, without ever leaving the hills of home.

There were early trickles, but true mass migration began in 1718, coming in waves thereafter to the end of the century, in rhythm with economic fluctuations. By the Revolutionary War, approximately a quarter million people had moved to the colonies from northern Ireland. It has been estimated from the census of 1790 that the Scots-Irish, as they came to be called in America, composed between ten and twenty percent of the entire American population, the largest ethnic group after the English.

At first they arrived in New England, but Congregationalists had no intention of allowing Presbyterianism into their midst. Most Scots-Irish thereafter landed in Philadelphia, where Quakers were more tolerant. In the Delaware Valley, the Scots-Irish mingled with Swedes and Finns. These groups had set an example, through relatively peaceful relations with the Indians, of adapting Old World traditions of log building and bear hunting to new circumstances. The Scots-Irish used the same strategy of adaptation, but it wasn't based on peaceful relations with Indians or most other people. Colonial governments quickly ushered them out of established settlements into the westward wilds because of their rowdy and bawdy behavior. "A settlement of five families from the North of Ireland gives me more trouble than fifty of any other people," wrote James Logan, the provincial secretary of Pennsylvania, himself from Ulster. Logan had invited an early group of Ulster Scots but regretted it by 1730.

From Pennsylvania, extended families traveled southward and settled the piedmont where it edged against the mountains all the way into Georgia. They traveled down the Great Valley and pushed against its western edge. Their very presence delineated the frontier. They were joined by the runaways from a lowland society in which indenture and slavery were entrenched, and by the outcasts who are always attracted to frontiers. Together they ignored the British king's treaties that reserved the Appalachians as Indian territory. As often as not, they squatted on land without securing legal title, and for good reason. Huge blocks of land were already owned by distant speculators, some of them thinking of minerals, and the price of a small farm was often too high. Conflicting land claims abounded. In some places, legal titles became so confused so early that even homesteaders who had paid taxes for years had their land sold from under them. From its birth, Appalachia held a large class of tenants and squatters. It was the first of many collisions between Appalachian fact and American fantasy.

Colonial administrators tried but failed to contain the stream of immigrants. And in truth, the new settlers were enormously useful as a buffer against Indians. The warrior culture of the Borderers supplied the Scots-Irish with fighting values. As passes into the southern mountains were discovered, American-born children of the first Scots-Irish streamed westward, pushing Indians before them and perfecting the American backwoods system that made today's nation possible.

This consisted most fundamentally of killing trees. The easiest way was to deaden them by girdling their trunks, cutting a circle that broke the transport lines of nutrients in the cambium just beneath the bark. Indians had employed this technique using stone axes. Corn could be planted around the leafless trunks for a first harvest. After a year or two, as falling branches and toppling trunks became a nuisance, the deadened trees were burned. It was much harder and more dangerous to chop down living trees, even with steel axes, but it yielded more usable ground and allowed more of the woody mass to be burned, which made cultivation easier. Expert axmen could lay trees down in parallel rows, to facilitate cutting them up. Branches were trimmed and logs were cut into lengths, and the best of them were pulled off for cabins and for fencing around crops and gardens to keep animals out.

After several months of drying, the slash was heaped up, and the logs were rolled or levered into piles. The backbreaking quality of this labor is unimaginable unless you've done it. Then there were days, perhaps weeks, of burning. Smoke thickened the air for miles. The tidy Germans insisted on grubbing out whatever stumps remained, but others let them rot.

Wood ashes ensured a flush of fertility for crops, but after four or five years, yields fell off and weeds thickened to the point that enormous amounts of hoeing were needed to control them. Fertilization of the soil was not a Scots-Irish tradition, nor was it practical, because the pigs and cattle that composed the first livestock herds mostly roamed the forest, dropping their manure in free range. Instead, new acreage was cleared. This might be nearby, in which case the cabin could be dismantled and dragged to the new spot. Or it might be across the next ridge, over to the next stream bottom, narrower and at a higher elevation, where the whole process started from scratch again. In this way, with astounding fecundity, mountaineers filled up one little creek valley after another throughout the Appalachians.

Hunting was integral to the backwoods system. Like most European peoples who came to America, the Scots-Irish had had little opportunity to hunt in their homeland—game was extirpated, or aristocrats monopolized the privilege. In Ireland, the Ulster Scots learned how to kill off the last wolves and deer. With the tremendous cultural flexibility that characterized them, they immediately adopted hunting in the New World as their own. Crops and livestock had to be protected from wild beasts. Venison, bear, wild turkey, and squirrel were essential foods, especially in winter. Skins provided the first profit from the frontier, the first commercial economy. They were also used for clothing. Leaving their wives to tend the corn, pioneers took off after the game, sometimes for months. Hunting soon became, like the music and dancing and drinking that the Scots-Irish brought with them, one of the passions of Appalachian life.

In the Revolutionary War, mountain men were George Washington's favorite soldiers, cool hands who fired crack shots from hidden places in the forest. Some historians attribute the winning of America to the Scots-Irish and their commitment to freedom from tyranny. They were also the new nation's first insurgents, when Washington's ungrateful attempt to tax a drink of great cultural consequence incited the Whiskey Rebellion.

Fighting Indians all the way, the Scots-Irish continued westward, across Ohio into Missouri and the Rocky Mountains, across the Ozarks into Texas and the Southwest. Their tradition of cattle herding merged with Spanish customs to evolve into the American cowboy. Some of them seemed incurably restless, moving on as soon as they had made a place safe for softer people. Others stayed within the Appalachians. Wherever they went, the Scots-Irish planted a culture based on a fierce sense of independence.

In the first half of the nineteenth century, roads and railroads gradually networked around but rarely through the Appalachians. Still, Appalachia was never as isolated as mainstream society pictured it. Mountaineers were connected to regional, national, and even international economies by many small, site-specific enterprises. Even though they made most of their own food, clothes, shelter, and tools; even though they were energy independent, using firewood year-round for everything from hog butchering to sugar mapling, they occasionally needed a little cash. Such things as salt to preserve meat, coffee, cloth, needles, and ammunition required cash flow. Services such as blacksmithing, milling, tanning, wheelwrighting, and shoemaking might be bartered for in some places but had to be paid for in others.

There were plenty of ways to earn cash. Seasonal jobs as day laborers for planters in the large valleys were usually available, but livestock was the largest source of income for most mountaineers. They raised pigs or cattle or domestic turkeys in the woodlands, which were used as a commons. Professional drovers took herds and flocks in the thousands to plantations and river towns. Other salable products of the land included corn whiskey and eggs from the farm, but also ginseng, charcoal, iron, bark, timber, coal, skins, and furs from the forest. And lots of wild meat for city tables.

In their contacts with the lowland world, mountaineers tended to reject outside influences, a practice that preserved their culture but over time left them bereft of strong legal and educational systems. They wanted to be left alone, and jealous concern for their own autonomy prompted fervent participation in local politics. Blocks of votes were sometimes delivered by kin groups. Yet where politics and land policies permitted, Appalachia before the Civil War came close to Thomas Jefferson's vision of democracy: a society of self-sufficient yeomen, living the kind of earthbound life Ralph and I were looking for. There was everywhere at least a tiny upper-class elite in the county seats to run things. This thread of class consciousness, the planters and the business and professional people in the valley towns, would later prove crucial to unraveling the Appalachian version of the Jeffersonian dream.

Despite poor roads, travelers entered the southern mountains and wrote about their passage. By the early 1800s, poverty, lawlessness, and individualism in the southern mountains were being noted. An idea of a

NATIONAL ARCHIVES AND RECORDS ADMINISTRATION, STILL PICTURE BRANCH, 95G-390771

Mountain farm family in the Jefferson National Forest in Smyth County, Virginia, 1939.

place called "Appalachia" was beginning to form, its name derived from Spanish and French mispronunciations of an Indian word that apparently referred to a tribe in northern Florida. But even though the mountains made an obvious separate kingdom, there was little sense of differentiation from the rest of America until the 1850s. As political conflicts over slavery escalated, mountain society formed an island of Unionist farmers in the Confederate plantation economy that lapped all around it. There were slaves in every Appalachian county by 1860, but few mountaineers outside the elite owned them. Union sentiment was strong, but there were also people who figured that if the government could take a body's slaves, it could take anything.

The Civil War gave a shattering blow to whatever idyll existed in Appalachia. Family members took opposite sides, sometimes even changing the spelling of their names, causing estrangement that persists to this day. Bushwhackers both blue and gray looted and burned, raped and assassinated throughout the mountains, leaving women and children destitute. Some of the feuds that made headlines a decade or two later originated in

Civil War atrocities between neighbors. Reconstruction in Appalachia was slowed by the resentment of political leaders in former Confederate states toward the Union sentiment in their mountainous parts.

But the most portentous result of the Civil War in Appalachia was the simple geography lesson learned by many soldiers who previously had known nothing of the mountains. Timber and coal quickened many a business instinct. Reconstruction and industrialization after the war required huge amounts of wood and energy. Union veterans of means, now comfortably back in New York, Philadelphia, and Baltimore, formed companies to survey land and buy it or the timber and mineral rights to it. Some of the large tracts still held by heirs of early speculators who had never lived on the land must have passed over fairly easily to them. For the rest, they hired merchants and officials in the county seats to act as contacts with mountain people.

Surveyors immediately ran into a widespread problem of unclear deeds. This made it easier to convince mountaineers that they were wise to take whatever money they could get for land or timber rights that they might not even be legally entitled to sell. Mountaineers had no reference point by which to understand that the sums offered were infinitesimal payments for the value. To them it seemed like wealth, and most of them spent it quickly.

As railroads penetrated the twisting valleys, timber and coal were wrenched out in prodigious quantities, in ways so devastating that outsiders prodded the government to step in and stop the destruction. In the half century after the Civil War, outside technology and capital drove the mountaineers to complete what they had started on a primitive scale in the previous century. Three hundred million years of evolution were thus overturned.

The coal wars of the mid-twentieth century brought Appalachia to the public eye with images of oppression and resistance. It was seen as a region apart. The 1960s brought the greatest surge of interest, as John Kennedy campaigned in West Virginia, and the War on Poverty was inaugurated. By the time Ralph and I entered Appalachia in 1971, its pattern of dichotomies had been engraved in symbol and reality: Proud individualism and abject victimization. Self-sufficiency and welfare dependence. Poverty in a land of staggering riches of water, timber, minerals, wildlife, scenery, and potential spirituality. The diamond-hard determination of coal miner's daughter Loretta Lynn and the comic shiftlessness of Snuffy Smith. The mountaineer is America's homegrown child of nature, savage in either a noble or a primitive way, depending on how you see humans in the context of wilderness. In this crazy quilt of blazing discrepancies and clashing paradoxes, my own love-hate affair with Appalachia seems of a piece.

We became acquainted with Appalachia not on the diluted western edge of the Shenandoah Valley, where we eventually settled down, but in unadulterated West Virginia. In the naive spring of our youth, we walked into a realtor's office in the valley town of Elkins. We had been married a year, during which time Ralph had studied maps to find the most remote area within a day's drive of where we were living. This happened, at the time, to be a small commune near College Park, Maryland. We were the last wave of flower children in the counterculture back-to-the-land movement of the 1960s. Sickened by the spread of roads, malls, and garish sprawl around us, we were instinctively drawn to the nearest mountains. Ralph had grown up in a rural area, but I was a product of cities and suburbs. The geography of my youth underwent its own Appalachian revolution.

We bought an old homestead, though the house was gone. An old-fashioned pink rosebush still sprawled over moldy boards and shards of canning jars. That was right above the spring, in which was rooted a venerable dogwood. Every time went there, we wondered if it was still alive. Eventually it died. From the old house site, the land dipped down to a saddle, with tiny meadows on each side. At first the view embraced all directions, because trees on the nearest slopes were small. You could look down into the hamlet of Valley Head and see the pom-pom-pruned trees that lined its one street. Now the forest has grown so tall that we can't see over it.

Early on, we met Parker Simmons, who had been born in the defunct house on our property in the 1890s. With him was Junior, fifty, the youngest of Parker's five children. Parker's wiry, wrinkled wife, Addie, always wore a turban wrapped around her hair. She took care of Ruth, the retarded and epileptic daughter. They all lived a mile down the road in a clapboard house that had seen better days. In true Appalachian fashion, they were very hospitable. Often we would eat with them, the table crowded with small, mismatched bowls of garden food and loaves of store-bought white bread. Afterward, Parker would rock on the part of the porch that wasn't rotted, while the latest batch of puppies poked their heads through the part that was, and he'd tell us stories.

From these we learned Appalachian manners. We learned how the real-estate agent had skinned us as well as the ailing, aging preacher who had owned the land just before us. We learned which of the neighbors were most likely to start fights, so we could be doubly careful not to run over their chickens as we drove up the road. We learned that whiskey was the only present that didn't insult poverty.

U.S. Forest Service, George Washington National Forest, Buena Vista, VA

Mountain family, probably in the northernmost section of George Washington National Forest, Virginia, 1920s.

Parker had a broad, weathered face. He had grown up on the ridges we could see, and Addie came from a few ridges farther. What I remember best are his hands. They were large and intricately gnarled, like the terrain. One hand lacked two fingertips, lost cutting trees. As a young man he had worked in the timber camps. There were stumps on our land, huge ones, big enough to host a tea party. We knew nothing of the forest then, except that we were driven to find it. Facing those stumps, for the first time I encountered what had been. Dimly at first, until years later it emerged into consciousness, grew an ache for what might have been. History haunts my understanding of Appalachia.

I had begun to wonder a bit about how we would fit in, but it was clear from the Simmonses that subsistence living could be good. In Appalachia, Mother Nature hands you life on a silver platter. From hazelnuts to grapevines to rose hips for vitamin C in the winter, I learned how a simple life on the land might actually be attained. But you needed seed money, and there were no jobs for us there. Jobs were what landed us in Virginia's Shenandoah Valley. When we found a piece of property that was in the mountains but still close enough to keep those jobs, we sold everything but the West Virginia property (never that) to raise money for it. Finally, we could proceed to implement our own version of the American backwoods system.

Our hundred acres are riven by two creeks that come together in the middle of the tract and by some wet-weather tributaries to them. If you trace these waterways on a topo map, you've drawn what looks like a Celtic rune. On the map the area is labeled "The Ridges." This led inevitably to the kind of name you might see on an upscale mailbox: RuneRidges. However, we knew rural America well enough by then not to put up a fancy mailbox. As it is, our plain metal tube gets clobbered regularly.

Unlike the West Virginia property, with its old fields, our hundred acres in Virginia are entirely wooded. Our trees are mostly white oaks, chestnut oaks, and white pines, with scarlet, black, and post oaks, red maples, black gums, dogwoods, and hickories, and with an occasional hemlock and birch scattered through. Witch hazel bushes hug the creek bottoms, blooming in unexpected sunbursts in November, a last kiss of summer. Wildflowers range from tiny and delicate to coarse and woody. Mountain laurel, greenbrier, huckleberries, and other shrubs form an undergrowth of varying height and thickness.

Some of our slopes are almost straight up and down, but there are also plateaus between the creeks. Old logging roads, their imprints softened by leaves and moss, run along our creek bottoms and into the national forest. Once we got lost among the rills of our own property—a heady feeling! We found the highest point—an elevation of about fifteen hundred feet—and talked about climbing up a four-pronged chestnut oak with boards and brackets to make a tree stand for the view. We're still talking about it.

It took a couple of years to sell the valley farmhouse we had fixed up for that purpose—with perfect timing, farm values dipped to their lowest rate in fifty years. We needed that money before we could build a house at the new place. So every weekend and every vacation for two years, we loaded up Sam the pickup truck with odds and ends from the farm and drove over to the property. We began by finding a flat site where the entry road forks, next to a stream. A friend gave us a big, old canvas tent. We clipped off branches and sawed down small trees to clear a place to put it up. We set up a kitchen, and a shower on a wooden pallet. We trampled the ground, shattered the lichens, crushed the moss, and bruised the trout lilies to death. And those were just the first casualties.

It didn't take long to reconnoiter a house site. A south-facing slope rose above a hollow, with a nearly flat plateau on top. It was almost exactly in the middle of the hundred acres. An old road passed near the site from the north, and we cut enough trees to make a spur off to the southern aspect of the plateau—rough, but good enough for old, beat-up Sam. Camped below in the tent, we chopped a shortcut up a piney slope to the house site. Behind it, we decided to begin by building a shop. There we could store tools and household utensils and experiment with building materials. Naturally we considered using our own trees for lumber. There was the essential rightness of it, but the logistics of making logs out of trees and lumber out of logs defeated us. Green oak boards purchased at the local mill were the heaviest, hardest to work, and cheapest alternative. Ralph set the shop on six locust posts, around which we poured extremely toxic chlordane. The shop was twelve by sixteen feet, with a loft just beneath the roof beams. Friends came over from the valley to help us put on a tar-paper roof.

Moving mattress and kitchen (the shower, by decree of gravity, stayed by the stream) up to the shop from the tent was cause for celebration. Lying in our loft bed, with the ceiling a bare foot above our heads, we watched a full moon rise over the mountain. Wood roaches scurried away when we shook the covers. Bats fluttered through the gable ends, their wings fanning our faces. That first morning, I awoke to find deer browsing around the edge of the clearing we had recently made. On another sleepy dawn, a gray fox clattered in the pots and pans, and I woke just enough to take in how catlike he was.

Finally, late one spring, the farm was sold and we moved into the shop for the summer. I had started freelancing by then, trying to teach myself ecology by writing about it, trying to teach myself writing by doing it. I worked on a manual typewriter on a table set in forest duff.

The shop stood on the edge of an acre that had been almost impenetrably dense with spindly Virginia pines before we cleared it. They grew so thickly they didn't have any branches, just green tussocks on top. I felt dwarfed when I walked through them. A local logger was willing to cut the pines for pulpwood and to actually pay us, never mind how little, for doing the hardest part of land clearing. Just rendering the pine slash off the garden and house site was all the reality check I needed: I was not meant to be a pioneer. Ralph chain-sawed each cantankerous limb, and I dragged them into piles thirty feet across for burning. With snow on the ground, we lit bonfires. After a couple of hours, each pile shrank and withdrew like a dying thing. The grass seed we threw in early spring sprouted green as emeralds.

When the pines were gone, two edges of the clearing emerged as straight, distinct lines. Oak trees press up from the forest side, then stop abruptly. A few reach branches out like rescuing arms over a cliff. In one place there is a long hump of earth, as if a plow had once turned it over. There was a clearing here, exactly here, once before. Harried and exhausted, I put aside the question of just how much history we were repeating.

A surveyor friend helped us lay off a driveway off one of the old roads. We put it up the south slope so snow would melt in winter. Ralph wrapped an orange ribbon on his cap and clambered thirty feet ahead through the underbrush. The surveyor sighted on him and waved him up- or downslope until he hit a ten percent grade. To cut the road, we hired a valley Mennonite whose religion prohibited him from owning a car but who drove a bulldozer for a living. He dammed a pond in the hollow below the house, too, and dug out the house basement from the dense shale soil. We hired other men with equipment to put in a septic system, dig out garden beds, and pile in the manure we had brought from the farm.

For weeks I listened to the bulldozer grinding, churning, growling along. The dozer would push at a tree, which would lean over slowly as if taking a bow; then there would be a crack as of splintering bones. Root masses ripped out of the earth quivered for many moments, and fine particles of soil dribbled away like blood. The men hit one another on the arms with their fists, winked, ran their machines with cigarettes dangling. I walked around trying to look tough and casual and competent, but I was terrified of the noise and the power. I wanted to burst into tears, cling to my husband, throw up. I beat the bushes ahead of the equipment, trying to scare off any turtles that might be crushed, but I was not always successful. I watched as the bulldozer spent an hour popping stumps out of the half acre where we planned the garden and the orchard. It would have taken Ralph and me months, if not years, to accomplish that hour's work. I wrote in my journal: Hooray for technology!

Living without electricity hadn't been a problem in summer, though I badly missed a phone, but for winter we wanted comfort. Power and phone lines arrived underground, along our third-of-a-mile-long driveway. Someone just a few ridges away advertised a mobile home in the paper. It was fairly clean and cheap, and we set it up right next to the house site. For reasons now unclear to me, Ralph named it the Taj Mahal. Our house design was simple enough that we drafted it ourselves on graph paper. Thinking ruefully of West Virginia, where an outhouse and most anything else you might want to do were not regulated, we were careful to meet all county permit requirements. A year and a half later, we sold the trailer and moved into the house. Parts of it we had built ourselves and other parts we had contracted out. We ended up with a passive solar- and wood-heated, two-story, wood-sided house. We had decided early that we didn't want a log cabin because of the dim interior and the hassle of hiding the wiring and plumbing along open walls. Later I came to realize that it would have been too intimate with traditions I wanted to change.

Maybe it was the shock of actually settling down, of finally committing to a place, that drove me to search for Appalachia. In the national forest just across our border, where Cross Mountain rises to the west, are some slippery, rocky slopes. It's not a long climb to the top, but it's hard going, scrabbling over stones where copperheads hide, sliding one step down on leaves slick as ice for every two steps up. Then, finally, we reach the blue vista that for so long has shaped our every desire: mountains beyond and beyond, mountains of dreams, dreams of mountains. What does it mean to live in them? What is this place I've chosen to call home?

Going back to the land came to mean, for me, going back to the forest. More than coal, more than moonshine, forests define Appalachia. To try to understand the place, I have focused on those forests, pondering their past, feeling their presence, anticipating their future. It's no surprise to find that society perceives them in contradictory ways. On the one hand, there are voices that praise the green growth that surged in the wake of destruction as the world's best example of natural resilience. Where whole mountain ranges were denuded in the early 1900s, before the end of that century there were forests of maturing trees covering some seventy percent of the mountains from Virginia to Georgia. Wildlife of many species is thriving. Life sprang back exuberantly in a clear demonstration of its irrepressible nature. Some see this as reassurance that what we have ravaged is repairable. Those who espouse this view don't reckon what has been lost, nor what the past means for the future.

On the other hand, other voices are filled with alarm for the forest's future because of air and water pollution and unchecked human sprawl. Many species of plants and animals are close to extinction. Scientists speak of forest declines affecting whole continents. Come the images of Armageddon, where instead of green rejuvenation there are black silhouettes of death. Such extremes embody the wrench and the promise I know now to expect from Appalachia, as I explore the rooms of my mansion, and the forests of my heart.

The Late Great Forest

Old Old Growth

Rage is not the proper emotion to feel in an old-growth forest. Awe, veneration, respect, humility—these are expected. But I wanted to pummel the furrowed bark with my fists, stamp my feet on the moldy ground, scream into the dappling canopy. I wanted to weep. The thought of forests lost so recently throughout the East was overwhelming.

It's not that the trees on this rocky Blue Ridge mountaintop in western North Carolina were huge and imperial, the charismatic megafloral equivalents of bears and wolves. On the contrary: they were stunted white oaks, forty feet tall and eighteen inches in diameter, yet they have been documented at 350 to 450 years old. Their limbs twined like Medusa's hair; their trunks were bearded by mosses. From them emanated a mysterious life of which we know almost nothing. They were living sculptures, the most perfect biological expression of which that ridge was capable. Once cut, half a millennium would pass before such trees appeared again, if ever.

This and a scattering of places like it are all that's left of the Great Forest, an old term for the original expanse of eastern woodland that met the first European settlers. It was said that a squirrel could travel from the Atlantic to the Mississippi without ever touching ground. My search for Appalachia began with a search for those primeval forests, out of a need to anchor myself in a past unsullied by history.

A few decades ago, everyone assumed that except for a handful of famous showcases, such as Joyce Kilmer Memorial Forest in North Carolina, all vestiges of the primeval eastern forest had been erased. Only stumps and legends were thought to persist. Then, in the late 1970s, researchers in the Pacific Northwest began to publish findings that showed that ancient forests were not just young forests grown old. Individual trees develop attributes distinctively different from those of their youth. Their bark becomes deeply fissured, offering habitat for dozens of rare lichen and moss species. Their structure changes, too, becoming increasingly complex over time and gradually creating an architecture of columnar trunks and baroque branches, stippled with deadwood. Being scientists, western researchers measured and quantified these structural characteristics. A handful of forestry professionals and environmentalists began to wonder what the new knowledge might reveal about the Great Forest. When they started to inspect eastern forests for old-growth characteristics, they found far more remnants than they ever imagined. Some estimates for old-growth patches across the East total as much as five million acres.

It's mostly the poorest timber, tiny patches on the stoniest lands and steepest slopes and in the wettest swamps, overlooked or rejected out of disgust or sheer inaccessibility. And it's hardly virgin forest, if the term means untouched by human impact of any kind. Even where timber wasn't commercially cut, almost every acre of original eastern forest has been changed by humans. Piecemeal logging took out the best of the most useful trees. Relentless arson and unfenced grazing by cattle and, worst of all, by rooting pigs were common, especially in the Appalachians. Extermination of native species such as buffalo, elk, passenger pigeons, wolves, and cougars extinguished entire cycles of forest life. There's no way to know what smaller, less visible species were trampled to extinction in the rush, just as unnamed species are being lost in rain forests today. Even though the eastern United States has been scrutinized for hundreds of years by scientists seeking new species, unknown kinds of soil invertebrates are still being found in Appalachian remnants of the Great Forest.

In the twentieth century, total fire suppression added another distortion to forest development. Insects and diseases introduced from other continents, of which chestnut blight is merely the best known, began a continuing attack on natural systems that never evolved defenses against them. Air pollution is damaging many species. Yet the tattered old-growth holdouts are the only hope for reinventing the world of the Great Forest. So I stood beneath the white oaks with Bob Zahner, trying to calm myself enough to take in the information he was imparting.

Long and lanky, with white hair swept back from a thin, thoughtful face, Bob looked the academic he was, albeit a renegade. He had taught forest ecology at the Universities of Michigan and Tennessee and at Clemson, all of them highly regarded forestry schools. He avoided their commodity orientation by working almost exclusively with graduate students engaged in pure research on ecological questions. Once safely retired, he criticized the manipulative approach of professional foresters in many articles and speeches. He advocated natural forests allowed to operate without massive human intrusion, and forestry that mimicked natural processes. He quickly became the guru of a burgeoning movement to discover and preserve the remnants of eastern old growth.

Bob's father was a lawyer in Atlanta; his mother came from an old South Carolina family. Like others of their class, they purchased a tract of land near the little resort town of Highlands, North Carolina, founded in 1875 to promote the summering of wealthy families far above the sultry lowlands. Highlands sits on a four-thousand-foot-high plateau in the Blue Ridge at the conjunction of North Carolina, South Carolina, and Georgia. Surrounding peaks rise above five thousand feet. Summer temperatures rarely top the seventies. Bob's parents remodeled the old farmhouse that came with the property into a mansion, adding wings, porches, and terraces. "My mother had a Scarlett O'Hara image of herself," Bob said. She created a garden of several acres based on the designs of Frederick Law Olmsted. There were statues beckoning on native rock benches, bowers hidden in deepest rhododendron shade, and Italian urns so big I could have climbed in. Bob and his wife, Glenda, also an expert botanist, are reclaiming the garden after decades of neglect.

Bob arrived on the plateau at the age of seven, and except for three years as a soldier in World War II, he has spent every summer of his life there. The farmhouse-mansion burned down years ago, but as a young man, waiting to get into Duke University on the GI Bill, Bob built a caretaker's house. It's a simple, wood-framed place; lacking electricity in the early days, he used only hand tools. He lived there year-round during several periods of his life, once for sixteen years, and considers it home. He came to know the area intimately, especially the nearby mountain called Whiteside. To visit Bob is to make a ritual visit to Whiteside Mountain. So we left the ancient white oaks, hoping to draw a sense of serenity from the solidity of this unusual mountain.

"The largest exposure of perpendicular, bare rock east of the Rockies," two naturalists wrote of Whiteside Mountain in 1883. Its two-thousand-foot cliffs above the Chattooga River are the most dramatic of the Cowee Range, which forms the eastern rim of the Highlands Plateau and the southern escarpment of the Blue Ridge Mountains. In Bob's boyhood there remained a thousand acres of what everyone called the Primeval Forest along the old trail to the cliffs. So magnificent was it that many of the most prominent botanists of the twentieth century came to study it. "I remember trees of several species there larger than the trees recognized as today's national champions," Bob said. But they were private property. Every one of them was cut in 1946, thirty years before the mountain was purchased by the federal government as part of Nantahala National Forest. "I resent that," Bob said, his characteristic mildness tempering my anger. Or maybe, as I gingerly followed him along cliffs too far off the trail to be imprisoned by the Forest Service handrails Bob hated, the mountain was working on me.

The big trees Bob remembered were not unusual. The Great Forest was full of behemoths. In 1770, George Washington was impressed by a sycamore along the Kanawha River measuring two inches short of forty-five feet in circumference. Such huge sycamores were often hollow, and some early explorers used them as homes for months at a time. Chestnut trees, which numbered one out of every four trees in much of the central and southern Appalachians, grew four to ten feet in diameter. White oaks were often six feet through the middle. The largest tree ever reported cut in West Virginia, in 1913, was a white oak more than thirteen feet thick at its base. Red oaks were smaller, averaging around four feet in diameter. Yellow poplars became legendary not so much for their diameters, which sometimes exceeded eight feet, but for heights approaching two hundred feet, the first third of which was generally free of limbs. The largest tree ever known to have been felled in Kentucky, in 1937, was a poplar nearly twelve feet in diameter. Black cherries and black walnuts were commonly four feet thick, beeches around three feet. Hemlocks in cool, wet ravines sometimes reached seven feet through, and it was the dark, wild hemlocks of Whiteside Mountain, at the foot of Highland Falls, that most impressed Bob.

The big trees of Whiteside's Primeval Forest either tapped or formed Bob's intuitive understanding of old forests. As an adult he girded his empathy with ecological knowledge. Yet the more he learned, the more he realized how little was known. Science has barely begun to glimpse the ecological essence of undisturbed forests. Just as their structure differs from that of young forests, so do their ecological processes, but these are immensely more difficult to measure. Nutrient cycling, energy allocation, regeneration, and other workings are so intricate that they are not yet and may never be fully understood. What is becoming increasingly clear is that old growth performs functions without which a forest may not be able to perpetuate itself. Scientists are beginning to wonder whether managed forests anywhere in the world can sustain long-term productivity without a complement of old growth.

"It's a hallucination," Bob said, referring not to the human belief in control but to the family of ruffed grouse that had just exploded from the underbrush. We were in a remnant of old growth that Bob had discovered downridge from Whiteside. From the slope on which we stood, we looked down into an airy, spacious, green and gold hollow where sun gleamed on brown trunks. The almost unbearably sweet, melting notes of a wood thrush flowed from some hidden place in the greenery. "For years, foresters and hunters have said that grouse live only in young forests," Bob said. "But grouse eat acorns. Oaks don't even start to produce good crops until they're around eighty years old. Grouse love old growth." Dozens of other species, from deer to deer mice, also depend on nuts from oaks, hickories, and beeches.

Wildlife was almost unbelievably abundant in the Great Forest. Many travelers remarked on the numbers of white-tailed deer. Between 1755 and 1773, around six hundred thousand deer skins were shipped to England from the one collecting port of Savannah, Georgia. While building the Wilderness Road through Cumberland Gap in 1775, Daniel Boone's party saw so many wild turkeys that the woods seemed full of one huge flock. The Knights of the Golden Horseshoe, as the members of Virginia governor Alexander Spotswood's 1719 Blue Ridge expedition were called, saw nearly half a dozen black bears a day as they rode horseback (and guzzled wine) up to Swift Run Gap.

Because of structural complexity, wildlife in old forests have a far greater array of habitats as well as food. One of the most crucial habitat components is standing and downed deadwood. Dams made of trunks and large fallen branches form pools for fish and catch nutrients that would otherwise pass through, carried away by rushing water. Soil is so shielded from erosion by layers of fallen leaves and twigs that streams draining ancient woods are among the purest waters ever tested. Large downed logs harbor the small mammals that eat and disperse a group of fungi, the mycorrhizae, that grow around root tips and help trees take up nutrients. Young trees fail to thrive without these fungi and often die. Downed logs remain damp enough through droughts to serve as refuges for amphibians, which are crucial to the food chain. In late fall, black bears look for trees big and old enough to have hollow spaces for denning fifty feet up or higher, accommodations that take centuries to produce.

As the ancient white oaks showed me, it's not the size of individual trees that counts but the age of the forest community. "Old growth" doesn't necessarily mean old trees, but an old forest, one that hasn't suffered any widespread leveling catastrophes in centuries. As a general rule of thumb, half of the trees should be at least half as old as they are likely to get—a complex and variable figure, highly dependent on site. This gives the canopy time to become nicked by storms and winds, droughts and floods, and insect infestations, which generally kill a small number of trees at a time. Like the sporadic twinkling of lightning bugs against a summer night, but on a longer time scale, these sudden bursts of light form a changing pattern across the forest. Wildflowers, shrubs, and subdominant trees fill the sunny spaces, resulting in a layered canopy of trees of all ages. Trees that have blown down often yank their roots out, mixing mineral soil with leaf humus and creating a terrain of pits and mounds.

With several other biologists, Bob Zahner worked out a general definition of eastern old growth that encompasses these characteristics. They are relatively simple external criteria, the kind that can be detected by a willing hiker with a trained eye. Another Bob, this one with the surname Leverett, began training his eye fifteen years ago. Like Bob Zahner, Bob Leverett soon discovered an instinct for it, which he honed to the level of an old-growth sleuth. He can scan a landscape and pick out the oldest sections of trees by the snaggly look of the canopy. He has identified dozens of previously unrecognized primary forest stands across the East and claims to hold the national record for stumbling and falling in old growth. This assertion was made publicly in Asheville, North Carolina, in 1993, at the first of a series of conferences on eastern old growth. Bob believes that natural forests are supremely important for environmental and human health. Identifying them so that they can be preserved and studied is one of his life goals. To do this better, he initiated the conference, which is where I met him.

Bob's thinning hair was belied by his fresh, open, youthful face. He was born in eastern Tennessee, his father a track maintenance man and later a manager for the railroads. For a while they lived in the coalfields of eastern Kentucky. He went to high school in northern Georgia. He could walk out his back door into the Cohutta Mountains, and often did. No one else he knew wanted to do that. He played football, and from the field he could see Big Frog Mountain. "My teammates didn't even know the right names of the mountains," he said. "I realized early on that revealing my interest in trees was not a good idea. When I think back about how the people I grew up with related to the forest, there's a big hole."

Bob's father had grown up in the Cohuttas and sometimes talked about the chestnut forests he remembered. When Bob was still very young, his parents bought a book about big trees in the national parks; he remembers pondering the pictures. He first visited the Great Smoky Mountains when he was nine and returned during adolescence when a rich uncle rented a cabin there. Forever afterward, the forests would pull him back. "Later, at Georgia Tech," he said, "I found I needed tree energy to survive. I don't know what it is, I'm not a Druid, but do I feel it? You bet. And whatever power trees have is distilled and concentrated in old growth." He married a woman of Cherokee descent. Together, they hold rituals in the forest to honor trees. Another of Bob's goals is to reintroduce Native American thought and practice into the mainstream of American culture.

But his special mission is documenting big trees. Obsession might be a better word, one that he readily admits to. For Bob, size is a means of understanding the genetic capability of trees and the personality of a species. He likes to compare statistics, to see how different kinds of trees respond to different kinds of habitats. He muses over the areas where each grows best and studies how they fare in marginal habitats, at the extremes of their tolerance. He was trained as an engineer and teaches computer science at the college level. "I'm anal retentive on accuracy," he said. "I've measured some trees fifty times. It's my way of communicating with them."

Finding what he believed was the tallest tree east of the Mississippi recently intensified his relationship with white pines. The tree was 207 feet high, with a modest girth of 11.7 feet. He was with a group of friends, and when he announced his findings, their cheer resounded through the forest. The fact that a few 200-footers still grew, and that they had found one, unified and vivified their collective vision of the Great Forest. Next time the group saw it, the tree was listing and had lost its top. A hurricane and heavy spring snows had broken off the top 36 feet. One man in the group wept. I hiked in with Bob on his third trip to the white pine. It had lost another 7 feet. Bob felt sad, but he knew that life can be hard for trees. He busied himself with measuring contenders for the title.

Measuring is not a cut-and-dried procedure. Determining girth is fairly simple: wrap a tape around the tree at exactly four and a half feet above the ground (a standard distance called breast height), do it again on the opposite side of the tree, and average the two measurements. Finding the height and crown spread, however, requires trigonometry. The simple fact that many trees lean, for example, so that the high point of the crown is seldom centered over the base, complicates the calculations. Recently Bob bought himself a Bushnell laser range finder, which eliminates the need for a two-hundred-foot tape measure. He sights on the top of a tree, and the range finder tells him the distance from his eye to it. Then he uses a clinometer to get the angle of that line to his horizontal (or "level") line of sight. This allows him to figure the length of the tree trunk from his straight line of sight to the top as the third leg of a triangle. He then sights on the base of the tree and repeats the procedure to calculate the rest of the trunk length. To sight on the top of the tree, he often has to back up a considerable distance. If foliage is too thick for good visibility, Bob returns in winter.

It didn't surprise Bob that most of the contenders for the status of tallest pine in the East grow in the Smokies. Many of the greatest trees of their kind are found in Great Smoky Mountains National Park, nurtured by annual rainfalls that approach rain-forest proportions and by relatively undisturbed soil. Because its rugged terrain delayed roads and rails until public opinion was strong enough to support the establishment of a park, more than one hundred thousand acres of the park's five hundred thousand were purchased before loggers could get to them. This is the largest Great Forest remnant in the Appalachians.

In the park's Albright Grove, I could pretend that the world was as it once had been. Black-throated blue and black-throated green warblers gave the air texture with their buzzy trills. Trickling water made an almost subliminal murmur. From far overhead, sunlight flowed through a dark fan of hemlock needles. There were many young trees, green and living. Even the huge, moss-draped logs on the forest floor gave no ambience of senescence. Rhododendron was just starting to reveal the pink inside its red buds. The ground held gaping pits and green-shrouded mounds. Trees were enormous, and many were broken, snapped off or uprooted by wind. A poplar that had lost a limb to wind thrust a remaining branch out, tensed like a muscular arm to maintain balance. Ferns grew out of a hole in the trunk eighty feet up. I looked up into a pointillist canvas in greens, but if I didn't watch the trail, snails crunched unpleasantly under my feet. I moved in an aura of high-pitched whining and wished that I had bug repellent.

The passion of both Bobs focuses on such pieces of forest as Albright Grove, which have been least affected by Euro-Americans. These are the East's primeval forests, or ancient forests, or primary forests—the terminology is not yet standardized. They are the measure by which to gauge how we've changed the rest of the landscape. The person who pioneered this concept of eastern old growth, whose work served as Bob Zahner's pathfinder and Bob Leverett's guide, was a scholarly, imperious woman named Emma Lucy Braun. She preferred to be called Lucy. No one dared do otherwise.

Lucy Braun was one of the most brilliant botanists in American history, ranking with William Bartram, Andre Michaux, and Asa Gray. She was born in Cincinnati in 1889 to affluent parents who were unusually strict and protective. Her mother had been a teacher, and she taught Lucy at home for the first three years. She instilled in Lucy her own passion for plants, which was manifested in a small herbarium. Both parents took

Lucy and her sister Annette walking in the woods to identify wildflowers. Lucy graduated with a Ph.D. from the University of Cincinnati in 1914, a time when few women ventured into the field, figuratively or literally. She taught at the university, becoming a professor of plant ecology by 1946, but she retired early to pursue her own research and writing.

In the course of her long career, Lucy named and described new species of plants, made major contributions to the understanding of plant distribution, and discovered and published a great deal of specific knowledge about specific plants. Building on her mother's work, she compiled a herbarium of nearly twelve thousand specimens, which she donated to the United States National Museum. She led a movement to conserve wild plants in Ohio through the establishment of parks and preserves. Remnants of the Ohio prairies were a particular love, but her primary interest was the new science of forest ecology.

From the mid-1920s through the 1940s, Lucy traveled sixty-five thousand miles to find the remaining original deciduous forests of the East. She always took Annette with her. The two sisters lived together, with Lucy as breadwinner and Annette as housekeeper, until Lucy died in 1971. Although Annette was five years older and had her own Ph.D. in entomology, Lucy totally dominated her. When Annette wanted to show a visitor drawings of a moth, Lucy would say, "Oh, they don't want to see pictures of your old bugs." She was consumed by her own work, and once she reached a conclusion, she believed herself infallible. When a prominent botanist came to consult her about his map of vegetation in the United States, she refused to see him because she didn't agree with his theories. Her only relaxation was reading mysteries. "All scientists read mysteries," she said.

The Braun sisters traveled by horse and buggy until Lucy bought her own Model T in 1930. That enabled her to reach remote areas of the Appalachians, where she loved the particular type of forest she named mixed mesophytic. Mesophytic refers to plants that live where there is enough but not too much water. She called it mixed to reflect the fact that no one or two tree species dominate the canopy, but six to eight out of a possible two dozen or more. Lucy drew the range of mixed mesophytic forests from the northern tip of Alabama across eastern Tennessee, Kentucky, and Ohio, encompassing the Cumberland and Allegheny Mountains and Plateau, and most of West Virginia into Pennsylvania.

Within that range, it was the coves that Lucy most sought. In those deltas of deep soil near the foot of mountain slopes, formed by millennia of deposition by streams coursing down the hollows, mixed mesophytic forests realize their full potential. Lucy felt them to be magnificent in both the size of individual trees and the diversity of tree species—yellow poplars, beeches, birches, buckeyes, basswoods, maples, magnolias, ashes, hemlocks, oaks, and the prettily named Carolina silverbells. She marveled at the lower canopy and ground cover of a thousand kinds of wildflowers, herbs, forbs, and shrubs. A quarter acre was likely to have seventy-five species of plants, compared with thirty in the average eastern woodland. The finest cove hardwoods she found grew in the Smokies.

With Annette beside her, Lucy lurched up the roughest mountain roads, stopping to ask people along the way if they knew of old trees. Initial distrust gave way to an assessment that the two city ladies were harmless, and once word to that effect got around, the mountain people helped them. "Oh," said a woman on Big Black Mountain in Kentucky, after first denying that there was a trail to the top, "you're the plant ladies living with the Mullins family. You're the ladies that take pictures of trees. Come along, I'll show you the trail."

Prohibition was still in effect, and moonshiners could be murderous. The sisters were careful to respect local ways. They never approached a still if they could help it, and once, suddenly sensing that they might have strayed too close, they retreated quickly over a divide into another valley. Lucy had been there ten years earlier and remembered that there was a steep sandstone rim, with a wooden ladder. This time the ladder was gone, and they had to make a wide detour, finally arriving at their lodge hours after dark. The management was much relieved to see them.

Where there were no roads, the sisters rode logging trains. Lucy noted that some of the last stands were being cut even as she studied them. Her knowledge culminated in her 1950 book, *Deciduous Forests of Eastern North America,* illustrated by her own excellent photographs. She continued to write on many aspects of ecology until her death and received many honors, but the book is her masterpiece. It was immediately recognized as a classic. In the half century since, only one of her beliefs has been seriously challenged: that coves served as unchanging refuges for deciduous species throughout all the glaciations. Recent pollen data show forests to be dynamic, capable of advancing and retreating in response to climate, and not as static as Lucy believed they were. Her book is still called the bible of the Great Forest.

In it, Lucy characterized nine broadly defined communities of trees, each with a dozen or more different associations of dominant trees and woody shrubs. Here are vignettes from every part of the Great Forest: The rustling beech and sugar maple woodlands that swept from Minnesota to New England. The hemlocks mixed with the towering white pines claimed by English kings for ship masts. The assemblages of river birch, sycamore, cottonwood, and elm that shadowed and cooled the banks of major waterways. The cypress-tupelo swamps along the southeastern coast and the Mississippi River that harbored bald cypress trees more than a thousand years old. The fragrant pine-oak woods that graced dry, shallow soils almost everywhere. The most widespread communities were the grassy woodlands of longleaf pine, with their handful of trees per acre and low understories of up to forty species per square meter. These once covered some ninety million acres of coastal plain and piedmont from Virginia to Texas. Less than five percent remains.

According to Lucy Braun's map, our West Virginia property lies just inside the eastern edge of the mixed mesophytic, near where it changes to oak-chestnut forests. True to its type, it gets around sixty inches of precipitation a year. "It's great country for growing hay, but terrible for making it," the county agricultural extension agent told us. This is the high end of average rainfall amounts for the central and southern Appalachians. In some sort of cosmic balance, the land in Virginia where we finally settled happens to lie at the low end. At thirty-four inches a year, our garden is in one of the drier places in the Appalachians. Mountains to the west wring out the moisture from most clouds before they reach us, casting a rain shadow. Our oak-chestnut region is adapted to a certain amount of drought. Not so our orchard trees. For years we lugged five-gallon buckets of water to them. Prickly pear cactus is common locally. Not very far west of us, Petersburg, West Virginia, recorded only ten inches of rain a year during the 1920s.

So the woods get dry, and fire comes to mind. More than once I have sprung from my chair in momentary terror when a column of smoke suddenly materialized in the view from my window. Then I remember that the Forest Service sent notice of plans to burn. Fire in the East probably never had as much influence as in the drier West, but it nonetheless played an important role in some places. The Great Smoky Mountains get up to eighty-six inches of precipitation at the highest elevations; fire has little chance there. Elsewhere, communities of oaks and pines on ridges and south slopes were maintained by low-intensity surface fires. These burned off fire-sensitive species such as sugar maples and opened the forest floor to sunlight, which helps oaks and pines sprout. Flammability along a single flank of mountain could range from sodden coves to desiccated slopes. The original fire pattern throughout the Appalachians must have been a mosaic of singed greens, blackened browns, and ash grays.

Now that I've come to fire and water, it's time to think about Cherokees.

Cherokees

"Going to water," Freeman Owle replied, after a moment of musing. I had asked him what was the most distinguishing characteristic of his people, the Eastern Band of Cherokees. We were sitting in the living room of Dewey Owle, Freeman's brother, on the Cherokee Reservation in western North Carolina. Freeman is a stocky man in his fifties, with a direct gaze and penetrating eyes. He taught school for fourteen years on the reservation and has a master's degree in social studies education from Western Carolina University. He is a stone carver and a speaker on Cherokee history to community organizations and schoolchildren around the region. We had been talking for hours, and he was ready to leave. He called for his five-year-old daughter to come in. Her long, blond ponytail bounced behind her as she raced through the door.

I've studied native cultures for years, and I learned long ago not to judge eastern Indians by their looks, but still, it was a shock. Native Americans in the East have coped with genocide for a much longer time than most western tribes. After the blatant killing and treaty-breaking came the more insidious forces of assimilation. It's almost incredible that traditions and descendants of eastern tribes survive at all. But they do, from the Passamaquoddys in Maine to the Choctaws in Mississippi. Many tribes even appear to be strengthening.

The foremost example of persistence beyond comprehension, of unconquerable devotion to place, is the Eastern Band of Cherokee

Indians. Cultural survival depends not on how torchbearers look but on what they believe. Besides, as Freeman's daughter tossed her blond head, I remembered what Rita Owle, Dewey's wife, had told their only child: "Your Cherokee heritage is fading, son. You better find you a good Cherokee wife." He did, and Rita's granddaughter looks as darkly Indian as anyone seeking a stereotype could demand.

North Carolina Museum of History

Jim Tail, fisherman, with river-cane basket and pole on the Cherokee Reservation in North Carolina, 1908.

Of the approximately ten thousand Eastern Cherokees on the tribal roll, it's said that anywhere from a couple hundred to a thousand are full-bloods. For the most part, these are elusive people; speaking mostly in Cherokee, they avoid contact with white society and maintain as much as they can of the old ways. As I have learned to expect from native peoples elsewhere, my phone calls trying to reach Cherokee traditionalists were never returned.

After the old Cherokee governing ethic of harmony through consensus broke down during the Civil War, various political factions sprang up. The Eastern Cherokee Defense League is one of the current expressions of conservative Cherokee values, including old ways of respecting the earth. Whenever I passed the league's office, it was, somewhat forlornly, closed. In the summer of 1996, the league had hosted, on the Cherokee Reservation, the seventh annual meeting of the Indigenous Environmental Network. Naturally, in a dichotomy applicable not only to Appalachia but to most Indian reservations, such conservatives are now called radicals by the mixed-blood, more acculturated tribal majority.

The tension of deciding which of the white ways should be accepted or rejected strums through every Native American society. Of all Indians, the Cherokees have been called the most accepting. From first contact, in every dimension of life, Cherokees took from white ways whatever they felt would work best to maintain their own autonomy. This ability to reflect white culture has led observers over the past century to predict the imminent demise of the Eastern Band.

Cherokees are an Iroquoian people who parted with their kin in the Great Lakes area either centuries or millennia earlier, depending on which theory you believe. The separation took place under unpleasant circumstances, if enduring enmity is any clue. Cherokees soon absorbed the Mississippian culture of the southeastern Indians, becoming mound builders, growing corn, and organizing around a central leader. They first appear in the historic record in 1540, when Hernando de Soto led a Spanish army of gold seekers north from Florida. De Soto visited a town on the Savannah River that was governed by a queen. The copper objects made there seemed to be mixed with gold. He seized the queen and forced her to guide his troops northward to where he had been told the metals were mined. The queen led him on a merry goose chase and eventually escaped.

De Soto turned west into rough, mountainous terrain. He was hospitably received in several villages, where he noticed lots of small dogs.

They were probably the ancestors of today's rat terriers. One village in western North Carolina presented de Soto with three hundred of them. The Indians treated them as pets and possibly used them for hunting. The Spaniards ate them. In every town, de Soto demanded tribute. He crossed the Mississippi River in 1541 but returned in 1542 after failing to find gold in Arkansas, Oklahoma, or Texas. While near the Mississippi, he died of fever. His men weighted his body with stones and sank it in the river to keep Indians from desecrating his remains.

Besides a reputation for white rapacity, de Soto and later Spanish expeditions left a legacy of European diseases. Isolated for thousands of years in North America, Indians never developed immunities to smallpox, influenza, or measles. It's thought that entire villages, even whole tribes, died out years before any English-speaking people arrived. Possibly spared to some extent by their location in the highest Appalachians, Cherokees moved down the streams to take over richer lands vacated by victims of disease. They next registered in white consciousness in the late 1600s, when Scots-Irish traders began to move through their domain. By the 1690s, at least one trader was living among Cherokees. No enterprising frontiersman could afford to ignore them: Cherokee land encompassed forty thousand square miles, from the upper Ohio River southward through West Virginia and across the mountainous parts of Virginia, North and South Carolina, Kentucky, Tennessee, Georgia, and Alabama. Their most ancient city was Kituhwa, near what is now Bryson City, North Carolina. The tribal capital was Chota, on the Little Tennessee River a few miles above the mouth of the Tellico River in southeastern Tennessee. There were sixty or seventy other towns, each with dozens of houses and acres of fields along river valleys. Before a smallpox epidemic devastated the Cherokees in the 1730s, there were around twenty-five thousand of them, the most numerous of all eastern tribes. They formed four geographically defined groups—Lower, Middle, Overhill, and Valley Towns—each distinguished by dialect and small differences in styles of pottery and toolmaking.

All their homeland was sacred to Cherokees, but some places were more sacred than others. It's hard to explain what makes a place sacred, but it's easy to feel it once you're there. Every place has a personality, arising from physical structure and life-forms. The different personalities of place attract different kinds of spirits. Any prominent or unusual feature of the landscape is likely to be the habitat of strong spirits. One of the highest mountains in the East, Clingman's Dome (6,642 feet), has a great outcropping of stones at the top. It was a place where Cherokees fasted and prayed. Balds were also special. So were springs and waterfalls. "Other things that make a place sacred," a Cherokee medicine person told an academic folklorist in 1985, "are what our grandfathers and their grandfathers before us have put there . . . or the ancientness of the grandfather trees, or the power of the plants."

The Cherokee homeland encompassed the greatest of the trees in the Great Forest. The eastern red cedar tree was held most sacred, because of its evergreen nature, its fragrance, and the striking color and fine-grained texture of its wood. The red stain came from the blood of an evil magician, who disturbed the daily course of the sun until two warriors killed him. They hung his severed head at the top of a tall cedar. For war dances, scalps were hung on cedar saplings. Like most Indians, Cherokees were enthralled by trees struck by lightning. The wood was believed to have mysterious properties, and splinters of it were used in rituals. The basswood tree was believed to be safe from lightning, so hunters sought its shelter during thunderstorms.

Yet it was not in trees that Cherokees found the dominant deity of the woods but in the crystalline flows that gathered among their roots. The Long Man was the god of rivers. He lay with his head in the mountains and his feet in the ocean. In the words of a sacred Cherokee formula, he held all things in his hands and bore down all before him. No soul slipped from his grasp. Always, he spoke. From the softest tinkling of a rivulet hidden in gnarly roots to the roar of a cataract over cliffs, the Long Man voiced the secrets of life. Because of him I listen closely to the tinkle and splash of my own creeks, but what I hear is white noise. In the Cherokee scheme of things, white is the color of peace, so maybe that's all I'm supposed to hear. Only a medicine person, trained through a lifetime to tune in to spiritual vibrations, can understand the Long Man.

The Long Man's aid was requested through prayer and fasting on every important occasion. Newborns were brought to a stream at four days old, the only time in their lives when the water ceremony did not include a dunking in cold mountain water. At each new moon, families fasted and went at daybreak to the river. They stood with toes just touching the water while a priest behind them prayed for each in turn.

Then they all plunged in and bathed. Sometimes, it was necessary to break a hole in the ice. "Going-to-water" rituals of purification were part of every tribal function. This made it peculiarly easy to convert Cherokees into Baptists, who insist on immersion.

Other odd parallels between Cherokees and Appalachian whites abound. Compared with other Native American societies, Cherokees were unusually individualistic, to the point of anarchy, in a way that meshed with the Scots-Irish brand of independence. They had a penchant for the kind of legalistic arguments characteristic of white society, at a time when land disputes were common. They believed in Little People, who were uncannily like leprechauns. The Little People lived in crevices between rocks and appeared bearing knowledge to those who fasted. The Cherokee code of blood revenge, which obligated a clan to repay in equal measure any injury done to one of its own, was the native way of feuding.

In one area, though, there was a chasm of difference. A prominent trader in the eighteenth century ridiculed Cherokee men for being ruled by a "petticoat" government. Another trader in the 1700s reported that Cherokee women sometimes beat their men within an inch of their lives. Women not only ruled the household but had political power as well. They dispensed punishment for transgressions of Cherokee law. They decided when to go to war and whether to torture, sell, or adopt the captives the warriors brought back. Some women accompanied their men to war. Men moved into the households of their mothers-in-law upon marriage. Children belonged to the mother's clan.

The source of women's power was agriculture. Corn was the tribe's staff of life, supplemented by beans, pumpkins, and yellow squash. Although men helped with the heavy work of preparing the fields, women were responsible for growing the crops. They bartered, sold, or gave away produce as they saw fit. Selu, the Corn Goddess, was a principal deity. She had provided corn to her family by rubbing her stomach, but when her son and his adopted brother, the Wild Boy, saw her do this, they feared her as a witch and cut off her head. Corn sprang up where her blood fell. Clearly, Selu had a forgiving nature.

In the lush Appalachians, where leafy green regeneration embodied female power, the freedom of Cherokee women extended to sex. Marriages could be casual, a sort of serial monogamy with equal choice for both partners. This was abhorrent to white males, despite the fact that it worked to their great advantage. It was easy for Cherokee women to enter into liaisons with white men. Cherokee women were tall, slender, and graceful and wore their hair so long that it sometimes touched the ground. When Cherokee women saw their soldier boyfriends besieged in forts by their own Cherokee relations, they sometimes smuggled in supplies and news. As the population of Cherokee males declined precipitously from warfare and disease, Cherokee women married the affluent traders who established stores and controlled the local economy. In fact, an early tribal law prohibited any trader from remaining permanently in Cherokee country unless he married into the tribe. By 1750, the resulting mixed-bloods, usually the only tribal members to get a white-style education, were becoming the arbiters of Cherokee destiny. Taking an Indian wife was acceptable for white frontiersmen, but rarely did a white woman marry an Indian.

In addition to agriculture, Cherokee women also practiced a wilderness horticulture. They cultivated persimmon trees, honey locusts, red mulberries, black cherries, chickasaw plums, black walnuts, butternuts, and other trees of the Great Forest into semidomestication. There is some evidence that they transplanted yaupon holly trees from the coast to their own villages. Yaupon holly is an evergreen tree native to the Atlantic coast from Virginia down to central Florida and along the Gulf coast to Texas. Its scientific name is *Ilex vomitoria*. Yes, vomit: for ceremonial purposes, the most distinguished Cherokee women brewed leaves, buds, and twigs into Black Drink, which induced throwing up. Purity was an obsession of many southeastern Indian tribes. They believed that the purity of your soul determined the success of your prayers to the spirit world. Just as going to water cleansed the outside, Black Drink cleansed the inside. It was drunk before many different kinds of rituals by adult males of high social standing.

But Black Drink wasn't just for throwing up. Men made it simply for socializing. In this secular role, it did not cause vomiting. Yaupon holly is the only caffeine-containing plant in the Southeast. Leaves were roasted before boiling, much like coffee beans. As implied by its name, Black Drink was dark, and it was said to have a mildly bitter taste comparable to coffee but most often likened to strong Oriental tea. In the mornings, before beginning the day's work, men would gather together and sit around drinking Black Drink and smoking tobacco. It must have been a regular coffee klatch.

Cherokee men were known for making beautiful tobacco pipes. They were also known for their war bows of oak, ash, and hickory, coated with bear oil for moisture protection. Like most men in Native American societies, Cherokees were hunters and warriors. They waged intermittent warfare with other southeastern Indian tribes, especially the Creeks, though they also traded with them. For hunting, men made blowguns by hollowing out tubes of river cane up to twelve feet long. Thistle down was used to fletch darts of locust. Boys were expert by age ten. The smallness of the dart obliged them to shoot at the eye of larger prey. They killed small prey such as rabbits, squirrels, waterfowl, and other birds at a distance of a hundred feet. Bows and arrows brought down deer and bears, which, along with fish, contributed much to the Cherokee diet. Fish were shot with bows and arrows or caught in clever water traps, hooked with bait, or dipped out with baskets. By the 1730s, guns replaced traditional weapons.

Like many other Indian tribes, the Cherokees channeled aggressive energies into a ball game, which evolved into lacrosse. In the old days, it was an elaborate ritual involving self-scarification and abstinence from sex and food. So rough was the game that it was called the "little brother of war." Disputes were sometimes settled by a game. A performance drew spectators from around the area, one of the earliest forms of the tourism that would eventually mean survival for Eastern Cherokees.

Men shaved their heads except for a patch in the back, which was ornamented with beads, feathers, and stained deer hairs. Earlobes were slit and stretched to an enormous size. Both sexes pricked gunpowder into their skin to tattoo pretty patterns.

Both sexes took quickly to a market economy. For men, trade with whites assumed some of the status and prestige that war had provided. Fur trading was initiated by the Spanish, expanded by the French, and dramatically intensified by the English. Beaver, bison, bear, and elk skins were all valuable, but deer skins were the backbone of commerce. The peak of the frantic hunting came in the 1740s and 1750s. Based on shipping records in the South Carolina port of Charleston, it's been estimated that Cherokees alone could have killed half a million deer during those two decades. A gun was valued at thirty-five skins, a hatchet at three, a calico petticoat at fourteen. By the end of the eighteenth century, bison, elk, and beavers were on the way to extinction throughout the East. Deer and bears were scarce enough that they could no longer be counted on as a food supply.

Getting skins to lowland traders meant canoeing downriver in long, shallow-draft boats that Cherokees cut and burned from the straight trunks of tulip-poplar trees. For overland treks, until horses became common in the mid-1700s, Cherokee men and women walked in long lines carrying large bundles of skins, in a practice aptly called burdening. Indian captives taken in tribal wars and runaway African slaves caught in the mountains constituted a sizable part of the wares of many trading parties. In return, Cherokees received blankets, iron kettles, steel needles, knives, scissors, cloth, earrings, vermilion paint—and rum. Getting drunk and reeling around town causing trouble became a young Cherokee male's way of challenging authority. As the Scots-Irish settled in the mountains, their stills ensured a steady supply of whiskey. Cherokee elders who couldn't control their young people shrugged and said simply that liquor made them do it.

Cherokee women sent corn, beans, chestnuts, and herbs, especially ginseng, to market. American ginseng is a small, shy perennial of moist woodlands with a fleshy root that is sometimes forked, resembling human form. It is closely related to Chinese ginseng. In the Orient, people have appreciated the healing properties of ginseng root for thousands of years. It is particularly valued as an aphrodisiac. Large quantities of the roots were and still are in great demand in China for tea. By 1750, a lucrative market for Appalachian ginseng began to develop. It helped finance the homesteading of many a mountaineer, red and white.

Cherokees had also been using ginseng, and many other herbs, for a long time. Ginseng needs years to mature and is susceptible to overharvesting. The foremost anthropologist of the Cherokees, James Mooney, wrote in 1900 that it was the tradition of medicine people to pass by three ginseng plants before harvesting the fourth. The Cherokee Museum broadens this guideline, in a contemporary display plaque, to include all plants that were harvested. In Freeman Owle's version, as we talked in Rita's living room that afternoon, this tradition also guided the harvest of animals. It must have been one of the first rules to break down.

Exploring the curative powers of plants seems to have been a joint venture between the sexes over many generations. Women provided botanical expertise, and men performed as shamans in healing rituals. But the new European diseases stumped them. Some shamans told their smallpox patients to undergo a sweat and then plunge into a cold river. This killed many sufferers instantly. It couldn't have done much for the faith of survivors, either. Finding new remedies takes time. Given the time, Cherokees might well have been able to cope. Their track record was excellent: they knew the medicinal uses of more than four hundred plants.

This was important knowledge. The Cherokees believed that long ago, animals found themselves cramped for room as human beings multiplied, and were besieged by the new hunting weapons that humans had devised. Those were the days when everyone still spoke the same language. Bears met in council and decided to try using human weapons in retaliation, but their long claws caught the bowstring and spoiled the shot. They refused to trim their claws, because then they couldn't climb trees to eat fruits and nuts, and they would starve. So they disbanded in confusion, and for this reason, Cherokees don't have to ask a bear's pardon when they kill one.

The deer in their council meeting came up with a better idea: to send crippling rheumatism to every hunter who killed one of them without asking their pardon first. They notified the nearest settlement of Indians and advised them how to behave properly when hunger forced humans to kill one of the deer tribe.

Next to meet were the fish and reptiles. They agreed to send nightmares of slimy snakes and decaying fish, without offering any possibility for pardon. Finally the birds, insects, and smaller animals came together, with the grubworm as chief of the council. One after another, the creatures denounced man's cruelty and injustice toward animals. They devised and named so many new sicknesses that human beings would surely have died off.

But plants were friendly to humans. When they heard what the animals had done, every kind of tree, shrub, forb, herb, grass, and moss agreed to furnish a cure for each sickness created by the vengeful animals. To put it another way, the Cherokee response to the diversity of the Great Forest was to become convinced of the beneficence of plants. They also learned something more. "The main lesson of Cherokee legends," Freeman Owle told me, "is an appreciation for all levels of life, no matter how small. Everything has its place."

It was the tiny water spider, for example, that secured the first fire for human use. Like most Native Americans, Cherokees depended heavily on fire. Whether Indians ruined huge acreages by careless burning, or purposely enhanced their environment, has been a hot topic among historians for many years. It was observed in the eighteenth century that Cherokees burned off brush and young trees to restore fertility to valley fields. If they were like other eastern Indians, they also set fires in fall and spring around their villages to kill off ticks. They burned to keep undergrowth down for easier traveling and sometimes used fire to drive deer toward waiting hunters. They burned some places regularly to keep them in blueberries, huckleberries, blackberries, raspberries, and wild strawberries. Undoubtedly, Cherokee use of fire changed parts of the Great Forest, especially along river valleys, from dense to open woods. Fire also kept many farmable acres cleared that would naturally have grown up in trees. And it encouraged the growth of river cane.

Cane was crucial to the old Cherokee way. Its diminishment from huge canebrakes that grew in the mountains to remnant patches mostly along the Atlantic and Gulf coasts today parallels the fall of Cherokee traditional life. River cane *(Arundinaria gigantea)* is a native, woody, perennial grass, closely related to the bamboo that is native to Asia. It grows in moist sites in woods and along stream banks from Virginia and the southern edges of Ohio, Indiana, and Illinois south to Florida and eastern Texas. Stems in the most fertile valley bottoms grew thirty feet high and three inches in diameter. Cherokee men used them for building houses. Cherokee women split the canes and dyed the splinters, then wove them into mats for sitting and sleeping and bowls for eating. The large, tight, exquisite storage baskets they nested together for market were a highly valued trade item from the earliest days of commerce. They're still pretty pricey in the Qualla Arts and Crafts store in the small town of Cherokee. Nowadays they're made from white oak splints by a method that Cherokees learned from Europeans, or from introduced Japanese honeysuckle, which has become a weed in eastern North America.

Cane was so abundant in parts of the Appalachians that herds of a hundred bison could graze in a single canebrake. Cane provided year-round forage for the livestock of early settlers, who didn't have to worry about making hay. It could recover from grazing if given a break but died if it didn't get one. When Cherokees finally began raising cattle, the pressure on river cane became fatal.

Women decided when to raise cattle, just as they decided which of the newly available crops to adopt. Peach trees from Spain were an immediate hit and were planted in large orchards that dominated village landscapes. Watermelons, sweet potatoes, yams, cowpeas, and sorghum followed. Pigs were assimilated early because they were so good at foraging on nuts in the forest. Horses were accepted because they were so valuable to men for hunting, trading, and raiding. Cattle were rejected for many years. At first they were scorned as "the white man's buffalo." Livestock ranged freely in those days, and cattle necessitated the extra job of fencing to keep them out of gardens. Besides, you took on the attributes of the creatures you ate, and who wanted to be dumb and plodding? It was Nancy Ward, the last of the Cherokee Beloved Women, who finally persuaded her people to raise cattle.

Beloved Women were matriarchs who had distinguished themselves, often in war. This was the case of Nancy Ward. At the age of seventeen, in 1755, Nancy accompanied her husband on a war party against the Creeks. It was her job to chew bullets, which increased their mangling power, and load them into guns. When her husband was killed, she grabbed up his weapon and fought in his place. The Cherokees won, and Nancy was acclaimed for her courage. She was said to have been awarded a Negro slave as her spoils of war, thereby becoming the first Cherokee slave owner. She also happened to be kin to the wealthiest, most prominent Cherokee leaders. She was therefore chosen at an unusually young age to fill a lifetime office that carried much influence at council meetings. Over the next half century, Nancy Ward became a famous participant in Cherokee negotiations with whites.

Nancy's home was Chota, capital of the Cherokee Nation. Chota was traditionally a town of sanctuary, where only peace reigned. Its color was white. Nancy wore ceremonial gowns of feathers from the breasts of swans, and her tribal responsibility was to preserve peace. She prepared Black Drink, danced friendship dances, and prayed as the protocol of various rituals demanded. Although she had proved herself violent enough to be a warrior—or maybe because of it—Nancy's every effort did indeed turn to peace.

Nancy was probably still too young to have achieved much prominence when Henry Timberlake visited Chota in 1761. He doesn't mention her by name in his memoirs, but he describes a priestess who flourished a swan's wing over a pot of Black Drink and "mumbled an ancient chant." Timberlake was a young Virginian serving in the British army during the French and Indian War. In a convoluted tale full of stupidity, he bravely offered himself as a hostage to the Cherokees to secure an alliance against the French. Like virtually all other Native Americans, Cherokees much preferred the French over the British, and by far over the Americans. Frenchmen lacked the land hunger of the others; they were trappers and traders and lived off the land like the Indians themselves. But like many other tribes, the Cherokee negotiated with any whites who promised help against traditional tribal enemies and bargains on trade goods. The English made such promises, but it wasn't long before the Cherokees fell out with them, offended by their arrogance. Timberlake's job was to patch things up.

As winter set in, he left the Long Island of the Holston (near Kingsport, Tennessee) and traveled south. Timberlake found the Cherokees neither as warlike nor as artistic as the northern Indians. They seemed to him strange and barbarous, but on some counts they were more reasonable than Europeans. The council house located in every village especially impressed him. A circular building of wood, fifty feet in diameter, it could seat five hundred people on benches raised one above the other, amphitheater style. In the middle was a sacred fire. Political discussions would often last for days, until a consensus was reached. The council house located in every village was situated on top of a mound and covered with earth, with "all the appearance of a small mountain at a little distance."

The only problem was the interior darkness. Light came in through a door and one small opening for smoke. Describing a feast in a council house, Timberlake conferred a judgment on Appalachian cooking that would echo through centuries of tourism: "After smoking, eatables were produced . . . though I cannot much commend their cookery, everything being greatly overdone." It wasn't really the food, though, that turned Timberlake off. "What contributed greatly to render this feast disgusting," he wrote, "was eating without knives and forks, and being obliged to grope from dish to dish in the dark."

A true patriot, Timberlake paid for much of the trip himself, including the requisite presents for the Cherokees. He tried without success to recover his expenses from the colonial government. Piecing his resources together, he took ship to England to try for reimbursement from the royal government as the war ended in 1765. Several Cherokees accompanied him to petition the king about white encroachments on Cherokee land. Wherever they went in England, the Cherokees drew crowds. Timberlake estimated that ten thousand people came to see them during a visit to Vauxhall Gardens. There, the Cherokees entertained themselves and the "gasping multitude" by plinking on an organ and a violin. Even the house where they stayed was mobbed and "much spoiled by the rabble" that came to see them. Timberlake tried to limit sightseers to "people of fashion," which was quite agreeable to the Indians. They were extremely proud and despised the lower class. In athletic diversions, they sometimes refused to compete with anyone but officers.

Poor Timberlake died while in London after publishing his memoirs, and I don't know if he ever got his money back. His legacy to the Cherokees is believed to be a son, though his memoirs don't mention a dalliance. One of his descendants married a descendant of Nancy Ward. Nancy's legacy is much more complex. As she came of age, Nancy watched the Cherokees wither from the strongest tribe in the Southeast to a devastated people on the verge of extinction. Chronic warfare, disease, and starvation assailed them. They picked the losing side not only in the French and Indian War (1755–63) but also in the American Revolution in the 1770s. American troops retaliated with a scorched-earth policy, burning three dozen towns and their surrounding cornfields, razing the orchards, and killing all the livestock. The Cherokees were repeatedly forced to sue for peace, which meant signing treaties ceding more and more land. They lost their self-sufficiency and depended on trade for survival.

After Daniel Boone pioneered the Wilderness Road through the Cumberland Gap into Kentucky in 1775, migrating whites squatted on Cherokee lands in defiance of law. The first treaty with the new federal government was signed in 1785. The ink on the parchment was hardly dry before states began to dispute federal authority over the Cherokees and their remaining lands. The states were eager to reduce Cherokees further and refused to protect them against squatting and other treaty violations. The federal government refused to confront the states. Factions within the Cherokee Nation split bitterly, even murderously, over what to do.

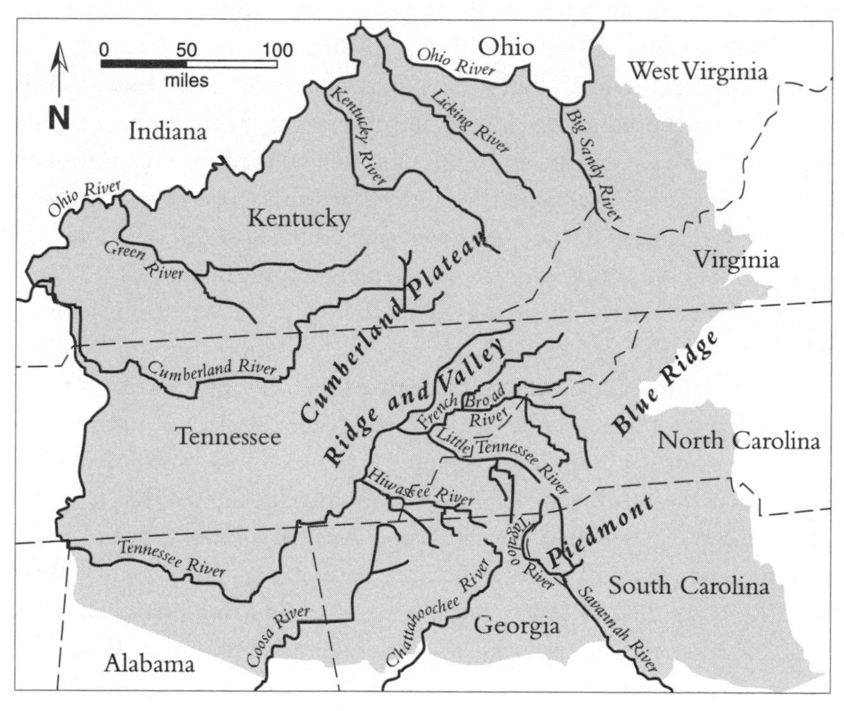

Territory held by Cherokees in 1720.

Nancy developed an unwavering policy of avoiding war between Cherokees and whites. She sent undercover warnings to white settlements of imminent Cherokee attacks. She resolved disputes involving whites, even with other tribes. One of her prerogatives as a Beloved Woman was to overturn the men's decision to torture a captive by the fiendishly ingenious methods that all Indians seemed to relish. One captive in a Cherokee town described a huge basket full of pine splinters resonant with turpentine. These were to be skewered into his skin and lit, one by one. Only fourteen years old at the time, he burst into tears.

A princess figured in his rescue, though in this case it wasn't Nancy Ward. Nancy did, however, pull a white woman from a more conventional death of burning at the stake. Before sending the woman home, Nancy asked to be taught how to make butter and cheese from cow's milk. She had acquired a few head of cattle in the hope of supplementing the dwindling supplies of meat from wild game. She also wanted to reduce the dependence on trade goods. Within a few decades, milk became an important nutrient for impoverished Cherokee children.

There is some confusion in the historical record as to whether Nancy was the daughter of an Indian or a white man. At any rate, shortly after her first husband was killed, she married a trader named Bryant Ward. It wasn't a lasting relationship, but they seemed to remain friends. One of several white traders she later helped to escape from Cherokee captivity was rumored to be her lover. She prepared Black Drink for the very warriors she was warning white settlers to prepare against.

Nancy may have been the first Cherokee leader to consciously acknowledge the terrible choice: accommodation or annihilation. Accommodation, apparent or real, seemed the only option for survival. It must also have seemed like treason. And Nancy spoke not just for herself but for most Cherokee women. Here was another paradox: they urged their men to become farmers like whites, even though it meant destroying their own role. Ambivalence in tribal memory, not to mention the emergence of male dominance, may explain why Nancy Ward is hardly remembered today. She's not even mentioned in *Unto These Hills,* the outdoor drama that is the premier presentation of Cherokee history to gawking tourists like me.

The play has been staged on a hillside above Cherokee every summer since 1950. Sourwood trees were in full bloom when I went, their long stems of lily-of-the-valley flowers forming white, arching sprays against the green of the forest. Wood thrushes were trilling so magnificently that I was a bit sorry when the preshow country music started up and drowned them out. It was a rousing play, full of the actions of men. The roar of rifle blanks startled the adults in the audience and made the children cry.

The most prominent feature of my immediate landscape is the place where the North Fork of the Shenandoah River breaches Little North

Mountain to enter the wide Shenandoah Valley. The silhouette of the mountain on the south side of the pass is long and knobby, like the backbone of a sleeping animal. It bends down to intersect the shining blue streak of river, then rises on the north side into a jagged line of cliffs. This pass is called Brock's Gap. It got that name, according to one of the local legends, because a small boy found there after an Indian raid could say only one word: Brock.

This was one of the first areas in the Alleghenies to be settled. Several families, including one named Brock, were homesteading there by at least the early 1750s. Just inside the pass is a little valley. Two rivers come together, and many acres of flat floodplain spread out between them. An abundance of river's-edge plants—tubers for eating, reeds for weaving—are native to the area. On the slopes above the pass there are hidden vantage points to observe the landscape at a point where animals of many kinds were bound to travel. The blandishments of Brock's Gap have attracted people for millennia. Projectile points of various styles, flakes, scrapers, and other stone tools keep coming up in fields and gardens along both rivers. Some date back nine thousand years, to the earliest days of human presence in eastern North America.

Our West Virginia land also looks down on river bottomland that yields evidence of long occupation. White people began to move in after the French and Indian War. From the middle of our meadow on the ridge, before the trees on the slope below grew too tall, we could see across the Tygart River Valley. On the opposite slope, rocks were laid out along the hillside to spell the name "Conley." They marked the massacre of a white family by Indians in 1777. The last Indian raid in the county was in 1791.

By then, the resistance of most eastern Indians to white settlement was entering its final phase. Cherokees made a lasting peace in 1798. In the early 1800s, they began a remarkable recovery. Women concentrated on rebuilding families. A brilliant mixed-blood named Sequoyah invented a syllabary, which enabled Cherokees to become literate in their own language almost overnight. A Cherokee newspaper was founded. A constitution was adopted, modeled on the U.S. Constitution and banning blood revenge. A traditional leader named Yonaguska persuaded his people to forswear spirituous liquors. Many Cherokees developed kinship ties and good relations with their immediate white neighbors. An elite few lived a plantation lifestyle supported by slavery. In the War of 1812 against the British, the Cherokees even picked the winning side. Unfortunately, it didn't do them a bit of good.

This was because of Andrew Jackson. The seventh president of the United States was the architect of the Indian Removal Act of 1830, which forced not just the Cherokees but also roughly one hundred thousand other Indians to leave their eastern homelands for unknown reservations across the Mississippi River. The first president from west of the Alleghenies, and the first to hold the kind of inaugural ball that left drunken men sick on the White House lawn, Jackson was enormously popular. In him, the backwoods population found its champion. He overthrew the effete elite, the British-aping aristocrats, and brought in the viewpoint of the common man. An entire era of American history—Jacksonian democracy (1824–52)—is named for him and his politics. It was a time of massive expansion, when democracy meant that common men should be able to get cheap land.

Jackson was one of those self-made men whose stories helped to generate the American dream. His parents arrived from northern Ireland a few years before he was born and settled in western North Carolina. They were poor homesteaders. Andrew's father died two months before his son's birth in 1767, apparently worn out by frontier work. Andrew's mother seems to have been fierce enough for two. "Girls are made for crying," she is said to have told a sobbing five-year-old Andrew. "Boys are made for fighting." By the time he was a teenager, Andrew had a reputation for being ready to fight at the drop of a thoughtless word. In later life, even his friends admitted that he was extremely irascible. That was understandable, given the fact that he suffered from rheumatism, recurrent malaria, constipation alternating with dysentery, and chronic pain from wounds sustained in duels.

Much of Jackson's public career was devoted to the single-minded pursuit of Indian removal. It wasn't that he hated Indians. Actually, he had relatively little interaction with them. His family was never attacked, though Indians were a danger when he traveled through the backwoods. It was the British who became Jackson's lifelong enemy. At the age of fourteen, he joined the American Revolutionary forces with his older brother, only to be captured immediately. Ordered to polish a British officer's boots, Andrew refused. The resulting saber scar across his cheek added much to his political image. The boys caught smallpox in prison, and Andrew's brother died. His mother managed to get Andrew back and nursed him for a short while. Then she left him to tend several wounded cousins aboard a British ship. She caught cholera and died there.

An orphan, Andrew lived with extended family until he got himself educated as a lawyer. Among his major subjects were cockfighting, card playing, horse racing, and gambling. After graduation, he bought a Negro girl and moved to the few cabins that then constituted Nashville, Tennessee, to work as a prosecuting attorney. It didn't take him long to become part of the ruling group. He married into a prominent family in typical Andrew style—eloping with a woman who was not yet divorced, which left them both vulnerable to duel-provoking charges of adultery. In his professional life, he was happy to accept payment in land. Through speculation, he amassed huge holdings, including land legally held by Cherokees. For decades before the Cherokees were forced out, Jackson was buying up claims and interest in their lands against the day that they would be dispossessed. By the time he died in 1845, he was a wealthy man.

His first military glory was acquired during the War of 1812, when he could revenge himself on the British. The Creeks had allied with the British and were attacking Americans in Alabama. As commander of the Tennessee militia, Jackson marched against them in 1814. After the first battle, a small Creek boy was found clinging to the body of his mother, who had been killed by Jackson's troops. Jackson adopted the boy and raised him as his own son until the boy died of tuberculosis in his early teens. At the Battle of Horseshoe Bend on the Tallapoosa River, Creeks were gaining the upper hand until the Cherokees, who had allied themselves with Jackson, swam across the river and routed their old Creek foes. Cherokees reminded Jackson of this assistance in the 1830s, when, despite the reluctance of many in his own party, he insisted on forcing eastern Indians to move west.

The Indian Removal Act was by no means universally supported. There was a lot of guilt over the treatment of Native Americans. Supreme Court Chief Justice John Marshall ruled in favor of Cherokees in an 1832 decision that should have vindicated their claims of landownership. But gold had just been found on Cherokee land in Georgia, and prospectors were not about to let a little thing like the law keep them from digging for it. "John Marshall has made his decision," Jackson is reported to have said. "Now let him enforce it." Instead, he sent the army to enforce the terms of a spurious agreement to move west signed by a few unofficial Cherokees. The majority of the tribe repudiated the document and refused to move.

In the spring of 1838, detachments of soldiers arrived at every Cherokee house. Sixteen thousand Cherokees were rounded up at bayonet point from the fields in which they were working and the cabins in which they were eating supper. Many turned for one last look at their farms to see them going up in smoke or being looted by the crowd following the army. On a forced march to Oklahoma that became known as the Trail of Tears, about a quarter of the Cherokees died.

It's not known exactly how many Cherokees fled in advance of the army to hide out at higher elevations; estimates range from one thousand to twenty-five hundred. They were the most traditional, full-blooded Cherokees, who lived in the remote Great Smoky Mountains of western North Carolina. For months they subsisted on toads, snakes, insects, berries, and the inner bark of trees. Some starved to death. The survivors became the nucleus of the Eastern Band of Cherokee. A handful of Cherokees escaped from the army en route and straggled back to join them. Among these were Freeman Owle's great-grandparents.

Freeman told me this during our conversation at his brother Dewey's house. Dewey's wife, Rita, had set up our interview. I had met Rita through a Cherokee friend of a Potawatomi friend—an Indian Old Girls' network. Rita herself doesn't have enough Cherokee blood to be enrolled in the tribe—you need one-sixteenth—but her husband and son do. She is active in tribal life, however, serving on various committees. After a back problem left her unable to continue doing office work, Rita concentrated on the beadwork she had been doing in her spare time. She regularly wins prizes at craft fairs. Dewey works full-time for the tribe as a chartered bus driver but carves small figures from wood in his spare time. He, too, wins prizes.

Rita has short, graying hair and a face with sweetness in it. She agreed to show me around the reservation, on the condition that I make a contribution to the Cherokee Children's Home. It was her way of ensuring against one more white person coming to the reservation to take and give nothing back.

It was Rita who took me to see *Unto These Hills.* "I think I've heard the name," she said when I mentioned Nancy Ward. The play ends in the 1840s, with Eastern Cherokees rallying behind the only completely white leader in their history, a man named William Holland Thomas. As a young teenager, William worked at a trading post near what is now the town of Cherokee in the Great Smoky Mountains. He caught the fancy of Cherokee leader Yonaguska, who dubbed him Little Will and adopted him. By the time Yonaguska died in 1839, Little Will had grown up to study law. He spent a lot of time in Washington, D.C., lobbying for the right of Eastern Cherokees to remain in their homeland. He also bought land for them, using Cherokee money but holding the deeds in his own name to prevent whites from swindling the Cherokees out of ownership. The purchases he made constitute much of the Cherokee Reservation today.

The day after the play, Rita also arranged an interview with Larry Blythe, the tribal forester. Larry was slim with dark eyes, hair, and mustache—just a touch of gray here and there. He worked in a small building set in back of a larger tribal administration complex. His office was lined with shelves of elk and caribou antlers, not trophies, but loose and imperfect ones, as if he had found them in the woods. There were hornet nests, cattle skulls, turtle shells, and a few antiques like a coffee grinder and a crosscut saw. A very large rattlesnake skin was mounted on a board. A painting depicted the seven Cherokee clans. A plaque announced: 1989 Intertribal Timber Council Eastern Regional Award.

Larry came to this job in 1983, after working in the same office earlier as a technician. His family history becomes hard to trace about four generations back, but he is probably related to James Blythe, the Cherokee who served as one of the first tribal foresters at the end of the nineteenth century. The years after the Civil War were full of struggle for Cherokees. Not only did the war leave them even more impoverished than other mountaineers, but their confused legal status between state and federal authority constantly threatened their existence. Their titles to land were often misplaced or stolen. What land they did have was not very productive; they barely grew enough to feed themselves and weren't interested in intensive new farming methods. There was no industry, and cars were just being invented, so there was hardly any tourism yet. By the 1880s, the Cherokees were failing to pay land taxes on several thousand acres of tribal common land. County sheriffs began advertising it for sale. Desperation gripped the tribe. To have endured so much, only to be destroyed for lack of a little cash flow! But what did the Cherokees have that could possibly generate income?

Trees.

The great Appalachian lumber boom arrived like a deus ex machina to save the Eastern Band. After the Civil War, railroads were laid into the mountains by enterprising capitalists from northern and midwestern cities. Railroads made lumbering possible on an industrial scale. At the 1893 Columbian Exposition in Chicago, sections from specimen trees on the Cherokee Reservation publicized the prime quality of Appalachian hardwood lumber. Timber agents approached Cherokees as well as other landowners throughout the Appalachians. Just like most other landowners, the Cherokees agreed to sell timber rights or, in some cases, the land itself. Cutting their part of the Great Forest provided money to pay back taxes and to buy food for the hungriest Cherokees.

The most valuable of all lumber trees were black walnuts, for the dark, rich furniture made from it. Walnuts were being heavily poached by white trespassers anyway—it had been one of the tribe's most serious problems for years—so they were the first to be sold. Other species soon followed. In 1906, the tribe sold thirty-three thousand acres of mixed hardwoods to a group of West Virginia speculators for $245,000, leaving the tribe with about fifty-six thousand acres. The speculators sold their chunk three years later for $630,000. Inevitably, such large amounts of money intensified the jurisdictional haggling between federal and state governments and the complexity of the bickering among the Cherokees themselves.

Most of the reservation was divided into individual tracts, called possessory holdings. These were much like private property, except that they couldn't be sold or bequeathed to anyone not enrolled in the tribe. The tribal council reserved timber and mineral rights but routinely issued permits allowing individuals to harvest timber on possessory tracts. Five thousand acres were retained by the tribe as common land. From this the tribal council sold large quantities of pulpwood. In the 1930s and 1940s, chestnut trees were cut and sold as a blight killed them off. For decades, working in sawmills both on and off the reservation provided the only steady wages for many Cherokees.

There were protests over the cutting of the trees. Traditional people must have spoken of sacred places, but their voices didn't carry. Virtually every acre of the reservation was thoroughly logged. Just as the last trees worth taking were finally gone, the Great Smoky Mountains National Park opened. The most heavily visited of all national parks, it attracts nine million people a year. Three-fourths of the tribe's annual income now derives from tourism, and a new casino promises much more. Some men capitalize on the crowds by standing on the sidewalks of traffic-clogged Cherokee every day through the summer, dressed in the head-to-foot eagle feather war bonnet of the Plains Indians. It is a costume totally foreign to Cherokees but makes for the right kind of Indian photo opportunity for tourists who don't know better.

There were no Plains Cherokees around when I returned to the reservation on a bleak and dreary December day. The leaves were all down, which made for better viewing on a tour through the tribal forest with Larry Blythe. We climbed into his worn four-wheel-drive truck and drove up a mountainside above Soco Valley. As we crossed the first stream, Larry said that it had once been dead, silted and muddied during the 1970s when tribal politics favored heavy logging. Politics could and often did change every few years with the outcome of tribal elections, and there was no long-term land-use plan. Larry described how he had worked for years to build political support for forest rehabilitation projects, such as closing roads so that he could drain and stabilize them, slowing down the harvest schedule, and making improvement cuts to favor tree species most valuable for lumber and wildlife. "There needs to be a healing process," he said.

For a couple of hours we jounced through the tribal reserve, easing under a downed tree across the road (just one more crease in the roof) and braking suddenly when a ruffed grouse flew in our way. The trees we passed were mostly small and young in thick stands, with lots of rhododendron. Larry groaned about how rhododendrons suppressed oak regeneration. He was trying to encourage the return of red oak, which was being shaded out by the red maple that had taken over after earlier cutting. In one place along a stream bottom, Larry said, "We cut out everything but the poplar. Now we see cherry, ash, oak coming back. But we do get a lot of negative response to clear-cutting, so we don't use it except for very specific goals."

Tribal members gather firewood, mushrooms, berries, salad greens, and medicinal plants from the reserve land, although most ginseng was picked out long ago. Fishing is popular, and so is hunting for squirrel, grouse, deer, turkey, and bear. As for sacred places, "I don't really know anything about them," Larry said. Freeman Owle had used almost exactly the same words, as well as the same end-of-conversation tone.

I understood that secrecy was necessary to protect the remaining sacred places from the kind of attention that drives spirits away. Clingman's Dome now sports a concrete ramp that barely accommodates trampling hordes of people. I don't need to trespass on the dwindling number of Cherokee sacred places, because I have my own. Brock's Gap surely qualified once. But the establishment of a bar right smack dab in the gap, with guns for sale hanging from strings just above eye level, has introduced a certain profanity, literal and figurative. On my own property are several small waterfalls, formed by steplike slabs of bedrock. Sometimes I go to one and sit for a while, just to watch the glistening drops of spray bounce around. Moss grows green and feathery near the water. I brush my hand over it, fingering the holy, probing for divinity. It's good to look for sacred places. It's even better to find them wherever you are.

Cutting the Trees

Appalachian mountaineers before the Civil War lived very like the Indians they so rudely replaced. It was a life close to the earth. Seasonal rhythms drove daily and yearly routines. Mountaineers eventually became less mobile than Indians but still traveled to specific places at certain times of year for berries, nuts, herbs, or forage for their animals. Clan loyalty was profound. Traditional ways were venerated, not questioned. Status arose from individual personality rather than structured hierarchy, although Indians placed group welfare higher than individual rights, while mountaineers did the reverse. Some mountaineers were driven by strong entrepreneurial instincts, but many others had little materialistic drive and did only as much work as was necessary to survive. It was just this lifestyle of minimum work and maximum leisure that most galled other Europeans about Indian occupation of the land. Later, it drew recriminations from missionaries to white Appalachia.

There was leisure for the men, that is. Unlike Cherokee culture, white Appalachia was deeply patriarchal. The mountain woman's work was never done, and it wasn't unusual for one man to wear out three wives bearing and rearing a dozen children each. But the major difference between the two cultures was spiritual. Cherokees and mountaineers were both ambivalent toward the natural world, feeling threatened by it even as they relied utterly upon it. Dependence led the Cherokees toward gratitude and reverence. It had something of the opposite effect on

Man on horseback inside this yellow poplar tree indicates its size and its wounds from repeated forest fires. Little Santeetlah Creek, North Carolina, 1916. This area is now part of Joyce Kilmer–Slickrock Wilderness.

mountaineers. They knew that they needed rugged terrain to maintain the seclusion they craved, and they needed forest products to survive. Yet like other Europeans who came to the New World, they feared the forest, and in fear is often an element of loathing. They saw the wilderness as a hostile force to be conquered, a thing to be used to suit themselves.

The Scots-Irish seemed little moved by the magnificence of the Great Forest. The Germans were just as brutal to the land, only neater and more law-abiding about it. The English had already swept away coastal pineries to build tobacco plantations run by slaves. They all took from the forest without thinking of anything but their own desires, certainly not thinking that there might be anything sacred there. In this the new Americans were solidly in the mainstream of Western thought. What is distinctive about Appalachia is not how it differed from the rest of the country, but how it distilled the American experience to moonshine clarity. And how long thc hangover is lasting.

After the first few decades in the mountains, the Presbyterianism that required well-trained and hard-to-get preachers withered. There was a shift to Baptist sects, led by homegrown ministers who sometimes couldn't read the Bible they banged. Literate or not, mountaineers revered the Bible. Tent revivals were added to the seasonal routine. Religion provided one of the few emotional outlets tolerated in a stoic and fatalistic culture. Today, every little community in Appalachia is likely to have two or more churches. Driving through, admiring the one-room white clapboard buildings with their pretty steeples, you might conclude that Appalachian people are all devout. This would be an error. Southern Appalachia ranks as having the highest percentage of "unchurched" people in America. The many tiny chapels testify not to universal attendance but to the contentiousness of congregations over small doctrinal matters.

Surely a spiritual emptiness in the woods contributed to the greatest of Appalachian paradoxes: attachment to place and complicity in its destruction. Mountaineers have been famous for their love of the mountains since the 1840s. In those days, many were caught up in the westward movement to Texas, Oklahoma, Kansas, and Nebraska, but some came back home when they found none of these landscapes to their liking. Throughout the twentieth century, during the many slumps in the coal industry, mountain families poured into the industrial cities of the Midwest. Sometimes they formed enclaves in blue-collar neighborhoods and visited back home every chance they got. During the Great Depression of the 1930s, many returned to chink up old cabins and grow desperation gardens. Somehow, this allegiance didn't translate into an ethic of land stewardship. There must have been individuals who cared deeply about their mountain land, but on a cultural level, sustainable practices didn't evolve. In this respect, Appalachia is a culture that failed. "We love the land," a historian at the University of Kentucky's Appalachian Center told me, "but only for what we can get from it."

I've spent my entire adult life in Appalachia, but I'll always be an outsider. I am unanchored by ancestry here, rooted only by my longing to belong. It is to the woods that I feel most bound. I walk through them slowly, stopping often, looking, listening. At first I was surprised by how noisy it was. Even in the most profoundly quiet moments, something is always going on. Drops of insect excrement and moisture fall in a constant, desultory rain. Insect wings brush leaves. Twigs break off and fall. Leaves whisper. In the forest, serenity is never silent.

For early settlers, a rustle in the leaves could be a turtle, a wild turkey, an Indian fitting an arrow. Wolves howled around the livestock. Would I be ambling along like this, never dreaming of danger from the forest, without the pioneer legacy? Could I head home to lounge on the deck with my feet up in a country less thoroughly tamed?

The clearing where we built our house turned out, to our surprise, to be nearly symmetrical. Before the pines were cut, we hadn't discerned the straight lines of the acre-sized patch in the midst of hardwoods. The low, moss-covered berm of earth around the edges underscores our guess: it was a plowed field, probably for corn. One time when we had Parker Simmons out at our West Virginia property, he pointed to a slope in a tiny hollow above a spring and said, "That grew corn." As it had been for Indians, corn was a staple of mountaineer life. It was grown the way Cherokees and native peoples all over the world have grown food, by slash-and-burn techniques that worked well for centuries where human populations were sparse. The unique Appalachian forest farming system developed by settlers was a masterful synthesis of Old and New Worlds. Trees on part of the most fertile land in creek bottoms and lower slopes were deadened by girdling and then burned. Row crops were planted. When yields declined after three or four years, the land might serve a few years more for pasture or hay cutting.

U.S. Forest Service, National Forests of North Carolina, Asheville, NC

Forest clearings for farming in the southern Appalachians being cultivated and abandoned in rapid succession higher and higher up the slopes. From Message from the president of the United States, transmitting a report of the secretary of agriculture in relation to the forests, rivers, and mountains of the southern Appalachian region, 1902.

Then it was left to grow back into forest. Tulip poplars or Virginia pines spring up quickly in abandoned fields, and nearly pure stands of them in the midst of an otherwise mixed forest usually indicate old fields. In less than sixty years, poplars in particular could refertilize the soil by the transport of nutrients to the surface through their roots and by the decomposition of their fallen leaves. Here was the weak point in the system: an absolute minimum of twenty years of reforestation was necessary before the soil began to recover. Used too soon, it was exhausted, grew ever sparser vegetation, and eroded. By the late 1800s, land was being reused too soon. Loss of landownership to outsiders was one reason. Another was a tremendous growth in population, combined with partible inheritance, the practice of dividing the family farm among all the children. Crop fields were pushed up slopes that were too steep for them. Gullies became common.

For several acres along a gentle bench of land beside our South Creek, one hollow over from the house, the trees are markedly spindly and sparse, with no undergrowth at all. The consulting forester who assessed our woods shortly after we bought them said that it had that cattle-grazed look. Most of a mountain farm typically remained in woods, and livestock was turned out in them. Mountainsides and ridge tops were used as a commons, where community members could graze their livestock for free. Cattle eat all manner of undergrowth. In the southern Appalachians, in wetlands and along streams, river cane provided rich green forage, even in winter. There were also tender saplings, whose demise slowly changed the pattern of forest regeneration. Tramping hooves compacted the soil, making it more difficult for seedlings to take root. Where animals gathered at watering places, they collapsed the stream banks.

National Archives and Records Administration, Still Picture Branch, 95G-247048

Cornfields on steep slopes of mountain farm in Knott County, Kentucky, 1930.

Beef cattle were an early commercial specialty of the mountain valleys here in my neighborhood, on the western fringe of the Shenandoah Valley. The meat fed troops fighting the Indians, French, and British. Farmers first raised their own animals, then began to buy lean cattle from professional drovers who gathered them in Kentucky and Ohio. These were fattened in cornfields in an early, innovative version of feedlots. The first herds of one to two hundred head that traveled to Richmond and Baltimore grew to thousands in the 1800s. Legend has it that the only woman known to work as a drover was Mrs. John Grattan, the wife of a local landowner. She moved cattle by horseback to Philadelphia from Brock's Gap, where the river breaks through the mountain, almost within sight of where I sit. She returned with goods to sell in her husband's store.

Maybe my bench along South Creek served as a cattle feedlot two centuries ago. More likely it was fenced when the free range closed a century ago, and livestock damage was concentrated. There are a few lengths of fence around the property, but I've heard them called pig fences. Two doubled strands of rusted wire braid together the tops and bottoms of short slats of wood. It wasn't cattle but pigs that provided the meat staple in the Appalachian diet, especially after deer and bears were shot out. Mountaineers recognized early that pigs were the best way to take advantage of a unique gift of the Appalachian larder: nuts. Chestnuts, acorns, walnuts, and hickory nuts provided a fantastically fattening source of food. Pigs love nuts and most everything else, including all the small animals whose habitat they root up. Pigs were by far the most numerous livestock in the woods. Every family raised them, notching the ears with their own brand. Pork was eaten fresh, salt-cured, and smoked. Lard flavored most meals. In their own words, mountain people used everything but the squeal. Even today, if you drive around in the autumn after cold weather has set in, you'll see gutted hogs hanging beside many a house and blackened kettles steaming over wood fires.

Pork was also marketable. By the mid-1800s, 150,000 hogs a year traveled the Buncombe Trail from farms in Tennessee and Kentucky along the French Broad River, through Asheville, North Carolina, to the lowland plantations of South Carolina and Georgia. Imagine the smell. Mules, horses, sheep, even turkeys and chickens were herded through the mountains to urban markets. Along the way, particularly where trails crossed rivers, commercial centers developed around stock stands.

To keep their animals from becoming wild and straying during the autumn months in the forest, farmers put salt out regularly. The places where they put it came to be called licks. Holes were sometimes augered in fallen tree trunks to hold the salt. Mountaineers used fire to stimulate grass for livestock grazing.

Fire and grazing are heavily implicated in one of Appalachia's foremost mysteries, the balds. Hundreds of these large, grassy or shrub-covered openings occur on mountaintops from Mount Rogers in Virginia southward. Cherokees incorporated them into legends. Mountaineers drove their livestock up to them for the summer, in a tradition of seasonal highland pasturage that dates back many centuries in Europe. No one is quite sure if the balds were there before people arrived, their trees destroyed by frost, lightning fire, or insects; if Indians cleared them off to attract game for hunting; or if whites did the same to make grazing lands.

At least some balds were definitely created by settlers, confusing the issue. The fact that balds in protected areas such as Great Smoky Mountains National Park are being invaded by forest growth is evidence that grazing at least maintained them, yet their many rare plants suited only to open areas hint at a long period of development. The latest theory is that during the era of glaciers, when the severe climate prevented tree growth, some of the resulting tundralike areas became favorite summer feeding grounds for herbivores, which then perpetuated the open conditions. There would have been the bison, deer, and elk known in historic times, but also ground sloths, musk oxen, mammoths, and mastodons.

Mastodon ribs served as tent poles and the vertebrae made seats for travelers at Big Bone Lick, Kentucky, in 1773. Natural salt springs and outcrops there and in several locations across the Appalachians had attracted animals for eons. They also attracted the attention of settlers, who depended on salt not only to gentle their kine but also to preserve meat through winter. Mining is just as much an Appalachian tradition as are farming and herding, and salt prompted some of the first diggings. Salt from the banks of the Kanawha River in West Virginia, famous for its reddish tinge due to iron, was being commercially produced by the 1790s. Two hundred thousand barrels were coming out of Saltville, Virginia, by the early 1800s. In Clay County, Kentucky, slaves were manufacturing 250,000 barrels a year by 1840.

Iron was essential for kettles to boil down salt brine, for hoes, axes, shovels, plows, barrel hoops, nails, wagon wheels, horseshoes, rifles, and cannonballs. There were many other kinds of mines—copper, lead, zinc, gold, silver, saltpeter, marble, slate, quartz, and porcelain clay—but until the ascendancy of coal, iron is what was mined in Appalachia. Iron ore occurs through much of the mountains. Early settlers were quick to take advantage of it, digging trenches on steep slopes so that there was less overburden to get through. Creeks provided the power to run oak-beam hammers that crushed the hunks of ore, and they also washed the dirt away. Limestone was mined locally to burn with the ore as a flux. The ore was smelted in forges and furnaces whose foundations remain by the score. At least two furnaces within an hour's drive of my house were built before the Revolutionary War. On the other side of Brock's Gap, Mr. Pennybacker built a furnace in 1837. My woods could have been cut several times over for charcoal, though for unknown reasons Mr. Pennybacker's furnace operated for only a year.

U.S. Forest Service, George Washington National Forest, Edinburgh, VA

Charcoal hearth, date unknown, George Washington National Forest, Virginia.

Charcoal provided the heat for smelting. Making it was a valued skill. Trees were cut in winter and seasoned until late spring. Accounts differ as to what kinds of trees were preferred—some liked hickories and hardwoods, others pines and hemlocks. Preferences aside, all trees were generally taken, and the woods were clear-cut. The hearth site was a flat space about forty feet in diameter freed of all brush, stumps, and roots and rendered as smooth and hard as possible. Four-foot lengths of wood were laid upright in tiers to form a mound around a central chimney, itself made of wood and about ten feet high. Air spaces were chinked with small pieces of wood. Leaves and duff from the forest floor were raked into piles, carried to the hearth in baskets, and packed over the mound to a depth of several inches. A shovelful of hot coals from the collier's cooking fire was placed on top of kindling in the chimney. An average hearth of about thirty cords of wood took nearly two weeks to char, during which time the collier lived in a temporary hut and tended the mound to make sure that no live flames broke out.

A good collier could produce up to forty bushels of charcoal from one cord of wood. It took somewhere around four hundred bushels, or roughly ten cords of wood, to produce one ton of pig iron. Most furnaces were small, producing a few hundred tons of pig iron a year, but there were quite a few large ones. One acre of forest could produce about forty cords every thirty years. Every year, in the vicinity of every furnace, from fifty to several hundred acres were clear-cut. It was common for furnaces to go out of business when all the trees within convenient hauling distance were cut. By the early 1800s, tens of thousands of acres had been cleared, crisscrossed with hauling roads, and pocked with mining pits and charcoal hearths. So highly valued was the iron that locally produced bars of it were used as currency.

Leather was as indispensable as iron, and trees were used to make it, too. Tannic acid from the bark of certain kinds of trees was used to tan leather until synthetic chemicals replaced it in the 1940s. Most towns of any size had a tannery. Bark peelers went out in April, just as the buds opened and the sap began to rise. For a few weeks, the bark was tender and pliable. Peelers were mostly local farmers, working their own woods or, after the Civil War, land owned by logging companies and other large holders. They cut the trees down, axed rings around them every four feet, and pried off the bark with a spud iron. The bark was stacked and hauled out when it was convenient to the farmer's schedule through the rest of the year.

U.S. Forest Service, George Washington National Forest, Bridgewater, VA

Remains of Callie Iron Furnace, Botetourt County, Virginia, 1983.

Bark was peeled in the highest, steepest, rockiest places that even mules couldn't reach. The young boys in the bark camps piled up man-sleds made of poles. The slopes were so steep that a wagon left untethered would roll over and kill the horses in front of it. To prevent this from happening, mountaineers used what they called a rough lock, a heavy chain wound through a wheel and a part of the wagon bed, to make the wheel drag. "I've seen ruts that big that rough locks tore out of the ground," said an elderly man near Brock's Gap, spreading his hands a couple of feet, when I talked with him about bark peeling in his youth.

U.S. Forest Service, George Washington National Forest, Bridgewater, VA

Five years' supply of tanbark (thirty-five thousand tons) for Lea & McVitty Tannery, Buena Vista, Virginia, 1939.

At least as early as the 1820s, cartloads of bark were being hauled from the Brock's Gap area to a local tannery. In the one year of 1890, well over a thousand tons of it were harvested from the same vicinity. There were still big trees then, and one good tree could yield a ton or more of bark, but trees as small as eight inches in diameter were also used. Until well into the twentieth century, after timber became scarce, it was customary to leave the naked logs to rot in the woods. The species good for bark weren't generally valuable for lumber. Hemlocks, red and black oaks, and chestnut trees were used to some extent, and after the chestnut blight arrived in the 1910s, the wood of chestnut trees was scavenged for its tannic extract. By far the most widely preferred species, though, was chestnut oak. "They got about all the chestnut oak around here," remembered the old man. "I reckon they about cleaned it out."

Contrary to the implications of this—that such heavy cutting must have wiped out the chestnut oak—chestnut oaks may have increased as a result of being cut so heavily. Many species of trees, especially conifers, don't sprout well from stumps, but chestnut oaks do so prolifically. The bark is fairly thick, so it was better than thin-skinned maple, hemlock, birch, or beech at withstanding the many fires of those days. It grows well on poor sites. A survey in 1940 found that chestnut oak was the single most abundant tree throughout all of western Virginia. My hundred acres are studded with three- and four-stemmed stump-sprouted chestnut oaks.

SPECIAL COLLECTIONS AND ARCHIVES, UNIVERSITY OF KENTUCKY LIBRARIES, PA91M2

Mouth of Beaver Creek, Floyd County, Kentucky, 1910. Logs heading down the Big Sandy to Catlettsburg, where a dollar a tree was the going price. Catlettsburg was at the time considered the largest hardwood market in the world.

Black walnut and black cherry were always the most prized species for furniture. Chestnut wood was used in fences and buildings because of its highly rot-resistant character. Tulip poplar and white oak were sawed into boards for construction and flooring. Farmers picked the trees they wanted and dragged them out with oxen or horses. Probably a dozen water-powered sawmills were operating in the eastern counties of West Virginia by 1775, and their number steadily increased. By the mid-1800s, mountaineers were cutting the best trees along major watercourses and floating them, tied into rafts, to settlements and sawmills downstream. Rafts were fastened together at first by poles and wooden pins, later by chains and nails. The largest rafts had over a hundred logs and sometimes carried a small shelter. Twenty- to fifty-foot oars were used for steering. Hundreds of boats made from tulip poplars carried cargoes of flour and whiskey.

It was dangerous work, and many logs were stranded and lost along the way, but it was lucrative. After loading themselves down with store-bought goods from the valley trading centers, mountain men walked back home. By the 1890s, logs were being floated out of most of the mountain counties throughout central and southern Appalachia. Logging their trees became an important seasonal source of income for many mountaineer families. Still, the forest was only dented, not broken; seventy-five percent of Appalachia remained forested in 1900.

The first timber scouts who traveled through the mountains on horseback after the Civil War represented lumber barons from the North. These businessmen had honed their pillaging skills in New England and the Great Lakes forests and were eager to exercise them elsewhere. Investors in Cincinnati, Philadelphia, New York, and even in Canada, Scotland, and England were attracted. The largest of the many companies that formed often bought land outright, but smaller companies preferred to buy only the right to cut trees and thereby avoid any involvement with land taxes. Fifty cents a foot across the stump was a good price, and many trees were sold for less than a dollar.

Industrial-strength lumbering began around 1880. At first it was selective. An 1889 deed in Kentucky specified, "40,000 poplar and whiteoak trees, each of said trees to measure not less than 30 inches in diameter under the bark, stump high, measuring three feet above the ground, without fire damage or blemish; and the grantee shall have two years after the date hereof to mark said trees with its brand." By 1895, the usual cutting limit was twenty-four inches on the stump. By 1900, it had dropped to twenty-one inches; by 1905, fourteen inches; and by 1930, trees ten inches on the stump were cut for lumber, even though handling such small logs resulted in losses for the mill.

Early contracts depended on the seller's delivering the trees to the mill. To get giants out of the interior forests before railroads came, tram roads of thick hardwood planks were laid across heavy stringers. This provided footing for draft animals. Wooden rails were added, and logs were loaded on trucks with iron wheels, still pulled by animals. Water remained the favorite transportation, and any choice trees remaining along rivers were quickly cut. To utilize streams too small to carry logs, mountaineers built splash dams. These were made of earth or saplings, some with a pole gate, that backed up water for several acres to a depth over a man's head. Logs were piled in the creekbed between dams. When a heavy rain came, the gates were pulled or the dams dynamited. The fierce ramming of water and logs scoured the streambanks. Our West Virginia property shows another technique: chestnut logs were laid as skids across a stream bottom so small that a fox could cross it and keep his paws dry. Worn down in the middle, the logs are otherwise still solid.

Forest Service Historic Photograph Collection, #55746, Special Collections, National Agricultural Library, Beltsville, MD

J. M. Henderson & Company's camp at the mouth of Pine Creek, Logan County, West Virginia, 1904. A big dam was planned at the junction of Big Island and Pine Creek (in middle distance) to carry the logs out in the winter floods.

Logs were caught by booms where the creeks entered large streams and held until huge piles accumulated for a drive. One of the most famous log-driving streams was the Greenbrier River of West Virginia. The St. Lawrence Boom and Manufacturing Company started buying tracts of white pines in Pocahontas County in 1874. By the mid-1880s, fifteen million board feet (a board foot is one foot square by one inch thick) of white pine and a million board feet of hemlock a year were being floated down to Ronceverte, followed by arks of logs a hundred feet long equipped with bunkhouses and kitchens. For the week or two of the drive, most of it spent soaked and chilled, men freed up logs caught along the banks and broke up logjams. Not all of it was lumber; pulp mills also began to utilize the smaller trees.

Ronceverte had one of the largest examples of the portable, circular-saw, steam-powered sawmills that facilitated early logging. Already by 1835, there were fifteen such mills in operation in West Virginia, and West Virginia was a microcosm of the rest of Appalachia. By 1880, most of the state's 472 mills were equipped with circular saws. In 1883, at 250 horsepower, the mill at Ronceverte was sawing 120,000 board feet per day. The next year it was converted to a more efficient band saw, capable of 250,000 feet per day. The Tygart River Lumber Co. was one of three band saws operating out of Millcreek, West Virginia, around 1900. Our property lies above the Tygart River, and it was probably for that company that Parker Simmons worked in his youth.

U.S. Forest Service, National Forests of North Carolina, Asheville, NC

Oxen hauling lumber, ca. 1920, Nantahala National Forest, North Carolina.

Railroads had begun to penetrate the mountains before the Civil War. The Baltimore and Ohio, Louisville and Nashville, Shenandoah Valley Railroad, Western North Carolina Railroad, and hundreds, perhaps thousands, of others are remembered now only in old songs, if at all. The lines moved deeper and deeper into Appalachia. Railroad owners often bought land along their way. Tracts of twenty thousand to three hundred thousand acres were accumulated, sold, and resold. Coal speculation was combined with lumber. Lumber capitalists financed logging spur lines off railroad branches, rails that could be picked up and moved as the cut progressed. After 1880, the Shay and Climax engines, with gearing systems that allowed much more flexible maneuvering on mountainsides, became widely available. Companies brought in sawmills, set up timber camps, and assembled logging crews from local farmers and from as far away as Pennsylvania. Many hundreds of boom towns popped up across Appalachia, and the systematic cutting of trees began.

U.S. Forest Service, National Forests of North Carolina, Asheville, NC

Eroded Appalachian mountain field. From Message from the president of the United States, transmitting a report of the secretary of agriculture in relation to the forests, rivers, and mountains of the southern Appalachian region, 1902.

So quickly did it progress that in 1899 the Appalachian National Park Association was organized by prominent citizens in Asheville,

U.S. Forest Service, National Forests of North Carolina, Asheville, NC

Sawmill on Wayah Creek, Nantahala National Forest, North Carolina, 1925.

North Carolina, with members from many states. It petitioned Congress for the preservation of the Great Smokies and the Black Mountains. In these ranges were the highest mountains in the East. The botanical richness of the forest silva, its rare natural beauty, the importance of headwater streams to mitigate floods and droughts, the health-restoring capacity of the mountains, and their central location within reach of millions were all cited as justification. In addition, the petition noted, "Easterners are entitled to a national park." The American Forestry Association, the National Board of Trade, the American Association for the Advancement of Science, and the Appalachian Mountain Club (a New England organization) passed resolutions in support. Congress responded by appropriating money to investigate the conditions of the southern Appalachians. Secretary of Agriculture James Wilson submitted the report to President Theodore Roosevelt in 1902.

The Geological Survey examined an area greater than five million acres between the New River Gap in Virginia and the Hiwassee River in western North Carolina and northern Georgia. Away from the railroads, the forest was still largely unbroken. There were places covered with a "spongy mass of humus sometimes a foot and more in thickness, and over this in turn a luxuriant growth of shrubs and flowers and ferns."

In the more settled regions, land had been cleared on slopes with a pitch of thirty and forty degrees. Gullies were visible for miles, and in the face of such erosion, the report noted that "hardwoods do not readily regain their footing." Woodlands connected with farms had already been mostly cut over, and were covered with second growth.

"The lumberman," continued the report, "is yearly going further in the forests. . . . Unnecessary damage to the forest and total lack of provision for a future crop is characteristic of the lumbering now carried on in this region. Logging operations have generally shown an inexcusable slovenliness." Cutting went on year-round instead of only when mountaineers could take time off from their farming, which was when the ground was frozen, so the loose earth was trampled and torn. It wasn't exactly clear-cutting, because at the time, only the most marketable trees were cut, but five or ten years later, others became worth getting. Trees were felled without concern for the saplings and seedlings they crushed. Trunks were dragged out any which way, gouging deep channels that rainstorms turned into rivulets of silt. On the highest and steepest slopes, logs were often rolled from top to bottom. A sixteen-foot-long, three-foot-wide log could gain enough momentum to crush even fair-sized trees and leave a track like a tornado.

Worst of all were the fires. Like the Cherokees, mountaineers burned the woods regularly. But whereas the Cherokees generally moved their villages after a generation or two, the mountaineers burned the same places through many generations. Fire scorched the butts of timber trees so that fungal rots could attack, diminishing the value for lumber. Fire consumed the leaf layer and exposed soil to the impact of raindrops. Eventually it destroyed the very forage plants that mountaineers wanted to encourage. Still, their fires tended to be low to the ground and not very intense. The heaviest impacts would have been around the farms; the fires were kept from spreading far by the moisture characteristic of Appalachian forests.

Loggers left treetops and branches scattered everywhere, and when these dried, they fueled much hotter, higher burns. Steam locomotives, skidders, loaders, and mills threw sparks constantly. The Geological Survey team found evidence of fire over more than four million acres in 1902; seventy-eight thousand acres had recently burned so severely that most of the trees had been killed. For many decades, fire scars were the

U.S. Forest Service, National Forests of North Carolina, Asheville, NC

Cutover slope of Mount Mitchell following wildfire, 1923. Red spruce were logged to supply wood for aircraft in World War I.

plague of the Appalachian hardwood lumber industry. The cycles of cutting and the subsequent fires shifted the former patterns of reproduction. Several oak species that prefer full sunlight for germinating seedlings and have relatively thick bark, particularly scarlet oak, began to compose a greater proportion of the forest. Clear-cuts became dominated by yellow poplars, which grew more densely than before. Hemlocks and red spruce, vulnerable to the drying out of logged soil, declined dramatically. In the southern Appalachians, rhododendrons and laurel crowded so thickly in some burned places that trees couldn't push through. Such places were called laurel hells. The 1902 report by the Geological Survey described whole mountainsides covered by scraggly forests choked with brush:

> In some cases, on steep, rocky slopes with thin soil, loss of humus has resulted in washing and leaching away of soils to such an extent as to destroy the forests entirely. Also storage of water from soils from which humus has been removed is far less perfect than in the original.

> [It is] a losing proposition to ask lumbermen to reduce present profits to insure a second crop of timber. The home and permanent interests of the lumberman are generally in another state or region, and his interest in these mountains begins and ends with the hope of profit. There is, however, no evidence that the native lumberman has in the past exhibited any different spirit.
>
> The rapid rate at which these lumbering operations have extended during the past few years and the still more rapid rate at which they are being extended at the present time . . . indicates that within less than a decade every mountain cove will have been invaded and robbed of its finest timber, and the last of the remnants of these grand primeval Appalachian forests will have been destroyed.

U.S. Forest Service, George Washington National Forest, Buena Vista, VA

Erosion gullies in the George Washington National Forest, Virginia, 1937.

And that's pretty much what happened. The movement for a national park in the Great Smokies didn't become effective for another quarter of a century. "Cut out and get out" was the way one lumberman described the prevailing attitude. There were outcries on a national level, but business interests prevailed in federal, state, and county governments—and in the woods. More than a billion board feet of lumber came out of the area now encompassed in Great Smoky Mountains National

Park. West Virginia was nearly denuded as more than eighty-five percent of its forestland was cut. The peak lumbering year was 1909, when hardwood lumber from mountain forests from Maryland to northern Georgia totaled four billion board feet. By 1930, this had fallen by almost half.

U.S. Forest Service, National Forests of North Carolina, Asheville, NC

Trainload of spruce logs crossing wooden trestle, Pisgah National Forest, North Carolina, 1922.

It wasn't only outside voices that were raised in protest. From one valley to the next, opinions differed. Where one locale might welcome a proposed railroad, the neighboring one might reject it. Farmers feared loss of livestock on the tracks, which did happen. Others objected to the smoke, noise, and hurrying that railroads brought, associating them with an undesirable northern way of life. But except for a Baptist preacher and novelist named Dr. A. E. Brown, few mountaineers seemed to give much thought to what was happening to the forest itself. In 1910, the Reverend Dr. Brown described "areas containing hundreds of acres of lands which used to be most fertile and valuable, and which are now practically worthless . . . those [people] left behind will have to bear the brunt of this."

The brunt consisted of collapse of their economic mainstay, traditional forest farming. There were no nut trees for pigs, and even if there had been, mountaineers didn't own much of the land anymore. They were now a dependent people. Their land was literally in smoking ruins around them. But not until decades later, after hundreds of thousands of strip-mined acres finally outraged a critical mass of mountaineers, did a native Appalachian movement for land protection arise.

Like timber, coal was exploited from the earliest days of settlement, but in a geographically restricted area. In the Cumberlands and Alleghenies of southern West Virginia, southwestern Virginia, and eastern Kentucky, coal has been mined since the 1790s. At first it was floated to market on rafts. By the 1830s, thousands of tons a year were being dug from the banks of the Cumberland River for use in iron foundries in Nashville. When development of the railroads made transportation easier, coal from the southern Appalachians became competitive with that from the Midwest, largely due to the comparatively low wages paid to mountaineer miners.

Special Collections and Archives, University of Kentucky Libraries, Harry and Anne Caudill Collection, "My Land Is Dying" folder

Attempt to control erosion on a strip mine in eastern Kentucky, ca. 1960s.

To obtain the mineral rights from owners of the lands, coal companies often used a type of deed known as a broad-form. It conveyed not only ownership of the coal but also the right to mine it in any way convenient. Many of the mountaineers who signed their spidery Xs couldn't read the large, much less the fine, print. The mines with which they were familiar were tunnels dug sideways into hillsides. Called drift mines, these

Special Collections and Archives, University of Kentucky Libraries, Harry and Anne Caudill Collection, "Strip Mining Photographs by Bob Gomel" folder

Strip mine, eastern Kentucky, ca. 1960s.

didn't involve wholesale removal of broad belts of earth, like mechanized strip mining later did. Even before the Civil War, though, mule-drawn steel scrapers were being used to strip away ground over a seam. A steam-powered shovel that could lift a cubic yard at a gulp was operating in eastern Kentucky by 1905.

During the 1930s, the federal Tennessee Valley Authority (TVA) built hydropower plants on the western boundary of the Appalachians. The demand for electricity soon exceeded capacity, and TVA built coal-burning plants as well. Appalachian strip mining increased dramatically. Whole mountains were leveled in layers, their trees pushed over by bulldozers, their creeks choked with silt and coal dust, their soil exposed to landslide rains. Family cemeteries were not spared. Sometimes an entire farm would be reduced to an island around the house, with everything else cut away around it. Mountaineers began to protest and caught the attention of the mainstream press. Scenes of Appalachian pathos filtered into the news. One of the most poignant was a picture of a tiny, bent woman named Widow Combs testifying before the Kentucky legislature in 1956, after being arrested for lying down in front of bulldozers.

Laws requiring reclamation of strip-mined land were finally passed in the 1970s. From our West Virginia meadow we can look over to green grass growing on giant steps notched into Elk Mountain, where a smoothly mounded silhouette used to be. Trees may never grow well there again, or on hundreds of thousands of other strip-mined acres.

The peak coal production years were the early 1920s. Thousands of mountaineer families moved to coal camps, where they met thousands of white and olive-skinned laborers imported from eastern Europe and black laborers enticed or kidnapped from the South. The life of the camps was smoky, dreary, and miserably poor, but it was a living for many. Then the Great Depression set in early and long in the coalfields, followed by a long-term, declining boom-and-bust rhythm. During booms, any remaining timber on the mountains was cut for mine posts. During busts, entire mountain communities moved out in search of jobs elsewhere. World War II demand for timber and new mines finished off nearly all that was left of the Great Forest.

It lay in pieces across the ragged mountains, its structure wrenched apart, its drainage system fouled, its foundation weakened. Ditto for mountain society. Whatever its brutalities, mountain life had been fulfilling, dignified, and tranquil. Most of all, in the bountiful, forgiving Appalachians it had had the great promise of sustainability. Left alone to mellow, maybe mountaineers would have come to see themselves reflected in the land more clearly. Adaptable as they were, maybe they would have been willing to change, to find a true harmony. As it is, their legacy of logging roads is slashed into my hillsides. In winter, snow whitens them like the buzzard down Indians used to stuff into wounds. In summer, I stroll down them and wonder, what was it like? What might have been, had history been gentler here? The Great Forest is so tormentingly close and so achingly unrecoverable. Never to hug a giant tree, never to hear a wolf howl in these humbled hills of mine, leaves me with an emptiness outlined by the harsh light of hindsight. Who is to blame—the callous mountaineers? The greedy capitalists and their furred and feathered wives? A heedless society? Even I, so far as I enjoy the fruits of all their labors, am complicit. But surely the pioneers could have sunk roots to produce something sweeter than this bitter aftertaste of frontier.

I hike past the stunted oaks on the old cattle loafing grounds and try to let my anger swirl away on the splashing current of South Creek. Remnants, regrets, and rage: these are the three Rs of the Appalachian past.

OUT OF THE CRADLE OF FORESTRY

POLITICIANS AND FEDERAL BUREAUCRATS CAME TO THE RESCUE OF THE devastated Appalachians. Through fair means and foul, they acquired nearly seven million acres in the name of the nation. It amounted to less than twenty percent of the mountains, but it proved enough to keep the wild heart of Appalachia beating.

Appalachian forests were hardly the first to be exploited. New England, the Great Lakes, and the South were all ravaged, but by a quirk of history it was timber destruction in the West that prompted the creation of forest reserves. After 1776, as the American government purchased or conquered the area west of the Appalachians, those lands became public domain. Various laws were enacted to survey them and make them available for purchase by farmers. No provision was made for timbering. Unauthorized logging on the public domain in the Old Southwest—Alabama and Mississippi—led to the Timber Trespass Act of 1831, the nation's first general law for forest conservation. The problem continued as waves of settlement moved west. Word began to filter back to the nation's capital about huge commercial operations stealing lumber from government land. Stories of fake claims, such as dragging a boat on wheels across dry land to qualify for swampland benefits, circulated in the halls of Congress.

The idea of forest reserves first surfaced in the 1870s. Then, as now, western interests resisted all efforts to protect land from exploitation. For decades, the democratic process made it possible to delay a decision through endless investigations, surveys, committees to gather information, and debates in Congress. It was only through political maneuvering that legislation was passed in 1891 authorizing the president to set aside forest reserves from the public domain. Within a year, President Benjamin Harrison had created fifteen reserves containing thirteen million acres. The idea of environmental conservation had been born, but it was still formless. No one knew what to do with forest reserves. For advice, Americans turned to the Germans.

Forestry as a science had been invented in eighteenth-century Germany, where woodlands were cut so destructively that they turned into heaths. Lacking wood even to keep warm, Germans were forced into rehabilitating their landscapes. They devised the practice of silviculture, the growing of trees for repeated harvests, with typical German obsession with precision and control. I can make this slur with impunity, because Germany happens to be the part of the Old World I come from.

American forestry was born in an Appalachian log cabin built in the fashion of Germany's Black Forest. It looked to me like a perfect blend of styles for the setting when I visited the Cradle of Forestry Historic Site in Pisgah National Forest near Asheville, North Carolina. A long, low visitor's center sat in front of breastlike little mountain peaks. A thunderstorm the night before had knocked out the power, and the displays on national forest history were pretty dim. A few glints of ambient light on a metallic surface caught my eye. It was an eight-foot circular saw, a relic of the Meadow River Lumber Company in Rainelle, West Virginia, which had once been the country's largest hardwood manufacturing plant.

I walked outside onto the Campus Trail. Intense sun blazed in small clearings along the way, but in the dense green of surrounding woods, it diffused into a golden haze. Although national forests originated in the West, the idea and practice of forestry as a way to manage them began here, on abused land bought for a song by a rich man. George Vanderbilt, of a fabulously wealthy railroad family, decided in the 1880s to make a showpiece estate in the southern mountains. Through agents, he purchased many different tracts of logged woods and abandoned farms that eventually totaled over a hundred thousand acres. Most of it lay in the still-forested mountains south of Asheville, but Vanderbilt also acquired 8,000 acres just outside the town on which to build the castle called

Biltmore House. "Except in a few inaccessible spots, there was not a tree left on the entire Biltmore estate that was fit for . . . lumber," wrote Vanderbilt's second forester, Carl Alwin Schenck, who arrived in 1895 from Darmstadt, near Germany's Black Forest.

But that's a little ahead of the story. The first forester Vanderbilt hired was Gifford Pinchot. Pinchot was one of a trio of men who established forestry in America, and the only one who wasn't German. Scion of a wealthy manufacturing family in Connecticut, he began his education in private academies in the Northeast. To pursue forestry, he traveled to Europe and found a German mentor, because there was no curriculum offered anywhere in the United States. When George Vanderbilt hired him, Pinchot became the first professional American forester.

Restless, always looking for new challenges, Pinchot stayed at Biltmore for only three years, just long enough to build wicker fences to control erosion and begin some selective harvesting. He then opened an office in New York City as a consultant. Corporate and individual owners of extensive forestlands in the Adirondacks and Pennsylvania paid him to prepare management plans. His experience convinced him that the federal government had an obligation to protect forests and other natural resources from exhaustion by the private sector. It was a crucial lesson for his later career.

Before he left Biltmore, through his connections in Germany, Pinchot recommended Schenck as his successor. Schenck held the position for fourteen years. Trained in Europe's woodlands, which have much less diversity of species and terrain, he tried various experiments to improve the unfamiliar Appalachian forest. Some of them failed completely, such as planting acorns to start an oak forest, which proved instead to be a highly successful means for fattening field mice. Whatever he learned, he passed on to his students.

One of Schenck's major accomplishments was the establishment of the first school of forestry in America. It was the black-topped Campus Trail of this school that I was now treading. In the shade, the temperature dropped to almost chilly. The path traveled through a scattered group of mountain cabins and farms that had once been part of a community called Pink Beds. The Scots-Irish term for flower was "pink," and they named this area for its rhododendron and mountain laurel blooms. Mixed among the older buildings were some that Schenck had built. They had the steep roofs and curved beams typical of his homeland and the dovetail corners and chestnut wood native to the Appalachians.

From 1898 to 1913, Schenck graduated more than three hundred students from a curriculum that was evenly divided between fieldwork and classroom study. Most of his students were the sons of wealthy landowners. They boarded in local homes or fixed up abandoned cabins for their summer months in the Cradle of Forestry, then known as Vanderbilt's Pisgah Forest (named for a biblical reference). Six days a week they attended lectures in the morning. The schoolhouse was set in a forest that was, when I visited, in the last blush of spring, with a few blossoms still smiling here and there. Glossy-leaved rhododendron and laurel were thick, and there were many kinds of trees in all stages of life. The schoolhouse was wood framed and sided, with desk pews and a handsome fireplace at the front.

Schenck taught selective tree cutting and thinning aimed at improving the growth of remaining trees. He clear-cut pines to favor hardwoods where possible, but also planted pines to cover eroding fields. He taught how to monitor pests and diseases and make harvesting decisions that saved as much timber as possible. He taught erosion control, measurement of lumber, and—most emphatically of all—the economics of harvesting. He believed in a system of privately owned forests and educated his students in a forestry designed to yield private profits. There was a little bit of graffiti above the schoolhouse fireplace: a dollar sign had been made out of the first letter of Schenck's name. It was here that the sons of timber barons learned to recalculate the bottom line from cut out and get out to cut and grow and cut again.

By showing how economical the practice of conservative forestry could be, Schenck hoped to smooth the ruffled feathers of lumber businessmen, whose feelings were hurt when the government accused them of irresponsible behavior. At the same time, Schenck was proposing the most breathtaking idea for an Appalachian national park that anyone has ever put forward: all lands above two thousand feet in elevation, from Philadelphia to Atlanta. Schenck's own estimate was fifty million acres. He envisioned government programs in timber conservation in which private owners would be invited to participate and showered with benefits if they did. To my everlasting regret, no one has ever paid the least attention to his idea.

After their morning lectures, Schenck's students grabbed a quick lunch at the commissary a hundred yards down the trail—cheese, crackers, and cans of meat and peaches. They spent the rest of the day in the field, applying in practice what Schenck taught in theory. Schenck was full of energy and enthusiasm, and his boys loved him. They also made the most out of being there. They were required to keep their own horses for transportation to their fieldwork, and they could easily ride down to the small town called Pisgah Forest and carry back a keg of beer. "In Schenck we trust / In booze we bust," declared more graffiti. In his memoirs, Schenck remarked upon the difference in alcohol habits between his own German countrymen and Americans. He noted particularly that although German peasants drank plenty of beer, it didn't interfere with their abilities as forest workers the way that moonshine rendered some mountaineers undependable.

I walked through the Hiram King home, built in 1882 and one of the original houses of the Pink Beds community. Mossy cedar shakes curled up from the roof. After Vanderbilt bought it, Schenck assigned the house to one of the rangers who guarded the estate against fire and poachers. The house was dark and cool, although it stood in bright sun at the edge of a tiny bit of lawn. The furnishings were elegantly simple. One room was filled with a quilting loom hung with a nearly finished spread, lovely and refined.

Farther down the trail was Schenck's office, a two-room building that was formerly half of a tobacco barn. Unfamiliar with the relatively mild climate of the Appalachians, Schenck insisted that mountain winters always had lots of snow, so his buildings had steep roofs to slough it off. His secretary and bookkeeper worked in the tiny front room, where an ancient typewriter remained. In the back was Schenck's desk, one of those that have cubbyholes at eye level. It was my last stop on the Campus Trail, and it left me with some faint vibration of the driving force of the man.

Schenck and Pinchot eventually fell out over points of forestry philosophy, and both of them dickered on and off with Bernhard E. Fernow, the third member of the first foresters trio. Fernow was a highly educated but thin-skinned Prussian who came to America in 1876 to attend one of this country's first forestry conferences. He fell in love with an American and stayed to marry his sweetheart. He gained experience in American forests by managing private woodlands such as Cooper Hewitt and Company's fifteen thousand acres in Pennsylvania, which were harvested for charcoal. In 1886, he was appointed chief of the Division of Forestry in the U.S. Department of Agriculture (USDA). He brought to that recently established division the idea of sustained yield, in which timber harvests are calculated not to exceed annual tree growth. It was largely through Fernow's efforts that the legislation to establish federal forest reserves finally passed through Congress.

Eventually, his Old World sensitivity to real and imagined slights rendered him unsuitable for rough-and-tumble American politics. After a dozen years in office, he was fired. Gifford Pinchot, who a few years earlier had left the Biltmore Estate to the ministrations of Carl Schenck, took Fernow's place as chief of the USDA Forestry Division in 1898.

President Theodore Roosevelt (1901-1909) is well known for his great crusade for the conservation of natural resources that so dramatically affected American politics at the close of the nineteenth century. But much of the advice that Roosevelt acted on came from his good friend and boxing partner Gifford Pinchot. Pinchot was the founder—would it be too metaphorical to say father?—of the U.S. Forest Service. Before he himself fell from political favor, after Roosevelt's term of office ended in 1909, Pinchot established the ranger system and the esprit de corps that still characterize the agency. He advertised cleverly and widely about the need for forest conservation, establishing it in the public mind as a good thing. He believed that the federal government should offer a model for private forestry, and developed programs that applied some of Schenck's ideas about enlisting private forest owners in cooperative management ventures with the government. Then, as now, private property rights were held up like the Holy Grail in arguments against laws governing timbering on private land.

In the tradition of Schenck, Pinchot believed that forests should be conserved in order to best produce whatever human society needed at the time. He once accompanied John Muir, the famous preservationist and founder of the Sierra Club, on a western trek. Muir argued passionately for leaving natural systems alone; Pinchot spoke with just as much ardor for using them efficiently. The tension between the two philosophies eventually broke up the friendship when the men took opposing sides in a controversy over building a dam in Hetch Hetchy Canyon in California.

The national forests that Pinchot organized after he became chief in 1898 were located in the West, because they were created from land already owned by the federal government. Nothing authorized the purchase of private lands for reserves, as was necessary in the Appalachians. Yet agitation for the purchase of public land in southern Appalachia and in the White Mountains of New Hampshire had begun soon after the 1891 law that established reserves in the public domain. By 1903, the Appalachian National Park Association changed its name to the Appalachian National Forest Reserve Association and reoriented its lobbying efforts.

During the first decade of the twentieth century, nearly fifty bills for an Appalachian forest reserve were introduced in Congress. Debates raged over states' rights and the constitutionality of federal land purchases. But Appalachian mountain lands were in such bad condition that one by one the states agreed to allow their purchase by the feds. The timber companies saw their chance to get rid of tracts from which they had already removed everything of potential value for the next half century or that remained so rugged and remote that they weren't worth the expense of cutting. These were called, by later historians, "the lands nobody wanted."

Arguments then grew heated over just how necessary forests really were for regulating stream flow and weather. The Asheville-based group promoting a forest reserve traveled to Washington to make a presentation to the House Agriculture Committee. They took a model: two six-foot-high mountains with slopes of thirty degrees and natural contours. One mountain was left bare. The other was covered with a layer of sponge about four inches thick, over which was spread moss stuck with small twigs of evergreens. Someone climbed a stepladder with a watering can. Drops that fell on the bare mountain ran off with a gush, showing how lowland rivers would be forced out of their banks. Drops on the covered mountain soaked in and ran out much more slowly. Gifford Pinchot used a similar technique at congressional committee meetings, pouring water alternately on a smooth picture of denuded lands and on a blotter.

Congress remained unconvinced until the floods of 1907. Millions of dollars worth of damage along the Monongahela and Ohio Rivers was traced back to the cutover conditions of the upper watershed in West Virginia. The West Virginia state legislature was the first to vote to approve federal purchase of private woodlands. Floods in other watersheds destroyed smaller valley towns and left ruinous cobble on valley bottom farms. Formerly navigable streams were silting up, and streams that once flowed dependably were drying up.

Problems originating in headwater areas affected many states, Forest Service Chief Pinchot pointed out, and it was in the national interest for the federal government to help resolve them. Pinchot was out of office by the time the Weeks Act of 1911 authorized federal purchase of forests to protect the headwaters of navigable streams, but the Forest Service he had organized was ready to act. The immediate goal was to acquire millions of acres in the southern Appalachians.

Not incidentally, the Weeks Act required the Forest Service to pay a form of tax to the counties in which the federal government owned land. The annual payment was to be five percent of timber sales. Otherwise, counties would lose all revenues from land that was purchased for the national forests. Five percent was soon changed to twenty-five percent, to provide greater compensation. But with the forests so depleted, it was years before many counties would realize money from Forest Service timber sales, and even then, the payments fluctuated too wildly for any kind of financial planning. Loss of income from taxes became a vocal complaint in some communities as Forest Service acreage began to accumulate.

Influenced by Pinchot's conviction that the people living closest to the national forests should be happy with them, the Forest Service decided at the beginning to purchase land only from willing sellers. It was a critical move. Condemnation to force transfer of ownership was used later by the National Park Service to establish the Great Smoky Mountains and Shenandoah National Parks. It was also used by the TVA to build dams that flooded thousands of family farms across the southwestern edge of Appalachia. Condemnation was a legal right of government that condemned those agencies to the undying hatred of the ousted mountain people. The Forest Service, however, advertised in local newspapers for willing sellers of land within areas it designated as purchase units.

The earliest Forest Service purchases were mostly high-elevation slopes and ridges above the larger watercourses, toward the goal of protecting navigable streams. In 1924, the Clarke-McNary Act approved federal purchase of land for timber production, enlarging the scope of acquisitions. Upon receiving offers to sell, Forest Service employees embarked on a lengthy process. First the land was surveyed and, if found suitable for purchase, recommended to the National Forest Commission, which met twice a year. Once approval was obtained, the task of clearing the legal title began.

Within two months of the passage of the Weeks Law in 1911, well over a million acres in the Appalachians had been offered to the Forest Service. Most were tracts of tens of thousands of acres from timber companies, but the first eastern national forest to be established came from George Vanderbilt's holdings. In 1916, President Woodrow Wilson proclaimed Pisgah Forest, where Pinchot and Schenck had made the first attempts at forestry, the Pisgah National Forest. Vanderbilt died before negotiations to sell his property were finalized, and his widow Edith completed the sale of 86,700 acres at a price of $5 an acre.

That was steep for the Forest Service. It bought millions of other acres for less. By the time the stock market crashed in 1929, just over four million acres in Appalachia were held by eight national forests. As ripples from the crash flattened even the Appalachian backwoods economy through the 1930s, rangers increasingly bought small tracts from people who were abandoning mountain farms. Decades later, former owners still looked back with resentment at the low prices the Forest Service had paid. Sometimes Forest Service officers bought farms that were being auctioned for nonpayment of taxes. This didn't sit well with some mountaineers, who muttered about a government conspiracy to get them out of the mountains.

They were exactly right. There was an entire agency created by President Franklin Roosevelt during the depression that was dedicated to removing people permanently from the poorest agricultural lands. Ownership of those lands was then to be diffused among other government agencies, for parks and national forests. The steep, eroded fields of Appalachia seemed a logical place to start. In 1934, the Agricultural Adjustment Administration sent out federal agents to buy most of the land in four mountain counties in Kentucky. Some of the agents were quite familiar with the country already because they had worked there for years as revenuers, searching out and destroying moonshine stills. Mountain families greeted the agents with suspicion. They showed reluctance to trust the government to provide a profitable farm in return for a poor one. And they were cautious about selling their land before their neighbors did, which would drive the price of their neighbors' land higher than their own. These factors scuttled the idea. The final result was the purchase of a few mountain farms, later to become Kentucky Ridge State Forest, and the displacement of hundreds of families who never got much compensation.

In other areas, there was no hesitation about selling. The Forest Service purchase records for Cross Mountain, where I live, echo the experience of thousands of Appalachian landowners. My hundred acres lie just inside a Forest Service purchase unit boundary. Behind it, up the eastern slope and cutting across the flank of Cross Mountain in a long rectangle, was a tract of about a thousand acres owned by a Mr. Riddel. Sometime during the 1920s, Mr. Riddel offered his land to what was then Shenandoah National Forest. Perhaps because it was swamped with work clearing land titles, the Forest Service failed to act promptly, and Mr. Riddel died. The file opens with a letter of January 1929, nine months before the stock market crashed. It is from the forest supervisor to Mr. Riddel's son, who lived in a small town twenty-five miles from Cross Mountain. The supervisor offered to buy the property from the Riddel estate at $4.25 an acre.

Things continued to move slowly, and the next several letters date from the summer of 1931. Just as the district ranger had secured the agreement of the several Riddel heirs to sell, the assistant regional forester reviewed the report on the Riddel land. The soil value for 450 acres of lower slope had been set too high, he decided. And while the 70 acres of "medium burn . . . is now recovering . . . we should not overlook the fact that burns on the upper slope will recover slowly." The little bit of merchantable timber was scattered in three different places, he noted, requiring three mills. He dropped the purchase price to $3.25 an acre. On the bottom of this official letter, the district ranger had penned, "Guess will not stand much chance to get this tract now." Chances must have looked even slimmer in 1933, when the Forest Service dropped the price to $2.75, apparently because of falling land values across the entire nation. In 1935, the sale was finally concluded at that price, but only after two conflicting ownership claims had been settled in court.

There is one more matter covered in the file. From the beginning, the Forest Service tried to accommodate people who lived on or near national forest lands. Moonshine stills, when discovered, were usually left strictly alone, despite the legal obligation of the Forest Service to report them. Many special-use permits were given out for free or for small fees to local people who were accustomed to making use of the woods. In 1942, the Forest Service granted a lifetime reservation of four acres from the Riddel land to Mr. J. A. Mumbert, unmarried. In return, Mr. Mumbert was required to take all reasonable precautions to prevent and suppress forest fire. His acreage was enclosed by a fence; the purpose of his request was for cultivation. I once stumbled across the remains of a split-rail chestnut fence that snaked straight up Cross Mountain, with locust trees and other signs of an old field on one side of it. The file ends with a notice that J. A. Mumbert died at 2:30 P.M. on February 13, 1949. "This reservation," the notice continues with irrefutable logic, "has, therefore, expired."

Other files near the Riddel folder told similar stories of overlapping land claims, with some disputes still ongoing, citing land grants from the 1700s as final authority. The story of the forest could be read from the survey descriptions. It was the practice to give diameters of the trees that served as corner markers between properties. I saw lots of six- and seven-inch white oaks and white pines mentioned in surveys from the 1920s, with an occasional three-inch yellow pine. Ten inches was the only double digit I encountered, until I finally spotted a white oak on top of rugged Shenandoah Mountain that was twenty-two inches.

Once land was acquired, the Forest Service put rangers in district offices. Rangers were a tough breed of men. In Gifford Pinchot's words, they had to be "thoroughly sound and able-bodied, capable of enduring hardships and of performing severe labor under trying conditions." Many mountaineers could meet those qualifications, plus they were "thoroughly familiar through long residence with the region," but few had the technical education required to pass the civil service exam. Most district rangers were outsiders and were met with indifference at best and hostility at worst. It was Forest Service policy for rangers to participate in community life, but what really helped improve relations was hiring local people as assistants, office workers, and field laborers. In another twist of Appalachian history, it was as firefighters that mountain men found their niche in the Forest Service.

The government made putting an end to forest fires its primary mission. In Appalachia, it proved to be a real mission, requiring nearly religious fervor to accomplish. Rangers had not counted on the

U.S. Forest Service, George Washington National Forest, Bridgewater, VA

Dry River District ranger of George Washington National Forest, 1928. Pistol is a .410 gauge issued to rangers for killing snakes.

mountaineers' profound attachment to fire, an attachment anchored many generations in the past. The old practice of burning land for pasture in the Old World was reinforced by Native American example in the New. In my library research, I came across a notice, meant to be nailed to a door or a tree in the Virginia mountains, dated April 1793. It offered a reward of $10 to anyone who, within thirty days, would give "certain information of the persons who lately set fire to that part of the Blue-Ridge which was the property of the late George William Fairfax." It continued:

> It is not only the duty, but the interest of the tenants upon the said land, to assist in detecting those unprincipled men, who, regardless of every moral and sacred obligation, are continually wasting and destroying the timber either by burning or by cutting: as it is only by care and attention in preserving the land and timber, that any of them can expect favours at a future day.

Beyond the greening up of pasture, beyond the killing of snakes and ticks, fire had another purpose. Burning someone's property was a favorite method of revenge. One of the first things we learned from

U.S. Forest Service,
George Washington National Forest, Buena Vista, VA

Forest Service fire lookout tower on Bald Mountain, Augusta County, Virginia, 1925. Guy wires from tower to trees are just detectable in photo. By 1934, this wooden tower had been replaced by a steel structure.

Parker Simmons, our elderly mentor in West Virginia, was not to post our land against hunting. "Somebody'll burn it down if you do," he said. That was all we needed to confirm a nascent feeling that absentee landowners like us ought not to post out families who had hunted our land for generations.

Before the Forest Service came, no one seemed to mind if fires burned far or deep. Fueled by the leftover debris from intermittent logging, fires raged every few years across the same woodlands. Each time, seedlings and young root sprouts were killed, until finally there were no more seeds and the roots died, leaving nothing to hold the soil. The Massanutten national forest purchase unit, thirty miles east of my place, was a famous example of an Appalachian burn.

Massanutten Mountain, now part of the George Washington National Forest, is an island of trees cleaving the intensely agricultural Shenandoah Valley. In 1912, a Forest Service assistant and his field helper carried out an assessment of seventeen thousand acres on Massanutten, owned by the Allegheny Ore and Iron Company (based in Coatesville, Pennsylvania, with an agent in nearby Shenandoah, Virginia). Allegheny had bought the property in 1902 from the Empire Steel and Iron Company.

The report's purpose was to describe the condition of the property being considered for purchase by the Forest Service. Exploitation went back many years. "Old coal hearths, together with mounds of earth and caved-in tunnels," notes the report, "are the remaining evidence of a former iron industry." With ore, charcoal, and limestone within easy reach, the furnace there, called Catherine, could operate independently of outside influences. Cannonballs were manufactured there for the Confederate Army. The 1912 report continued:

> There has been hardly a month contractors were not engaged in getting out whatever mercantile products could be found; lumber, staves, ties and bark have been cut, until now there is not more than 60,000 board feet of merchantable timber remaining. . . . There is practically no mature timber left, except a very few culled patches of five or ten acres, or less, where for one reason or another, a clear cutting was not made. . . . The tract has not been protected, and has been burned over repeatedly. Only in the coves and on the lower slopes has the moisture been sufficient to afford any adequate protection to the second growth. On the ridges and upper slopes, fires have prevented satisfactory restocking. . . . The ridges are often bare of tree growth. . . . Farmers living near say that during the wet seasons the streams are much higher, and floods are more numerous than they were fifteen to twenty years ago, when the mountain supported a fair stand of timber.

A price of $6 an acre was originally asked, but the company gave the Forest Service an option for six months at $1.25 an acre, starting from the date of the report. Because the tract was the single largest body of land in the 150,000-acre Massanutten purchase unit, the Forest Service considered it vital for establishing a national forest in the area. The report concluded that about one thousand acres contained young timber that was not now merchantable but that would be of value in twenty-five years—that is, if fire didn't kill the young trees. Fires were recorded in 1887, 1897, 1904, and 1912 on just one section of the mountain. Virtually every wildfire on Massanutten and other mountains was caused either purposely or accidentally by people.

"It is very probable," stated another study of Massanutten five years later, "that the productive capacity of forest soils throughout most of this region has been greatly decreased by repeated fires, so that the present forest growth is poorer in composition and quality than it once was." Fifteen years later still, the forest supervisor would say of Massanutten that it "has been considered more or less a joke so far as timber is concerned; some folks have even gone so far as to ask the ranger how he found trees large enough to post fire notices on . . . there would have to be a special sign made for the Massanutten, as the present signs would go all the way around the tree and overlap and no one could read them."

It was fires like those at Massanutten that the Forest Service aimed to stop, and it was at Massanutten that the system, quickly copied by other national forests, was created to defeat them. The headquarters of the Massanutten district was in the tiny town of Woodstock. The national forest examiner for the district in the early years was E. D. Clark. His secretary, Helen W. Gordon, described her boss in 1929 as "a man small in stature, but of inexhaustible energy. From early morning until far into the night he gave the best of his mind and heart to the business of bringing the gospel of forest conservation to an untutored public." His office was so dusty she compared it to the Sahara Desert.

Clark and other rangers throughout the Appalachians hired local fire wardens to patrol small areas. A salary of $50 a month made the job attractive. Wardens went out on horseback into all the national forests. At first they had neither towers nor telephones. Organizing a fire-fighting crew of twenty men under those conditions was difficult. One of Clark's most important tasks at Massanutten was the political maneuvering necessary to overcome the distrust of the locally run Farmers Mutual Telephone System. This key organization suspected that the government would use its lines without paying and refused to allow any connections. It took Clark more than a decade, but with a single-minded dedication that typified forest rangers, Clark had built several towers by 1926 and linked them all by telephone lines.

Convincing mountaineers that they shouldn't set fires took a lot of exhortation. It wasn't uncommon for local men to threaten rangers with wildfires if such traditional uses as hunting and grazing were restricted. Rangers persevered. By lecturing in schools, using the new moving pictures, and handing out literature, rangers gradually succeeded in persuading mountaineers to suppress their urge to burn. Also in the early years, the Forest Service took on the job of policing the woods against poachers who violated the new game laws being passed by the states. Some national forests inaugurated programs to buy or raise breeding stock of depleted game species such as native white-tailed deer, wild turkey, and ruffed grouse. In the 1930s, national forests throughout the Appalachians formalized a system of cooperation with state game agencies.

U.S. Forest Service, George Washington National Forest, Buena Vista, VA

Forest Service ranger inspecting a "Special Use Resident" permit in northern section of George Washington National Forest, Virginia, 1928.

There are several notable exceptions to the generalization that mountaineers didn't become rangers. One was a native of northern Georgia named W. Arthur Woody. He was not a poor mountaineer—he bought, sold, and rented farms as well as worked his own—he just preferred to go barefoot unless he was on the rockiest ground. Restocking the forest with trees and wildlife was his purpose in life, one that he said he gained from watching his father kill the last deer in his entire region. He started as a national forest laborer in 1912 and became district ranger in 1918; he retired in 1945. His sons, a nephew, and a grandson all became foresters. Woody used a bloodhound to track fire setters, and he caught them, too. It was a Georgia thing: Ranger Nicholson of nearby

NATIONAL ARCHIVES AND RECORDS ADMINISTRATION, STILL PICTURE BRANCH, 95G-344061

W. Arthur Woody, mountaineer and Forest Service ranger in northern Georgia from 1918 to 1945, in 1937.

Rabun County also used a bloodhound. After word about the dog got around, a known local firebug, who burned every spring to green up pasture for his stock, was overheard to answer when asked if he was going to burn again that year: "No sir, not me. I don't want any bloodhound tearing the seat out of my britches."

By the 1930s, the Forest Service had established a significant presence in the Appalachians. Although fires were still frequent compared with other regions of the country and were sometimes set by the very men who fought them for the extra pay they meant, the repetitive burnings were coming under control. Protected areas were beginning to grow up in young trees. So obsessed was the Forest Service with fire control that it suppressed its own research showing that some kinds of fires at certain times could be useful to humans without unduly harming forest life. Later, in a masterful and unrelenting public relations campaign, the Forest Service used Smokey the Bear to symbolize the pitiless effects of fire. On a sticky, hot day a few years ago at a campground in southwestern Virginia, I shook hands with Smokey, a poor ranger smothered in synthetic fur.

Rangers and their staff worked hard, but there weren't enough men to carry out all the restorative projects that needed doing. It took the Great Depression and the social programs of the New Deal in the 1930s to really put the eastern national forests on their feet. One of President Franklin Roosevelt's earliest and dearest efforts to help America recover was the Civilian Conservation Corps, known as the CCC. Its purpose was to conserve the natural resources of the country—timber, soil, and water—by providing employment and training for jobless, unmarried young men. To make sure that there was plenty of national forest land for the men to work on, tens of millions of dollars were appropriated for land purchases.

U.S. FOREST SERVICE, GEORGE WASHINGTON NATIONAL FOREST, BRIDGEWATER, VA

Men on the road to the first Civilian Conservation Corps camp in the nation, Camp Roosevelt on Massanutten Mountain in Virginia's Shenandoah Valley, April 1933.

From 1933 until 1942, when Congress abolished it because of World War II, three million men between the ages of seventeen and twenty-three worked for the CCC. They lived in work camps and received a base pay of $30 per month, $25 of which they were required to send home to their families. They were encouraged to spend the rest in nearby towns, to bolster local economies. In Appalachian national forests, the presence of so many young men in a countryside famous for moonshine inevitably set off a few incidents, but on the whole the program was widely liked.

Appropriately enough, given the extent of its degradation, Massanutten Mountain was the site of the first CCC camp. Young men arrived at nearby train stations on the tops of boxcars, sometimes a hundred at a time. Some wore shoes; some did not. Camp Roosevelt held

U.S. Forest Service, George Washington National Forest, Bridgewater, VA

First day at Camp Roosevelt, 1933. Clearing and carrying poles to set up tents.

three hundred men, and many other camps, including a few "black camps" for African Americans, sprang up across the mountains. At first the men lived in tents. Snowstorms caved them in. Simple wooden barracks became the norm. Daily life was structured and full of hard labor. The men built fire towers, telephone lines, picnic tables, overlooks, trails, and campgrounds with wells, fireplaces, and privies. They piled up boulders and brush piles in erosion ditches to stop the force of water. They thinned out thousands of acres of choked stands of young trees. They dug up all the gooseberry and currant bushes they could find to eliminate them as a reservoir of blister rust, a fungus that killed white pines. Whatever other timber improvement projects the rangers could devise, the CCCers did it. In some national forests with nurseries, they planted hundreds of thousands of seedling trees.

The CCC also built many, many miles of roads. During a cold winter in Monongahela National Forest in West Virginia, the CCCers had to build fires to get the road equipment going. Without this kind of labor, the national forests would not look as they do today. Although social improvement policies in the 1960s and later created valuable programs such as Job Corps, Youth Conservation Corps, and Senior Conservation Employment, none ever approached the impact of the CCC.

Entry into World War II in 1941 ushered in another era. For one thing, CCCers had to go fight. For another, funding for national forest

U.S. Forest Service, George Washington National Forest, Bridgewater, VA

Returning tools at close of day's work, CCC Camp Roosevelt, George Washington National Forest, Virginia, ca. 1933.

land acquisitions nearly stopped and was not renewed by Republican administrations after the war. With something over five million acres, the Appalachian national forests had acquired more or less their current configuration. Funding increased under the Democratic administrations of John F. Kennedy and Lyndon B. Johnson in the 1960s but never reached previous levels. Most of the tracts that were purchased after the war were concentrated in the badly cutover and mined lands of the Daniel Boone National Forest in eastern Kentucky, which in 1966 became the last national forest to be established in the Appalachians.

The 1964 Land and Water Conservation Fund Act provided funds for the eventual purchase of several hundred thousand additional acres by various national forests, but these were lands with specific recreational value. Mostly, the Forest Service has come to emphasize land exchanges instead of purchases to acquire key tracts and smooth out borders. Periodically, some private property ideologue comes up with the idea of selling national forest land *back* to private owners, but mercifully little has ever come of that.

American participation in World War II also meant that the national forests had to provide war materiel. Although the volume of timber

U.S. Forest Service, George Washington National Forest, Buena Vista, VA

Erosion control by CCCers in Amherst County, Virginia, 1939.

harvest had dropped far below the peak reached in 1909, wood products never completely stopped coming out of Appalachia, including the national forests. True to its roots, the Forest Service has always been bound and determined to get out the cut. Forest Service policy favored small, portable sawmills that local people could afford to run with family and a few hired hands. During the war, the annual amount of board feet cut in national forests throughout the South increased from less than 100 billion board feet to nearly 250 billion. Most of it was sold in bids of less than $500. Most of whatever old growth was left went to build bridges, barracks, boats, aircraft, and above all, packing crates to ship supplies overseas. The last of the dead chestnut trees, killed by blight, was cut for extract to tan the leather that went into soldiers' boots.

The war stimulated a cutting boom in the national forests that continued for decades. As the veterans returned and started families, an enormous demand for housing drove up the value of trees. The timber industry began to pressure the Forest Service to make more wood available. By the 1960s, the Forest Service was tripling and quadrupling its cut. Amounts and methods of cutting were mandated by high-level administrators, removing some of the district rangers' autonomy and their ability to let the immediate community have a say in land-use decisions. The latent suspicion of local people toward the government men waxed accordingly.

U.S. Forest Service, National Forests of North Carolina, Asheville, NC

Ranger John Waslik supervising loading onto truck, ca. 1940s, Nantahala National Forest, North Carolina.

Even the acceleration in cutting caused by the war was estimated at less than overall annual timber growth, because of all the second-growth trees not yet mature enough to harvest. The remarkable resurgence of Appalachian forests—shrunken and distorted in every dimension from the original, but full of potential timber trees—was well under way. The Forest Service had taken the least productive lands plagued with the most destructive abuses and through dedicated care had made that land productive again. The question that became increasingly insistent after the war was, what exactly should the national forests produce?

Of course, trees were also maturing on the approximately twenty million acres of mountain forests from Virginia to northern Georgia that were and still are held in private hands. All this talk about the national forests of Appalachia shouldn't obscure the fact that they manage less than twenty percent of the region's forested land and supply only about ten percent of its timber harvest. Whatever influence the national forests have had in pumping dollars into local economies and change into local traditions, their presence in the context of timber has always been modest. Today, no communities anywhere in Appalachia depend economically on national forest timber, and fewer than a dozen counties out of nearly two hundred in the Appalachian region are more than half owned by national forests. The wood products industry is alive and well on private lands, and for the last couple of decades it has constituted a fairly stable five percent of the regional economy. The tourism dollars brought in by the public lands amount to considerably more.

Operations of the Cherry River Boom and Lumber Company on North Fork Gauley River, West Virginia, 1940.

Private lands are generally at lower elevations with more productive soils than national forests. They got little of the nurturing that national forests received from the CCC, but they did benefit from fire suppression and other timber improvement programs that the federal government subsidized through state forestry agencies. Appalachian states have relied on these voluntary programs as the preferred alternative to regulating the cutting of timber on private lands, with debatable results. Attempts to pass federal laws governing private harvests have never gotten very far. Anyway, it wasn't the cutting of trees on private land that ignited the next major controversy in the continuing saga of Appalachian forests and knocked off the white hat that the Forest Service saw itself as wearing. It has been a rocky philosophical journey for the Forest Service to realize that it shouldn't try to compete with what private lands can provide but should offer what they can't—such as old trees.

On private lands, trees tend to get cut when they reach a size that will bring economic returns. On national forests, however, large swaths of land may be categorized as unsuitable for harvest because of steepness or thin soil. Other tracts simply haven't come into a cycle of cutting.

Across the Appalachian national forests, millions of acres of recovering Great Forest are growing toward old growth. The ecological implications of this are profound, but they weren't clearly recognized until the 1980s, and then not by the Forest Service.

The earliest product of the national forests to be recognized as unique was access to nature. Private property owners couldn't be expected to open their gates to ever-growing multitudes. The postwar baby-boom generation was much more affluent than its depression-era parents and also had more leisure. Most importantly, it had automobiles. Baby boomers liked to get into the great outdoors, and more and more of the millions who lived in the Mid-Atlantic and the Southeast got into the Appalachians. By the first Earth Day—April 22, 1970—the rise of interest in the natural environment across the nation was reflected in a tenfold increase in visitation to all national forests since World War II. A diffuse but powerful force called "outdoor recreation" was emerging to challenge the supremacy of timber as the major value of national forest lands.

Like logging and mining, tourism has been part of Appalachian life since frontier days. But never had so many people thronged to Appalachia to enjoy the rivers, trails, campgrounds, roads, and views that were available to them in the national forests. Many visitors must have been impressed enough to decide that it would be a good place to live. In a reversal of the out-migration characteristic of Appalachia through the earlier twentieth century, its population surged by nearly a third from 1970 to 1990. Those were years of rapid change. Congress passed the Payments in Lieu of Taxes Act to increase and diversify the revenues that counties received from the national forests. Satellite dishes made TV reception possible in the most remote hollows. A burgeoning service economy helped to reduce the region's poverty rate by almost half. Like me, many of the people I know moved here during those two decades.

We brought new ideas about how land should look and what it should be used for. We felt that the public lands belonged to us as much as they did to people who had lived there longer. Often, we have found ourselves at uncomfortable odds with native people. But in the first big showdown with the Forest Service over clear-cutting, one that changed the future of all national forests, traditional residents and outsiders agreed. Together, their voices began to carry over the increasingly defensive growl of the Timber Beast that stepped out of the Cradle of Forestry.

THE FOREST TODAY

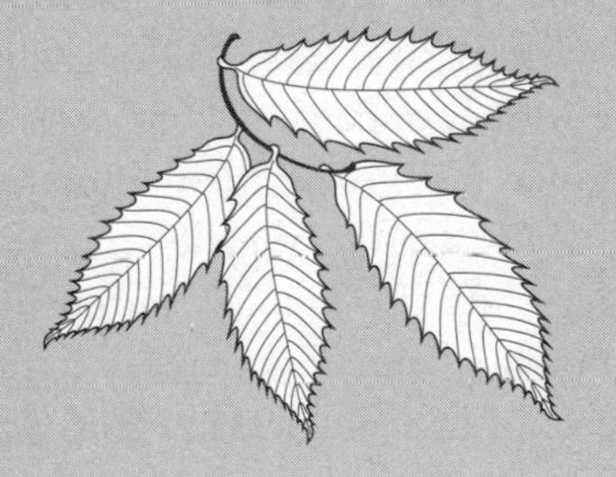

Profiles in Controversy

MONONGAHELA NATIONAL FOREST, WEST VIRGINIA

In the following profiles of federally owned lands in central and southern Appalachia, certain aspects of each are essential for an understanding of the whole picture. First is size. The Monongahela National Forest, known locally as the Mon, contains 909,084 acres in the north-central section of West Virginia. Just giving the number of acres can be quite misleading, though. No eastern national forest stretches unbroken into the blue mountain haze. Each is riddled with private ownership gaps, called inholdings. Inholdings are often devoted to nonforest uses, which can make the maintenance of ecological integrity difficult on the adjoining public land. The best way to assess a national forest's cohesiveness is by comparing the acreage within its proclamation boundary—the total area within which it is authorized to purchase land—with actual acreage held. The Mon's proclamation boundary includes 1.6 million acres. It owns fifty-seven percent of this area, a high quotient for an Appalachian national forest. As in other national forests, most of the private inholdings are concentrated in the valley bottoms, but some are scattered across even the highest ridges.

Another peculiarity of national forest ownership is reserved or outstanding mineral rights. The tradition of selling off rights to attributes of the land, such as timber and coal, affects national forest as well as private land. The contemporary equivalents of timber and coal are gas and oil.

Private or corporate owners control the gas and oil rights on a third of the Mon's acreage. Outstanding coal rights are held on a little less than a quarter of it.

A year or two after we bought our property in West Virginia, where we look across the Tygart River valley into the western slopes of the Mon, a representative of a gas company came to visit us where we were living near Washington, D.C. He presented us with a gas lease that the title-search lawyer in Elkins had, in his own words, "forgotten to mention." To our relief, the company let the lease lapse. A few years later, we arrived for a weekend visit to find stakes with orange ties marching across the meadow. We pulled them up. That was at least a decade ago, and nothing has happened yet, so I'm beginning to relax my guard.

The Mon straddles the divide, called the Allegheny Front, between the Ridge and Valley topography to the east and the Allegheny Plateau to the west. Because the Allegheny Front intersects many eastward-traveling, rain-bearing clouds, in what is called a rain shadow effect, rainfall on the eastern side of the forest averages only half of the sixty inches a year received by the western side. The Mon's elevation ranges from 900 feet to the 4,861-foot summit of Spruce Knob, the highest mountain in West Virginia. About seventy-five tree species occur; the most economically valuable are the oaks, black cherry, and ash. The Mon is known for its fine hardwoods and sells roughly thirty million board feet a year, for something like $7.5 million. For most of the 1990s, an average of fifty-three hundred acres have been harvested every year, thirteen hundred of them by clear-cutting. That's about a third of the thirty-seven hundred acres being clear-cut every year in the late 1960s and early 1970s.

In 1964, the Forest Service changed its approach to harvesting timber. Previously, selection cutting, called uneven-aged management, had been the preferred method. Rangers walked through the woods assessing and marking individual trees to be cut. But research in Forest Service experimental forests seemed to imply that selective cutting, which leaves many standing trees, would suppress the regeneration of the shade-intolerant species that need sun to sprout, such as the highly valuable oaks and tulip poplars. Instead, shade-tolerant species, such as the less valuable maples, would come to dominate. Unless carefully done, selective harvesting also leaves economically worthless, defective, and diseased trees to compete with and retard more desirable young growth. And it involves more frequent human disturbance of the same woods than clear-cutting, which removes all merchantable timber for at least several decades.

At the same time that it adopted clear-cutting, the Forest Service began to place much heavier emphasis on timber production. Wood was in great demand as the consumer society expanded in the decades after World War II, and the lumber industry, having rapidly cut its own woodlands, lobbied for access to federal timber. The national forests were directed to set timber sale goals. Job promotion depended on meeting them. Clear-cutting, called even-aged management because it results in a block of trees all the same age, quickly gained most favored status in most national forests.

The technique of clear-cutting developed in eighteenth-century Germany, where valuable trees had been removed and defective ones left behind for so long that the forests offered little benefit to anyone, human or animal. Clear-cutting to get rid of all the clutter, and replanting when necessary to ensure desirable regeneration, became common in the nineteenth century. By the early 1900s, pervasive problems with impoverished soils and stunted, disease-prone trees cast suspicion on clear-cutting, and it gradually fell from favor. It is little used in Germany today, and some states ban it. Germans now prefer to cut in ways that are *Naturnahe,* close to nature. German foresters visiting the United States have been appalled to find their early mistakes being repeated here.

American loggers in the Mon objected at first to the Forest Service requirement that they clear-cut, because they were used to taking out only the most valuable timber and coming back for more at shorter intervals than clear-cutting would allow. But the market for pulp and low-value wood began to expand as technology found uses for them. Mechanization of logging continued to make it easier to handle large quantities. Clear-cutting was soon hailed as the most economical way to harvest. It was also promoted as the best means to provide all the other functions of the national forests demanded by various forest users.

Rangers in the Appalachians reasoned that since so much of the forest had been cut at roughly the same time, in the early decades of the twentieth century, the new growth was all approximately the same age. Large blocks had to be cut out of it to allow the establishment of different age groups. Even-aged stands of various ages, chockablock through the forest, would assure the diversity of products legally required by the

Multiple Use–Sustained Yield Act of 1960: outdoor recreation, range, timber, watershed, and wildlife. By fortunate coincidence, clear-cuts were especially good for deer, the favorite game species, because of the constant availability of tender new browse.

The problem was that clear-cuts look like hell. Huge, rectangular expanses of barren land gashed with logging roads and bereft of everything but stumps and dead limbs are not pretty. They look as if they could not possibly be good for anything but logging convenience. With more and more people entering the national forests for drives, picnics, and hikes, the way the woods looked became an issue. So did the erosion and the loss of wildlife habitat that clear-cutting caused. Clear-cuts began to provoke protests in national forests all over the country through the 1960s and into the early 1970s. Public sentiment simmered and occasionally came to a boil in an alphabet soup of laws such as NEPA (National Environmental Policy Act of 1969) and RRPA (Renewable Resources Planning Act of 1974).

When a 550-acre experiment in even-aged management appeared on the Mon within sight of a golf club in Richwood, West Virginia, public opinion crystallized in a lawsuit. A local politician found his favorite wild turkey hunting spot ruined. He had friends in the Izaak Walton League, a sportsmen's conservation organization named after the seventeenth-century English author of the literary classic *The Compleat Angler.* It was this group that took the lead in bringing suit against the Forest Service. The league was joined by a recently formed state-level group, the West Virginia Highlands Conservancy, which advocated tourism and the scenic views that stimulated it. Two large, national-level environmental organizations also joined—the Sierra Club, which didn't have a chapter in West Virginia until 1984, and the Natural Resources Defense Council. And for perhaps the first time, the voices of plain mountain people sounded, too, calling for protection of the forest. Many of the local opponents to the clear-cutting were older folks who had seen the devastation of the land that became the Mon, when it was called the Great Burn and the Great Brush Patch. They didn't like clear-cutting because it reminded them of those days.

In 1973 the judge ruled that the Forest Service had violated the Organic Act of 1897, the original law setting out the guidelines by which public forests should be managed. The Organic Act stipulated that trees could be sold and cut only if they were dead, mature, or large, and only when marked. Few of these conditions were met by clear-cutting. The loss of the lawsuit practically shut down the national forest timber program. Industry and the Forest Service scrambled to lobby Congress to repeal or amend the Organic Act. In 1976, the National Forest Management Act legalized clear-cutting under certain restrictions of size and placement. It also required the national forests to produce comprehensive land-use plans and to solicit public participation in the planning process.

The Forest Service took the law and ran with it. In the Mon, clear-cuts got much smaller but more widespread, erupting like patches of mange on the skin of the mountains. In 1993, the Sierra Club helped inaugurate a new genre of books with the publication of a parody of the coffee-table format. *Clearcut, the Tragedy of Industrial Forestry,* is composed of hundreds of oversized photos of desolate forests, from Alaska to Maine to Texas, on private lands as well as public. One of the pictures was taken in the Mon. In it, twenty-four acres of brown stand out from a matrix of green forest. The gray trunks of trees too small to be worth hauling away lie in random heaps like bodies after an explosion. The two roads created to truck logs out, called skid trails, are open slashes through the hillside.

When I saw it nearly ten years after the cut, the scene hadn't changed much. The contours of the skid trails were slightly softened by grass, and the small tree trunks on the ground had decayed or been covered by blackberry bushes. The clear-cut began at the edge of a dirt Forest Service road and ran down a steep slope on Middle Mountain. It was spring, and the green of the new leaves still glowed with the yellow brilliance of fresh growth, not yet deepened into the humid blue of high summer.

At my feet, coltsfoot plants had gone to seed, poking their thick, dandelion-like heads up along the road's edge like a crowd of gray-haired old people. Behind them were hay-scented ferns mixed with blooming violets. Then the blackberry bushes took over as ground cover, with some striped maple saplings scattered throughout. Nowhere was there the dense, chest-high thicket of young trees I had expected from the moist climate. The rawness of the early cut was gone, but the scene felt empty, strained, somehow not right. It disturbed me to be there. I remembered a scientific paper I had read recently, in which the researcher compared old-growth stands with clear-cuts of various ages. He concluded that clear-cutting disrupted the herbaceous understory of the richest Appalachian forests so severely that many species of wildflowers had not restored themselves nearly a century after the cutting occurred. He concluded they were unlikely ever to recover under repeated cycles of clear-cutting.

The opening created by the cut in the Mon offered one of the only outlooks to a view of Shavers Mountain in the west. Along the several swells of mountain within view, I saw six other similar scoops out of the forest cover.

"What do you see when you look at this clear-cut?" I asked Gary Bustamente, the Mon's silviculturalist, over the sandwiches we were eating for lunch. Gary had arrived at the Mon shortly after this centerfold clear-cut was begun. He had thirty years' experience with the Forest Service in Montana, Wisconsin, and Missouri, but his hair was still as brown as his eyes. He had a nice smile. For most of his career, he worked in timber sales.

"I see a successful clear-cut here," he said, "although admittedly the natural regeneration is pretty sparse." Regrowth of trees was so poor that a few years after the cut, the Forest Service set out four-foot-high white plastic tubes with red oak saplings inside them, at the rate of fifty an acre. "This whole area is known for deer problems," Gary said. "There hadn't been any harvests around here in many years, and when these cuts went in they drew all the deer for miles." Deer ate any oaks that might have germinated and many of the maple sprouts, as well as other young plants struggling to get a purchase. "Oaks wouldn't survive without help," Gary said, "but I'm really encouraged by the success of these." Tender sprays of reddish leaves spilled over the tops of the tubes.

Right across the road, in a classic Appalachian conjunction, was Laurel Fork South, a legally designated wilderness area within the Mon, which meant that it was protected from all timber cutting. The trees were mostly beeches, some maples and ashes, wild cherry, and an occasional mountain magnolia in full bloom. They were not very large, being at least second growth, but they created a rustling forest canopy. A wood thrush played a flute somewhere in the dappled shade.

"How long will it be before the clear-cut begins to have a canopy like this?" I asked Gary.

"I typically expect canopy closure in about fifteen years," he said. It was hard to imagine.

On the way back from the clear-cut, we passed a couple of timber harvests in process. Forced by public opinion to minimize clear-cutting, the Forest Service was experimenting with alternative methods. One of the most widely used of these is called shelterwood cutting. The theory of a shelterwood cut is that trees are logged in successive stages rather than all at once, to stimulate and protect the young growth of desirable tree species. Some large trees are left standing after the first cut, depending on species, size, and the goals of the timber manager. Trees left behind are harvested at a later date, usually no more than five to ten years in the future, but sometimes longer, depending on circumstances. In practice, shelterwood cuts can range from virtual clear-cuts, with only a few scuffed and sorry trees remaining per acre, to cuts that leave what still looks like a forest. The variants of shelterwood cutting that I saw in the Mon were very small—two to three acres. The mature cherry trees had been taken out, because they live only eighty to one hundred years and then die and are lost for timber. About forty square feet of basal area—the total amount of space that tree trunks take up on the ground—had been left per acre. Young wild cherries, beeches, and maples formed an open, airy stand. "We're still learning," Gary said. "We don't know whether the remaining trees will suffer a high rate of blowdown, or how the remaining canopy will affect regeneration. But we have to manage. That's our job."

There's more to the Mon besides timber cutting, of course. Because it lies near the southern limit of the Ice Age glaciers, plants native to northern conditions were able to survive right next to southern plants at the northern end of their tolerance. This conjunction of northern and southern ecosystems fosters unusual communities such as sphagnum bogs, heath and shale barrens, grassy plains, and cranberry thickets. More than two hundred species of migrating or nesting birds have been documented in the Mon, and seventy-eight species of fish. Eleven species of plants and animals are listed on the federal Threatened and Endangered Species List, one of the lowest numbers for any of the Appalachian national forests; fifty other species are considered rare or sensitive. White-tailed deer, black bears, wild turkeys, and squirrels are heavily hunted—one of the predominant uses of national forests by local people. The number of people who use a national forest every year is a hard statistic to get; the best estimate for the Mon is three million, many of them from the Washington, D.C., metropolitan area. Like all the Appalachian public lands, the Mon is within a day's drive of one-third of the population of the United States, now pushing toward three hundred million.

GEORGE WASHINGTON NATIONAL FOREST, VIRGINIA

Even closer to Washington, D.C., and absorbing even more visitors, is the George Washington National Forest, on whose eastern edge I am ensconced. The Mon and the George Washington share about thirty miles of common border in West Virginia, where the George Washington covers one hundred thousand acres. In Virginia, it covers one million acres. Within its proclamation boundaries, the George Washington owns sixty-two percent of the land, making it both the largest and the least fragmented of all Appalachian national forests. Agricultural livestock businesses and expanding towns dominate the eastern border of the George Washington; to the west are mostly small farms.

Two hundred thousand acres of the George Washington have outstanding mineral rights. Even more significant in the George Washington is the fact that a national forest can lease whatever mineral rights it does own. During the early 1980s, after scientific reports predicting gas and oil reserves in the area were published, there was a flurry of corporate interest, and the George Washington leased the rights to 725,000 acres. On the boundary of our land with the George Washington is a feature called Yellow Spring. The trickle of water is filled with orange floc from the sulfur that signals the presence of gas. On a hike past it one day, I found half a dozen big efts, the red-spotted, land-based, subadult form of the eastern newt, drowned in the spring. They lay neatly packed beside one another as if in a mass suicide—a mystery I have never figured out.

Just like our West Virginia property, our tract here had a gas lease outstanding when we bought it, but at least this time we knew about it. Again, we were lucky; after a few years, the company let it lapse. Prices for natural gas had fallen, and a test well in our area proved to be a dry hole. The amount of land leased by the George Washington greatly declined.

As a result of the Monongahela lawsuit, the Forest Service was forced to intensify its planning. All national forests had to inaugurate a ten- to fifteen-year cycle of composing and then revising comprehensive land-use plans. As part of the planning process, national forest administrators were required to ask for public input. Like the other Appalachian forests, the George Washington published its first plan in the mid-1980s. All the plans received a tumultuous response from the public, but the George Washington's was the most reviled. In it, George Washington staff had doubled the amount of cutting and quadrupled the road building projected over the next fifty years. Eighty-four percent of George Washington land was judged suitable for logging.

Fifteen loggers, plus Westvaco, the biggest timber company in the area, wrote in support of the plan, although one logger worried that there wouldn't be enough purchasers for the increased timber on the market. Letters against the plan filled three thick notebooks. Dozens of municipal, state, and federal agencies; dozens of hiking, horseback-riding, and rod and gun clubs; and almost a thousand individuals wrote in protest. The Central Virginia Hang Gliding Association wanted a commitment in the plan for ten launching sites. The Augusta County Bird Club protested the public subsidy of the timber industry represented by the logging roads built by the Forest Service. The Environmental Protection Agency complained that the impact of erosion on groundwater quality from timber cutting had not been fully considered. Each group and almost every individual expressed some nuance of view, but all agreed on one thing: the plan called for far too much clear-cutting and road building.

Eighteen appeals were filed against the plan by individuals, timber organizations, environmental groups, and coalitions of various interests. After a couple years trying to resolve the conflicts, the chief of the Forest Service told the George Washington's staff to ditch the plan and write a new one, paying more attention to legal requirements and public demands this time. After endless rounds of public meetings in airless rooms where the temperature was often driven up by emotion, the new plan was finally issued in 1993. The amount of land judged suitable for timbering dropped to thirty-three percent of the George Washington. The number of appeals dropped to thirteen, and this time the chief denied them all. In an uneasy truce, only one of the individuals has sued so far, not over the plan itself but over specific timber sales.

The George Washington is the driest of the Appalachian forests, being mostly on the east side of the Allegheny Front. Because of its droughtiness and its steep, stony slopes, it has the least amount of recuperative capacity. There is little of the Mon's high-quality, second-growth hardwood lumber. Most timber from the George Washington is ground up as pulpwood to make paper. Beginning in the late 1980s, the total number of acres harvested annually declined dramatically, from around six thousand acres to about two thousand by the late 1990s. The number of acres harvested by clear-cutting fell from nearly all to a couple hundred a year.

For me, the forest is a cloak, sweeping down around my shoulders from the top of Cross Mountain. From my deck I can see two clear-cuts, holes in my cloak where the wind blows through. One of our first summers here, a chain saw buzzed continuously, like a mosquito you couldn't swat. The logging trucks were a menace on our narrow dirt road. Now the dogwoods along the cut edges are responding to the increase in sunlight, blooming white like a necklace of pearls on the bosom of the mountain. The population of deer has grown noticeably. There's no question that a disturbance in the forest can serve various ecological purposes. The question is how well the disturbance fits into the natural pattern of the place. In the Appalachians, the kind of storm that knocks down many acres of trees all at once, the way clear-cutting does, doesn't happen very often. And no natural force ever removes all the woody debris from the recycling processes of natural regeneration.

The George Washington has eleven species on or proposed for the federal Threatened and Endangered Species List. It seems to have been the first Appalachian national forest to stock trout in its streams, beginning in 1931 when the CCC was available to help repair damaged fish habitat. White-tailed deer were also stocked in the 1930s. Deer were so scarce then that seeing one was an event; they have since become abundant, especially on Cross Mountain. In fact, there are so many deer that the district ranger complained that they ate too many of the upcoming young trees. In some places, the forest undergrowth has been mostly nibbled away to the height of a deer's easy reach, leaving a visible browse line. We've given up planting ornamentals around the house because the deer invariably eat them.

Eighty thousand hunters come to the George Washington every year, the bulk of them in late November during the two weeks of the deer gun season. From the traffic on our normally tranquil road, it seems like a lot of them come to Cross Mountain. Because there's so much public land immediately accessible, and because we don't want unknown hordes shooting around the house, we posted our property. So far, no one has threatened to burn it down.

Almost every year we find evidence of poaching—someone hunting out of season, trespassing, or both. One morning I was interviewing someone on the phone and heard a shot that sounded very, very close. It had taken a lot of time to track down the person I was talking to, so I continued. That afternoon, my husband found footprints in the snow all over our property, coming right up behind the shop. Another time, the chain we used as a gate was snipped and stolen. Other times we've found shotgun casings, shot-up trees, deer gut piles, and most recently, a nice, new hunting stand securely nailed into an oak. The most memorable artifact of all was a full deerskin stuffed with straw and mounted on a two-by-four frame. It was set in a brushy spot near the road. We could only guess that someone was playing a joke on hunters who shoot from their trucks, which is illegal but common around here.

JEFFERSON NATIONAL FOREST, VIRGINIA

The Jefferson National Forest, extending from the southern border of the George Washington through the southwestern Virginia mountains just barely into Kentucky and Tennessee, was one of the first national forests to attempt the restocking of most of the favorite game animals. In 1917, elk were imported from Yellowstone National Park to replace the native animals that had been hunted to extinction. A few of the park elk survived and reproduced, and in 1935 more were brought in. Until they were poached out in the 1970s, these and a similarly small introduced herd in Pennsylvania were the only wild eastern elk. Like the other Appalachian national forests, the Jefferson also brought in beavers, white-tailed deer, and wild turkeys from out-of-state sources in the 1920s and 1930s. These animals thrived enough to overcome the effects of poaching. The first deer season on the Jefferson opened in 1945.

Twenty-eight species are listed as endangered or threatened in the Jefferson, four more are proposed, and several hundred are considered sensitive, requiring special habitats. The largest category of endangered animals is mussels. These small, shelled creatures constitute one of the specialties of southern Appalachia. They thrived in the formerly silt-free gravels at the bottom of once clear rivers. Slightly wetter and warmer than the George Washington, the Jefferson occupies part of seven highly biologically diverse watersheds: the James, Roanoke, New, Holston, Clinch, Big Sandy, and Cumberland Rivers.

Salamanders are another Appalachian specialty, and the Jefferson has the most concentrated area of woodland salamander biodiversity in the world: a two-thousand-acre segment of the Mount Rogers National Recreation Area has twenty known salamander species. No one knows why this is such a hot spot of salamander evolution, except that it seems to perfectly suit the salamander preference for cool moisture.

It's plenty cool on Mount Rogers, which at 5,729 feet is Virginia's highest mountain. Just below the peak are five thousand acres of stone outcrops and rhododendron thickets, sometimes referred to as the northernmost of the southern Appalachian balds, although it was known to be created by logging, burning, and grazing. The 360-degree vista you get from standing on some of the rocks up there is spectacular. Misty mountain ranges hang in ever paler reflection of one another until they merge with the sky. It's just the kind of scenery that attracts tourists. Established in 1966, Mount Rogers was not the first national recreation area in the Appalachians (the Spruce Knob–Seneca Rocks area in the Mon came nine months earlier), but it was probably the most contested.

National recreation areas were conceived by a presidential council in the early 1960s, in response to a jump of more than nine hundred percent in visitation to national forests from 1945 to 1960. The Mount Rogers area was expected not only to help satisfy the recreational demand of millions but also to benefit local economies through tourism. Intense recreational development was planned—nine hundred campsites, almost as many day-use facilities, reservoirs, a winter sports center and a fifty-five-mile scenic highway. However, the Jefferson owned only 85,000 acres of the 154,000 proposed for the area. In a reversal of its long-standing policy, the Forest Service initiated condemnation proceedings against a total of 6,500 acres in two sites where resorts were planned. Full-time residents on fifteen parcels did not want to sell at any price.

This represented an infinitesimal amount of displacement compared with that caused by the Tennessee Valley Authority and the two Appalachian national parks. Thousands of families had been displaced by those agencies in the 1930s, with hardly any recourse and little public notice, but mountaineers had learned a thing or two since then. Local citizens around Mount Rogers organized to oppose the Forest Service. They publicized their opinions in newspapers and special newsletters. Eventually, several national environmental groups, including the Sierra

Club, sided with them against the use of condemnation and the intensity of planned development. By 1980, the Forest Service was forced to abandon many of its proposals and drastically scale down its acquisition plans. Dispersed recreation, such as hiking and backpacking, became the management principle at Mount Rogers.

At 714,518 acres, the Jefferson owns forty-three percent of the 1.6 million acres within its proclamation boundary. Private mineral rights underlie twelve percent of forestland, mostly in the Clinch Ranger District, the western and most isolated part of the Jefferson. Clinch District lies partly along Virginia's border with Kentucky, in the heart of coal-mining country. The coal companies in these parts sold to the national forest only those lands that they knew did *not* have rich seams. The oddly flat tops and stepped silhouettes of the mountains give away the strip mines. Coal dust from the trucks in front of you blackens your windshield when you drive through, and if it starts to drizzle and you turn your wipers on, it takes forever to get the smear out of your view.

The Jefferson has gas, manganese, sand, gravel, limestone, lead, zinc, gypsum, and iron. As in the George Washington, iron mining has a long history. Fenwick Mines near New Castle in Craig County is a relatively contemporary site, having opened in 1900 and continued until 1924. Several large open pits, many small ones, and a deep mine two hundred feet down, with a mile of tunnels running from it, were dug to get at the ore. Around the mines, a company town of three hundred people spread out over two square miles. In addition to residences, there was an ore washer to remove sand and clay, a dynamo for power, a commissary, a hospital, a school for fifty children, an engine house for the locomotive, a playhouse, a superintendent's house, and a mule barn. There were three neighborhoods: native whites within the town proper, African Americans and Italians at the edges. There was a white church and a black church.

"I've been told this is the black cemetery, but I don't think so because this is on the white side of the tracks," Mike Barber said. We were strolling through a grove of Virginia pines, which had perhaps been planted—no one was exactly sure. There was little undergrowth except greenbrier. Around us were depressions in the ground, some with stones almost buried, some without. Whatever inscriptions might have identified the stones had worn away. Mike was the archaeologist for the

Jefferson and the George Washington National Forests, which are administered together from the same headquarters in Roanoke. When he joined the Forest Service in 1977, in the early years of its cultural resources program, he was responsible for five national forests in four states. With a full beard and gray hair flowing loose down his back, he did not look like a typical Forest Service employee. He walked with a colleague along the banks of several mysterious trenches, trying to figure out their function and noting whether the pipes that stuck out in places had threads or not. The industrial history demonstrated by Fenwick Mines certainly qualified it for the National Register of Historic Places, Mike said. It was just a matter of getting to the paperwork.

Yucca plants lined part of the road, a sign of old homesites. The land had strange contours, with inexplicable dips and bumps. Talus piles were unexpected lumps like tumors, camouflaged with trees that were mature but not really big. Many trees had fallen over, unable to push roots into the compacted soil. A sinkhole rimmed with mountain laurel was an old test mine. The Virginia pines, some of them as much as a foot and a half in diameter, gave way to scarlet oak and spindly poplars as far into the woods as I could see. The district ranger thought that there was enough wood here to schedule a timber sale, although he planned to avoid the areas of archaeological interest.

Old pieces of cement and pipe lay in the stream, and a bed of silt was settled above a broken dam. Dollops of silt lay in the streambed below it. Looking downstream, with ferns arching over the banks and sun lighting the pine needles with a warm afternoon glow, I could have taken a postcard kind of picture. The creek had eroded a talus bank to make a pretty little waterfall. Downstream, beavers had taken advantage of the uneven ground and disturbed hydrology left by mining to create a wetlands. It was a lovely, peaceful scene. In fact, Fenwick Mines has been added to the Watchable Wildlife program and has a self-guided trail with an interpretive leaflet that waxes eloquent about the abundant wildlife. "How do human activities benefit our landscape in a long-term way?" asks the leaflet, without a trace of rhetorical sarcasm.

PISGAH NATIONAL FOREST, NORTH CAROLINA

The Clovis point filled my palm, and though it was made from cold, lifeless stone, it seemed somehow to glow. The fluorescent light of the basement storage room in the Asheville, North Carolina, office building brought out the stone's greenish gray luminosity. It was a spear point, large and heavy enough to launch at a mammoth and perfectly made, without a chip to mar the edge. Fourteen thousand years ago, someone probably regretted losing it in what is now the Pisgah National Forest.

The Pisgah may be considered the most historic of the Appalachian national forests, containing as it does the Cradle of Forestry. It also boasts the first land purchase completed by the Forest Service in the East after the Weeks Act of 1911: 8,113 acres on Curtis Creek in McDowell County, bought from the Burke-McDowell Company. Five hundred acres of the land were described as "fire killed." Most of the tulip poplar had been cut, and the chestnut trees and chestnut oaks were being logged as the sale was completed. As the decades passed and the forest grew back, Curtis Creek became a popular fishing and camping spot. On some of the dry western slopes, old-growth researchers are finding stands of old trees overlooked by the early loggers.

The Pisgah owns 504,790 acres, or forty-seven percent of its 1,076,711-acre proclamation boundary. It lies in the Blue Ridge geological province, which widens from a few narrow ridges in Virginia to a broad complex of ranges in North Carolina. By this point in the Appalachians, gorges and waterfalls are becoming impressive, as at Linville Falls along the Blue Ridge Parkway. White-water canoeing and rafting, popular in Virginia and West Virginia, have become big business in western North Carolina.

Minerals and gems abound in the Pisgah: olivine, feldspar, mica, quartz, emerald, kyanite, apatite, tourmaline, beryl, gold, amethyst, ruby, sapphire, limestone, even uranium. Because of record-keeping idiosyncracies, it proved impossible to get an account of the acreage of outstanding and reserved mineral rights for either the Pisgah or the Nantahala National Forest, although one report referred to "many areas."

The Pisgah and Nantahala National Forests are administered jointly, and one land management plan addresses both. Only four appeals were filed against the first plan in 1987, compared with the George Washington's eighteen, but they were thorough enough to cause the plan to be amended. One of the major points made by the appellants was the lack of Forest Service concern for old growth. The Pisgah National Forest contains the largest remaining segment of unprotected old growth in the

U.S. Forest Service, National Forests of North Carolina, Asheville, NC

Felling a sugar maple in Big Ivy, Pisgah National Forest, 1950. All sugar maples over 12 inches in diameter were being cut at the time because of "sapstreak disease."

Appalachians, scattered in remnant stands within fourteen thousand acres in the Big Ivy watershed, east of Barnardsville.

Big Ivy, so-called because in local parlance mountain laurel is known as ivy, came to the attention of Karin Heiman in 1990, while she was working as a botanist for the National Forests of North Carolina. Hired to identify areas of plant diversity, Heiman quickly became mired in timber politics and believes that she was fired because of it. She began an appeal founded on the word "whistle-blower" but put it on hold so that she could earn a living doing field research, which involves a lot of travel.

A small strawberry blond with eyes the cool blue of a mountain stream, Karin was sunburned from fieldwork when we met for a hike in Big Ivy. The Forest Service had been logging in Big Ivy for several decades and was planning to do more. Heiman and others had documented over fifty rare plant and animal species there, some of them with hearteningly healthy populations. Fringed orchids and bead lilies bowed over the trail in front of us. A shield fern draped itself twenty feet up in a lightning crack in a northern red oak. In the lushest places grew every fanciful form of leaf, every imaginable elegance of blossom. The annual growth rings on the stump of a fallen hemlock numbered close to three hundred.

Karin stepped almost unconsciously out of her way to touch the largest trees in passing. After she came to know Big Ivy, she made its preservation a personal crusade. "It's been hard to get the local people involved," she said. She spoke softly, with a barely discernible cadence from her origins in the upper Midwest. "But we have interested a few."

The amended management plan required old-growth inventories in both forests. Estimates in 1995 identified a total of 98,000 acres of trees over one hundred years of age. The computer data were not thoroughly verified on the ground, and significant parts of Big Ivy escaped the inventory. "What generally gets on the old-growth inventories," Karin said, "is legally designated wilderness areas where no cutting is allowed anyway. Those tend to be high, rocky ridges where old growth can't get near as diverse as in Big Ivy, or may not ever develop true old-growth characteristics." To address the concern for old growth, planners in the Pisgah and Nantahala set up a network of small, medium, and large patches designated for old-growth restoration across both forests, for a total of nearly 170,000 acres. Although it remains to be seen exactly how much protection a designated old-growth patch will receive, environmentalists consider the patch system a model for old-growth planning on other national forests. The old-growth patch in Big Ivy is 3,273 acres, about twenty-three percent of the area.

Appalachian people have always collected plants from the mountains, and the tradition continues today by the truckful. Some national forests require permits to collect some species, but there is no standardized record-keeping system and no good way to enforce it anyway. The great variety of plant life in both the Pisgah and the Nantahala makes them particularly inviting. A surge of demand for herbal remedies has driven up the number of people harvesting ginseng and goldenseal. Moss, ferns, and galax are increasingly sought for floral arrangements (galax loses its skunky smell upon drying). Grapevines are cut for wreaths. Rhododendron, azalea, and other flowering plants are dug for ornamentals and often sold to nursery wholesalers. Mushrooms and berries are picked by the bucket. The garlicky-onion taste of ramps is valued as a spring tonic by many thousands of people and celebrated in annual festivals.

By far the most intensive collecting anywhere takes place on about a thousand acres on top of Roan Mountain, near the Tennessee state line. One of the few red spruce–Fraser fir forests that is characteristic of the highest elevations survives there. In a good year, up to a million four- to six-inch Fraser fir seedlings are pulled out of Roan Mountain's soft, mossy ground. People pay the Forest Service $96 per thousand and transfer them to private nursery beds. After two years, the foot-high seedlings are transplanted to fields for another eight years, fertilized, manicured, and then sold across the nation for Christmas trees. The popularity of the procedure has ballooned in recent years in proportion to the decline of burley tobacco, which used to be the economic mainstay of Mitchell County. The Forest Service samples plots before and after the sale, to monitor the harvest.

Parts of both the Pisgah and the Nantahala National Forests adjoin the Great Smoky Mountains National Park. In all of them, you are apt to run into small, scattered populations of wild pigs, or rather their unmistakable sign—the forest floor turned over as if by a herd of plows.

NANTAHALA NATIONAL FOREST, NORTH CAROLINA

In the Cheoah District of Nantahala National Forest, a wealthy Englishman established a private game reserve about 1900. He shipped and railroaded European bears, elk, and Russian wild pigs into fenced enclosures. The pigs escaped to the woods and mated with the domestic swine that still ranged freely in the mountains. Their wily, elusive progeny made for good hunting. Because of their habit of rooting up and eating endangered species, which is contrary to the more stringent rules in national parks, the pigs have been trapped for years by park rangers in the Great Smoky Mountains National Park and released into neighboring Cheoah District. Originally, the National Park Service simply wanted to eradicate the pigs, but local hunters protested. For a while, the hunters volunteered to help the park move pigs. At first, hundreds of pigs a year were relocated, and hundreds of pigs were weighed in at game checking stations. Average size was 150 to 200 pounds, but animals over 500 pounds have been documented. Over a period of years, the numbers relocated and shot have declined to dozens.

At 528,223 acres, the Nantahala owns only thirty-nine percent of its proclamation boundary. It is particularly splintered by private landholdings around half a dozen communities. Of these, Franklin and Highlands have been growing second homes for more than a century. In recent decades, the pace has accelerated. The outlines of privately owned ridges are defined not by waving, endless silhouettes of trees but by staccato dashes of rooflines and chimneys.

What may be the best-known remnant of old growth in the East is located in the Nantahala: Joyce Kilmer Memorial Forest. More than a hundred species of trees, and specimens over three hundred years old, survive on thirty-eight hundred acres saved from imminent logging. It was dedicated in 1936. Joyce Kilmer, author of the poem that begins "I think that I shall never see/A poem lovely as a tree," was born in New Jersey, died in France during World War I, and never, so far as I know, visited the place later named for him. Fifty thousand other people do each year. Nonetheless, the Horse Cove Campground just outside the Memorial Forest wasn't full when we stayed there several years ago, despite the fact that it's a particularly beautiful campground. A pine needle bed pad beside a tumbling stream with rhododendrons bowing over it was like a picture, except for the clear-cutting going on right up to the border of the Joyce Kilmer–Slickrock Wilderness Area, where cutting has to stop by authority of law.

The combined harvests of the Nantahala and Pisgah average just under four thousand acres a year. Clear-cutting accounts for less than ten percent of the harvest, a substantial reduction from the 1980s. The two forests lose more money on timber sales than any of the other Appalachian national forests, amounting to either a few hundred thousand dollars or millions, depending on whether the Forest Service or environmentalists are doing the figuring. Below-cost sales, in which the Forest Service spends more to prepare a logging road or administer a sale than the sale brings in, is a common feature of most national forests but is especially characteristic of the Appalachians. Logging is more expensive on national forest land there because terrain is steeper, distances to roads are greater, and trees per acre are fewer, compared with private land. The Forest Service tries to compensate and make logging more attractive by various inducements, such as building roads.

The Pisgah and Nantahala National Forests encompass the greatest elevational change of all Appalachian national forests, providing the most diverse range of habitats and creatures. *Nantahala* is a Cherokee word meaning "land of the noonday sun," referring to the Nantahala River Gorge, where the sun reaches the valley floor only at midday. A total of twenty-two plants and animals are on the Threatened and Endangered Species List. Nearly three hundred more plants are categorized as sensitive, including more than fifty kinds of mosses.

Insects are notable in the national forests of North Carolina, though not for good reasons. The balsam woolly adelgid, accidentally introduced from Europe, has killed many if not most of the older Fraser firs that occur on high peaks such as Roan Mountain, although the Forest Service maintains that there are still enough firs to produce the cones that produce the seedlings that sustain local Christmas tree growers. An isolated infestation of gypsy moths, another introduced tree killer that has been making its way south from Massachusetts since 1869, reached the southern tip of the Nantahala in the 1980s. It was eradicated by a chemical insecticide called Dimilin. Hopes are rising that the moth may not, after all, become the scourge of the Appalachians—not because of Dimilin, but because of a fungus that attacks the gypsy moth caterpillars.

The cliffs of Whiteside Mountain, where I trekked with Bob Zahner, are within the Nantahala National Forest, and the area is famous for waterfalls. At 411 feet, Whitewater Falls is the highest east of the Mississippi River. At Dry Falls, I walked behind the roaring torrent without getting wet, to verify its name. The Nantahala and Pisgah have between them more than thirty thousand acres of lakes and reservoirs, maintained for hydropower and flood control by the Tennessee Valley Authority, Nantahala Power and Light, and the Aluminum Company of America. At 480 feet, the dam at Fontana Lake in the Nantahala, along the boundary with Great Smoky Mountains National Park, is the highest in the East. For twenty-nine miles, Fontana water curls into mountain hollows, where morning fog becomes snagged like skeins of gray wool. The availability of so much water in the Pisgah and Nantahala boosts their recreational draw; together, the two forests may host as many as twenty million visitors a year.

In Fontana and other such lakes, heavy drawdowns of water for electricity from August to December destroy crucial shoreline habitat and reduce possibilities for fish and wildlife. Nonetheless, migrating waterfowl sometimes use them for resting. Some friends of mine saw a young bald eagle while they were swimming in Santeetlah Lake, near the Joyce

Kilmer Memorial Forest. A human family was playing along the shore, and they had a yapping little poodle. Suddenly, my friends said, the yapping stopped. They looked up and saw a huge brown bird carrying the dog away across the lake. The bird had trouble rising, and after a couple hundred yards dropped the dog into the water, where he struggled for a few moments and then disappeared. The people on the shore were yelling and crying.

SUMTER NATIONAL FOREST, SOUTH CAROLINA

There are no artificial lakes in the headwaters of the Chattooga River, although from my outlook above its course, the mountains swelled up through an ocean of clouds like standing waves. Rising in North Carolina, the Chattooga's southward flow forms the boundary between South Carolina and Georgia. Three different national forests in these three states cover parts of its watershed. The Chattooga is the largest and longest free-flowing mountain river in the Southeast, dropping half a mile over the fifty-seven miles of its protected length. Many people have drowned trying to run its rapids. Its white water formed the background for the most notorious novel ever written about Appalachia, James Dickey's 1970 book, *Deliverance,* which was made into a movie.

In South Carolina, the Chattooga forms the western border of the Andrew Pickens Ranger District of Sumter National Forest. The presence of the river is the salient feature of the only district of this national forest that lies in the Appalachians. The Pickens was named after a general who forced the Cherokees out of the area with a treaty in 1792. The district has 80,151 acres, or sixty-two percent of its proclamation boundary.

In 1974, Congress authorized purchase of a corridor up to one mile wide along the river. There was little furor over the purchase of sixty-two hundred acres of private land in forty-seven tracts, but there was plenty when the Forest Service closed several jeep trails down to the river. The roads were closed to restore the character of the forty miles of river designated as "wild." In response, locals torched parts of the national forest. As visitors to the river have increased to more than a hundred thousand a year, some of the local people, few of whom ride the river, continue to express their resentment in less incendiary ways about Forest Service management for what they see as special-interest and minority groups.

CHATTAHOOCHEE NATIONAL FOREST, GEORGIA

On the road to Clayton, Georgia, I passed a tourist trap named Gold City, where I was invited to pan for gold. It was the only remnant I saw in northern Georgia of the 1828 gold rush that pushed the Cherokees onto the Trail of Tears. Traces of old mines can still be found farther south near Dahlonega. Some $17 million worth of gold was extracted from the region before 1849, when the big strike in California moved all the action to the West. There's still occasional interest in gold mining, especially when the price of gold goes up. Mining of any sort couldn't be very promising in the area, though, since only fifty-two thousand acres of the Chattahoochee National Forest have outstanding or reserved rights.

This national forest contains 749,418 acres, which constitute forty-seven percent of its proclamation area. The Chattahoochee, a Cherokee word meaning "flowering rock," covers some of the southernmost reaches of the Appalachians into the foothills of the Georgia piedmont. Hickories and white and red oaks still grow at higher elevations, but shortleaf, Virginia, white, pitch, and loblolly pines are much more common than in the north.

Just outside of Clayton I drove down a long, long slope toward what looked like great walls of mountains. Kudzu swallowed the orange clay of the road banks. I passed the Rabun Gap–Nacoochee School, an imposing red brick building, where Eliot Wigginton started an Appalachian renaissance by sending his students out to interview mountaineers. They asked about hog dressing, snake handling, corn shucking, gourd banjos, and "other affairs of plain living." The Foxfire project began in 1966 as a way to motivate students. It succeeded, growing into a student publishing enterprise with book sales in the millions.

Within sight of the school stands Rabun Bald, which at 4,696 feet misses being Georgia's highest mountain by less than a hundred feet. In 1775, William Bartram, one of America's first and most appreciative botanists, passed through Rabun Gap on his tour of the Southeast. His journal notes many a "charming vale," "delightful brook," and "sublimely high forest." Bartram's route into the mountains from the lowlands of South Carolina was marked by volunteers in the 1980s as the Bartram Trail. It runs for thirty-seven miles through the Chattahoochee, from the West Fork of the Chattooga River over the summit of Rabun Bald, and continues into North Carolina. References in Bartram's journal to waterfalls, rivers, and mountaintops were used to plot the trail as closely as possible to his actual route.

Brasstown Bald is Georgia's highest mountain, also located within the Chattahoochee, but Springer Mountain (3,782 feet) is better known because of the Appalachian Trail, which runs through most of the Appalachian national forests. The trail begins at Springer Mountain. Or you could say that it ends there, but it makes much more sense to begin in the south in early spring and hike north twenty-one hundred miles to Maine in pace with summer's arrival in the high country. The ruggedness of the trail's seventy-nine miles in the Chattahoochee takes many hikers by surprise.

Every part of the Chattahoochee is within a couple hours' drive of Atlanta and its multiplying suburbs. Estimates of the number of annual visitors to the Chattahoochee range close to ten million. Tens of millions receive their drinking water from the forest. Living on the Chattahoochee are fourteen species of plants and animals that are federally listed as threatened or endangered; another twenty live so close by that it is assumed that populations continue into the national forest.

The Chattahoochee provides twenty-five percent of the timber volume sold in northern Georgia and calls itself the primary provider of quality hardwoods in the state. Harvest statistics include the much smaller Oconee National Forest in central Georgia, with which the Chattahoochee is jointly administered, but most of the seven to eight thousand acres cut per year in the 1990s came from the Chattahoochee. By the early 1990s, the number of acres being clear-cut each year had dropped to less than a hundred, from a high of five to six thousand acres a decade earlier. At the same time, the number of acres being cut as "salvage and sanitation" went from less than fifty to around three thousand a year. Many national forests across the country showed the same trend and gave the same reasons: protection of forest health, such as cuts that would retard the spread of destructive southern pine beetles, and cuts that would remove the woody fuel for a rampaging fire.

The Armuchee Ranger District in the northwest corner of Georgia is separated from the rest of the Chattahoochee by several major highways and busy towns. It is roughly shaped like an arrow that points southwest toward the Talladega National Forest in Alabama. The last of the Appalachian Mountains can be found there, but the Talladega is about seventy-five miles away, a long distance for most plants and animals to travel in search of dependable forest cover. So I'm turning north here to stay within the reasonable possibility of contiguous forest afforded by public ownership of land.

CHEROKEE NATIONAL FOREST, TENNESSEE

The Cherokee National Forest runs along Tennessee's eastern edge from Georgia to Virginia, except in the middle, where the Great Smoky Mountains National Park lies. The Cherokee has common borders with the Chattahoochee, Nantahala, Pisgah, and Jefferson National Forests. The 633,483 acres of the Cherokee therefore serve to link many of the southern Appalachian national forests and the park into a large, if deeply fissured, block of public land. The Cherokee holds fifty-three percent within its proclamation boundary.

Like all the lands it adjoins, the Cherokee was cut over and burned during the heyday of lumbering. In addition, it has at its southeastern limit the area known as Copper Basin, once ranked as the largest manmade biological desert in the country. Copper was discovered there in 1843. By the early 1900s, sulfuric acid fumes from copper processing and fuel wood cutting to feed the furnaces had stripped all vegetation from thirty-two thousand acres. Mounds of soil washed away with the more than sixty inches of rain that fell every year, and tons of silt are still moving down the Ocoee River, which drains the basin. On average, three feet of soil was lost across the area.

A change in mining technology in 1912 made it possible to recover the sulfuric acid before it was vented in fumes. The acid was then sold for a profit to the fertilizer industry. In the 1930s, a coalition of county, state, and federal agencies, private industries, and educational institutions began a partnership to reclaim the site. More than sixteen million trees have been planted; acid-tolerant grass and legume seeds have been spread by helicopter. The brown earth is now speckled with green.

The Ocoee River Gorge, downstream from Copper Basin, was the venue for the 1996 Olympic slalom canoe and kayak events. The chasm is narrow and nearly perpendicular. Driving in and out of deep shade and bright sun made it almost painful to keep an eye on the bustle under way at all the scenic pull-offs in preparation for the games when I passed through. The river course had a smooth rock bottom broken by jumbles of bouldery rapids, over which an absolutely transparent river flowed like liquid glass. Later I learned that some of the rapids were fake. The Forest Service had hired a firm to modify fourteen features in the channel, which involved drilling anchor bolts four inches deep into adjacent rock. Rebar, plastic mesh, and colorized concrete were layered over them.

The clarity of the water owes something to the fact that it is almost sterile along part of its course, because the concentration of heavy metals in the runoff from Copper Basin has killed aquatic life. This is a shame, because rivers in the Cherokee have more aquatic species than any other national forest in the country. In part, this is due to the variety of stream habitats, with waters of different temperatures and chemistries that issue from forests of differing slopes, elevations, and aspects. Plus the rocky barriers to movement up and down the rivers fostered local specializations. It's likely that a couple of mussel or fish species lived only in the upper Ocoee and nowhere else and are now extinct. There's no way to ever know for sure, because no one inventoried the original aquatic species before mining started in Copper Basin.

One hundred fifty-eight species of native fish have been documented in the Cherokee, as well as seventy mammals and nearly three hundred birds. Fish and mussels have engaging names like blue shiner, frecklebelly madtom, amber darter, and Alabama moccasinshell. A total of thirty-five aquatic and terrestrial species are on the federal Threatened and Endangered Species List; more than two hundred others are considered sensitive.

The Conasauga River is particularly rich in endemic fishes, with eleven of them endangered, threatened, or sensitive, plus six species of endangered mussels. When Cherokee forest managers recently proposed to cut more than five hundred acres of trees spread over ninety-three hundred acres in the Conasauga watershed, environmentalists objected even though no clear-cutting was involved. Why take the chance, they argued, of letting silt carried by rain from the logging roads degrade the river bottom? As on other national forests, lawsuits and appeals caused the amount of timber harvested in the Cherokee to drop sharply in the 1990s, from more than three thousand to less than one thousand acres. The proportion of those acres harvested by clear-cutting also dropped.

The Cherokee priestess Nancy Ward is not altogether forgotten. Her grave is located near the western edge of the Cherokee National Forest, just off Route 441. A parking lot for a dozen cars was empty on a Friday afternoon when I drove in. A long cement walkway with railings curved up a small rise through a pasture. At the top was a single large cedar, the tree most sacred to the Cherokees. Beneath it were three mounds of rocks, each with a headstone, enclosed in a low iron fence. The marker for Nancy's brother was a natural stone, blank except for blotches of bright orange lichen. Her son's marker was inscribed, "Five Killer Pvt. Morgan Jr.'s Cherokee Indians War of 1812." On Nancy's stone was a plaque:

> In memory of Nancy Ward, princess and prophetess of the Cherokee Nation, the Pocahontas of Tennessee, the constant friend of the American pioneer. Born 1738 died 1822. Erected by the Nancy Ward Chapter of the Daughters of the American Revolution 1923.

Maybe the DAR didn't realize that pots and pans had been buried in Nancy's grave in thoroughly heathen fashion and that Nancy's last official missive to her people urged that no more land be sold to whites. There was a heat-hazed view to the mountains from her grave, over meadows in which hay bales had just been rolled up. In between the drone of logging trucks and recreational campers on the road, there was the sound of cicadas. Several bundles of plastic and dried flowers and a plastic American flag decorated Nancy's grave. Her monument was beaded along the top with pebbles from the nearby river, a practice that I had heard was a customary homage. I walked down to the riverbank to pick a contribution, but the slope was waist-high with poison ivy, and I had shorts on.

DANIEL BOONE NATIONAL FOREST, KENTUCKY

There was a traffic jam on the Wilderness Road. A line of nose-to-tail coaches streamed up and over Cumberland Gap, heading toward the promise of Kentucky bluegrass country. It was a sweaty July day. Sun beat down through the wide, ragged opening the new road made through the forest. Toppled trees were wilting. Dirt in their root balls dried up and blew away in a fine, parching dust. My throat was gritty with it, and my stomach was growling. And I didn't have air-conditioning.

A little travail on the trail keeps you humble. When I finally got clear of road construction and zoomed down a four-lane highway into Middlesboro, a small city in the Cumberland Mountains, I was relieved to see that the bluegrass had delivered early on its promise: a fast-food strip, with Arby's, Roy Rogers, McDonald's, Long John Silver, and more. For this the pioneers had braved Indian warfare and worked themselves into early graves. It looked good to me just then, as I expect it would have to them.

Daniel Boone and thirty axmen spent three weeks in 1775 cutting a 208-mile horse trail through this remarkably convenient set of mountain gaps, feasting on the abundant wild turkey as they went. Over the next two decades, two hundred thousand people traveled an average of ten miles a day on the route into America's Midwest. They ate what game they could get, and cooked the meager corn they carried with them over fires that threw uneasy shadows across the trail. At first they poured through Cumberland Gap into flatter farmland, passing on through the deeply cloven foothills of the escarpment of the Cumberland Plateau, which forms the western border of Appalachia. These hills were settled when the press of migration slackened in the early 1800s, as new highways in other places relegated the Wilderness Road to a backwater. The settlers here were often mountaineers from farther east and north.

The forest that Daniel Boone chopped through lay in the heart of what Lucy Braun would later name the mixed mesophytic forest, the most biologically diverse temperate woodland in the world. The national forest named after Boone has 691,000 acres, which represent thirty-five percent of its proclamation boundary, the most fragmented of all the Appalachian national forests. The Boone is situated west of the most productive coal-mining country; still, seventy percent of its acreage has outstanding rights. Seven deep coal mines are in operation. Oil and gas companies have been interested in eastern Kentucky since the early 1900s and still hold dozens of leases on the forest.

Lying as far west as it does, the Boone is not contiguous with any other national forest. Its own disjunct Redbird Ranger District, a few valleys east of the main body of the Boone, is tantalizingly close to the Jefferson National Forest's Clinch Ranger District in Virginia, which itself is just a few ridges away from the main body of the Jefferson.

The Boone is dominated by a wide variety of hardwoods: scarlet oak, northern red oak, basswood, beech, yellow poplar, sugar and red maples, and birch on north and east slopes and in coves, with hickory and white and chestnut oaks on west slopes. On dry south slopes and ridges there are shortleaf, pitch, and Virginia pines in small, pure groups,

Special Collections and Archives, University of Kentucky Libraries, PA91M2

Hauling a log near Troublesome Creek, Perry County, Kentucky, 1930.

as well as mixed with hardwoods. These pines form the northernmost habitat of the red-cockaded woodpecker, which is one of thirty-seven threatened and endangered species in the Boone, the most of any Appalachian national forest.

Red-cockaded woodpeckers usually nest in old longleaf, shortleaf, or slash pines that grow farther south and lower in elevation. The pines must be old enough—roughly a century—to develop red-heart fungus, which softens the heartwood and makes excavating a nest cavity easier. In lowland forests, years of suppressing the natural lightning fires allowed the hardwood understory to grow up around the pines. When hardwood crowns reach the level of nesting cavities, they ruin the habitat for woodpeckers, which prefer open spaces to keep watch for predators. The Forest Service began regularly burning areas inhabited by red-cockaded woodpeckers to keep them in pines.

But in the Boone, where pines are mixed with hardwoods, woodpeckers forage on hardwoods for insects. They nest in Virginia pines, a tree that is able to grow on depleted, eroded mountain land but is the most fire-sensitive of the pines. So when the Boone began to follow the practice of national forests to the south by cutting out oaks and burning, pines available for nesting were killed. Dense shrubbery grew up, which had to be burned every three years, killing more pines. The artificial cavities made by the Forest Service killed more trees yet. An academic researcher went to every known woodpecker colony in Kentucky in front of the chain saws and counted sixteen birds. Afterward, there were four.

In less than a decade, beginning in the late 1980s, the Boone reduced the number of acres harvested annually for timber from between four and five thousand to less than two thousand. All harvesting was done by clear-cutting until 1990, when shelterwood methods were adopted. But the most lucrative crop that the Boone produces these days is not one that the Forest Service can manage. After California, Kentucky is the country's leading supplier of homegrown marijuana, and most of it comes from the Boone. Dope is the economic mainstay of several counties around the national forest. Local car dealers enjoy big cash sales every fall after the crop is harvested. A banker found that his assets declined by $5 million when he asked depositors to complete tax forms for cash deposits over $10,000.

A study of drug-producing regions of the world sponsored by the United Nations likened the attitudes and behavior of pot growers in Kentucky to those of the poorest peasants in Third World countries. Like poverty, violence, or at least the threat of it, is also associated with illegal drugs. One Kentucky grower tied native poisonous copperhead snakes to his plants, which proved their mettle by biting a state trooper. At least one wildlife researcher at a local university canceled a project in the Boone because of potential danger to his students.

There were no marijuana plants on Cromer Ridge, off Interstate 75 between the towns of London and Mount Vernon. There were no plants of any kind in the middle of that red sandstone moonscape. This privately owned hundred acres within the Boone may have been the first off-highway-vehicle (OHV) playground in the East, with an early version called dune buggies gouging out mud holes and jumps as early as 1974. Manufacturers of OHVs soon expanded into various designs of open-sided two-, three-, and four-wheeled machines capable of roaring across almost any kind of terrain. At Cromer Ridge, they had created gullies fifteen feet deep and wide enough for a tractor trailer. I walked past islands of bruised trees sliding down the cliffs. "Get visible," yelled the friend who had taken me there, as we heard motors approaching. A pack of four-wheelers zipped by, driven by kids that looked younger than twelve years old.

OHVs are popular in all the national forests, despite controversy over their destructive impact. More than five million people visit the Boone every year, and a lot of them like to ride OHVs. Most forests restrict

OHVs to designated, clearly marked trails, but the Boone is by far the most generous. More than eighty percent of it is open not only for trail use by OHV's but cross-country, too. The resulting degradation has prompted Boone administrators to propose a change in policy even before the next round of forest plan revisions comes due.

In a slow version of OHV erosion, the natural forces of wind and weather over the last seventy million years have sculpted eighty large arches in the Boone's Red River Gorge Geological Area, near Winchester. This is the largest concentration of arches east of Utah. The sandstone span at the Natural Arch Scenic Area near Somerset is more than a hundred feet wide and sixty feet high. The Boone is further distinguished by cliffs. The nearly perpendicular walls blasted by highway construction through the rugged little mountains looked amazingly to me like the natural bluffs of the area. But at the base of some of the natural formations are cavelike indentations, called rock shelters. Pioneers followed the example of eons of Indians and used them as houses until they could build something better.

BIG SOUTH FORK NATIONAL RIVER AND RECREATION AREA, KENTUCKY AND TENNESSEE

South of the Daniel Boone National Forest lies the Big South Fork National River and Recreation Area. It is part of the national park system but has attributes that straddle the division between park and national forest. It allows hunting, like a national forest, but prohibits timbering, like a national park. Deer, turkeys, squirrels, and rabbits are popular game. Bear hunting is prohibited because bears are rare, having been cleared out through logging and hunting by the 1920s. Twelve adult female bears, some with cubs, were brought from the Great Smoky Mountains National Park in the mid-1990s, tranquilized, given radio collars, and hauled by stretcher to winter dens searched out by park wildlife biologists. Women carried the cubs under their shirts, then smeared them with Vaporub to cover the human scent from handling. Getting the bears into the dens was a trip in itself. Within a couple of years, half the bears died or disappeared, but the other six remained, and a few of them were seen with cubs.

The Big South Fork was authorized in 1974 to contain 123,000 acres; to date, its administrators have acquired over 113,000 acres, a handful of them from unwilling sellers. Most of the acreage extends into Tennessee. Just under a million visitors a year enjoy the scenic gorges cut by the Big South Fork on its way to the Cumberland River, and many of them float the fork and its tributaries in winter and early spring, when the flow is more reliable than in summer.

The river depends on rainfall for life, yet every rain washes in death as well. Toxic heavy metals leach from more than a hundred abandoned coal shafts and from spoil piles visible along the shoreline. Fishing is good in places throughout the Big South Fork system, but the mine drainage is a microcosm of a persistent water quality problem throughout coal-mining country. Heavy metals occur naturally and for the most part harmlessly in the ground, but when dug up and exposed to oxygen, they become soluble in water. Iron precipitates into a mat called yellow boy that strangles the stream bottoms. The only way known to retrieve a stream from the grip of yellow boy is to put new sediment on top and start a whole new aquatic community. The park is sponsoring a major study to identify the worst of its mine drainages and to find ways to deal with the particular circumstances of each.

GREAT SMOKY MOUNTAINS (NORTH CAROLINA AND TENNESSEE) AND SHENANDOAH (VIRGINIA) NATIONAL PARKS

In contradistinction to the bearlessness of Big South Fork, the bears of Great Smoky Mountains National Park, just eighty miles southeast as the crow flies, constitute the second thickest population of black bears known anywhere. Shenandoah National Park, three hundred miles to the north, ranks first. Bears are the stars of Appalachian recovery. They have always been the trophy animal of Appalachia, a tradition that shows no sign of weakening. Bear hunting continued mercilessly even as industrial logging destroyed bear habitat. Then chestnut blight wiped out the bears' richest source of food. Bears disappeared from most of Appalachia, holding on only in the craggiest, most isolated heights, the kind of areas being purchased by the federal government. It's been estimated that when Congress authorized the two Appalachian parks in 1926, fifty to two hundred bears roamed the 520,000 acres of the Great Smokies. At only 195,000 acres, with more roads available to hunters, Shenandoah had far fewer, possibly none at all.

Hunting of all sorts was first restricted, then prohibited, when the parks were established. Logging stopped, and wildfires were extinguished. The Blue Ridge locations of both parks are among the most productive sites in all the Appalachians, and although the chestnuts were gone, other food supplies for bears grew up rapidly after the forest was protected. Up to six hundred bears are estimated today in Shenandoah, as many as two bears per square mile. In the Great Smokies, bears aren't quite as thick but still total in excess of seven hundred animals.

By the 1970s, bears in both parks had learned to forage in trash cans and campsites for the easy meals available there. They were encouraged to approach humans because people hand-fed them. A photo opportunity with a bear became a tourist coup. There is a Park Service legend—I've not been able to track down its actual source—about tourist stupidity with regard to bears: A parent smeared a child's cheek with jelly to entice a bear's cute pink tongue. The big white teeth that entered the picture and bit the child's face came as a surprise.

Like national parks out west, the two Appalachian parks have evolved a bear policy over decades of experience. Park rangers now take much time and trouble to minimize human contact with bears, and it's working. Relations between the species are usually peaceful.

Ralph and I had stopped at a spring beside the trail to Gregory Bald in Great Smoky Mountains National Park, when I heard a slight scuffling noise a few hundred feet upslope. A very large black bear was just visible in the undergrowth. After the first surge of adrenaline subsided, I said, "Hello Mr. Bear," softly but loud enough for him to hear, to make sure that our presence was known. But he was already well aware of us and seemed to be waiting patiently for us to leave, maybe so he could drink from the pool beside the trail. Clearly, he had chosen the distance between us, and we never decreased it. We walked slowly away up the trail, watching him amble just as slowly toward the spring as we went, until the trail curved over a hip of mountain and he was out of sight. I restrained myself from yipping with joy over this calm and mutually respectful encounter. For once, a wild animal had not run away from me.

The protection that national parks offer, which made this bear willing to show himself, sharply distinguishes parks from national forests. With the exception of sport fishing and scientific collecting, extractions of plants or animals from most parks are prohibited. Both Great Smoky

Mountains and Shenandoah National Parks serve as refuges for bears and other species, plant as well as animal, that would otherwise be consumed in some way or other by humans in the surrounding countryside.

Both parks are heavily visited; at nine million a year, the Great Smokies get more tourists than any other national park in the country. Both parks suffer equally from winds that blow from the west, carrying industrial pollutants across political boundaries to damage the forests. And both parks are involved in conflicts with some of the local residents.

The two Appalachian parks represent the dark side of public land acquisitions. Each of them contained hundreds of families, many of whom did not want to move. It was actually the state governments that condemned land from unwilling sellers and donated it for the national parks, but it is the federal government, and particularly the National Park Service, that bears the brunt of local blame.

Promoters of the parks—local judges, doctors, real-estate agents, and other members of the upper-middle-class elite who controlled the valley towns—allied with a wide variety of outside interests, including schoolchildren who contributed their pennies toward the purchase of parkland. Local park advocates touted the solace of "virgin woods" for teeming urban masses and the benefits of tourism for local economies. They utilized mythic images of "eighteenth-century-like" mountain folk to justify removing "a few" people. Mountain residents were portrayed as illiterate and uncouth people with lives that were stunted or, better yet, grotesquely deformed by social isolation. They were called squatters on the land and abusers of it. The 1933 book *Hollow Folk,* the most notorious scholarly work on Appalachia, manipulated and possibly even falsified data to highlight filth and ignorance in mountain life.

Shenandoah National Park is now heavily forested, but in the 1920s, one-third of it was pasture. Prosperous farmers from lowlands on both sides of the mountains owned large tracts of land and ran their cattle up to thrive on cool green meadows every summer. As late as 1927, Virginia's Blue Ridge was recognized as a prime beef-producing area. The people who lived there were mostly small landowners and legal tenants who helped mind other people's cattle. They occupied log cabins but also clapboard houses. Most of them grew corn and garden vegetables and kept a few head of livestock, in the typical subsistence lifestyle, but there were also storekeepers and tradesmen. Until the tanbark industry turned to synthetic chemicals, followed by the chestnut tree blight that deprived them of nuts to sell as well as feed for livestock, mountain people made what money they needed from the forest left by the loggers.

They also earned seasonal wages at Skyland, a resort on Stony Man Mountain. George Freeman Pollock came to Stony Man in 1886 to examine a copper mine his father owned there, but it was the scenery that most engaged his attention. A hotel at Black Rock Springs, 45 miles to the south, had already been in operation since about 1830, but Pollock had grown up in Washington, D.C., and knew he could attract an affluent clientele. He built several bark-covered cabins on Stony Man in the 1890s, personally throwing a rattlesnake out the back window of one of them before he ushered in his first customers. By 1910, Pollock's "dude ranch and resort" was so large it had its own post office. Skyland provided a handy place for natives to market home-grown produce and white oak baskets (mostly made by men), and to exchange pleasantries with outsiders.

Archaeological excavations of old homesteads in Shenandoah document a people who participated in the twentieth century just as much as they wanted to. Coke bottles, Bakelite toys, a 1931 calendar featuring the artwork of Maxfield Parrish, and a metal ray gun testify to a familiarity with modernity. A number of men from the back hollows fought in World War I. Evidence of terracing, a method for protecting land from erosion that is rarely found elsewhere in Appalachia, shows concern for more efficient farming. Mountain people did marry cousins more frequently than did people in the lowlands, but that is a misleading indicator of social isolation. About a third of the mountain people could read, although, as one elderly man said in a taped interview, it didn't occur to anyone to read the contracts the government gave them to sign. But they understood what the coming of thousands of outsiders and the loss of lumbering jobs might do to them, not to mention dispossession of their own homes.

Park promoters and representatives of state and federal governments lied repeatedly to the mountain people in both parks, telling them that they would not have to move. In the Great Smokies, the Park Service did grant lifetime leases, but "they made hit so difficult to stay we had to leave," said Mr. McGaha, whom I met in the Cataloochee Campground in the park one damp and buggy July evening. Cataloochee was once the largest community in the Great Smokies, twice as big as the more famous village in Cades Cove. Mr. McGaha had been in seventh grade at the

Beech Grove School, up the road from the campsite where we stood talking, when his parents moved out in the 1930s with their ten children. He still spoke in mountain dialect, using the old form "hit" for "it." Cutting of green wood was prohibited as soon as the park came in; only deadwood could be used for heating and cooking, Mr. McGaha said, but the Park Service wouldn't let people cut up the dead trees in their backyards.

"You had to haul hit from the deep woods," said Mr. McGaha, "and if you made too big a mess getting hit out, you got fined." When my husband and I go camping, we travel light, and we didn't have a chair to offer the old gentleman. He leaned against the car and was so soft-spoken that we leaned toward him to hear. I asked if he was bitter toward the park. "Oh, no, hit was the best thing that could have happened," he said. "I don't believe in this first cousin marriage, and there was too much of hit."

In Shenandoah, lifetime leases were harder to get. Most families did not own the land they lived on, which reduced their eligibility for compensation. They were evicted, some forcibly, and their possessions removed. Like the Cherokees at the beginning of the Trail of Tears, some mountaineers saw their homes burned by the government to prevent their return. A photograph of the Shenandoah removal shows two burly men carrying a woman, who is obviously struggling against them, across a snow-covered field. She was five months pregnant at the time. Some people were resettled on farms and others in government-built, rambler-style houses around park borders. They were saddled with mortgages and other foreign monthly bills. Few remained in their resettlement homes, though many stayed in the area.

The legacy of bitterness lives on. Poaching by some residents around park borders is one manifestation of hostility and is a chronic problem in both parks. Shenandoah, a long, thin park more easily accessible than the Great Smokies, closes parts of the popular Skyline Drive on fall and winter nights to reduce poachers' entry into the park. Although Shenandoah is not authorized to purchase land and can acquire it only through donation, paranoia about park expansion is rife. When Shenandoah administrators initiated a study of land borders in the early 1990s to identify ecological and recreational problems, the public meetings they held to explain it were tense with emotion. Opponents commandeered an international symbol to make their point: a stick-on label of a circle containing a capital P for park, with a slash through it. Infants who couldn't yet walk sported them.

A group of descendants organized themselves into a group called the Children of Shenandoah to urge the park to revise its historical interpretation of mountain culture. They asked that park videos and publications show the richer side of mountain life, instead of presenting all mountain people as pitifully uneducated, poor, and abusive to the land. They asked for acknowledgment that the park dealt badly with them. Park officials agreed to consider their suggestions.

In the Great Smokies, descendants of mountaineers near Hazel Creek, on the other side of the park from Cataloochee, asked that a road be built to family cemeteries that were landlocked in the park when Fontana Lake was created. To make the reservoir, the Tennessee Valley Authority flooded an existing road and promised to replace it with a new thirty-mile route. Only nine miles were ever built, because the steepness of the terrain required extensive blasting and bulldozing, and the expense became enormous. Park officials also opposed a new road because construction would expose the underlying Anakeesta rock, which is extremely acidic and could leach heavy metals into streams in the same way that coal mines cause acid drainage. Once or twice a year, the park charters a boat and arranges to transport family members to the graves. A group of descendants pursued a lawsuit up to the Supreme Court, but the case was dismissed because cemeteries were never mentioned in the original agreement to build a replacement road.

Despite their historical and biological similarities, as pieces in the ecological jigsaw puzzle of Appalachia the two parks are very different. Great Smoky Mountains National Park is almost as large as the average Appalachian national forest. Most important of all, logging was halted before it swept through the entire park. Over a hundred thousand acres of some of the greatest trees of the Great Forest remain in the Great Smokies, the largest amount of ancient forest in the Appalachians. This is the core of Appalachian wilderness.

Shenandoah National Park is, comparatively, one of Appalachia's ecological extremities. Not only is it much smaller, but what acreage it has is stretched along the hundred miles of Skyline Drive, making it no more than a ribbon of protected land. It is embedded in private lands rather than almost surrounded by national forests, as are the Great Smokies. Shenandoah has virtually no old growth. To preserve a forest remnant for guests at Skyland, George Freeman Pollock's wife paid

$1,000 in 1920 to save a hundred of the largest hemlocks in the Limberlost area from the advance of sawyers. Limberlost is now Shenandoah's premier old growth.

BLUE RIDGE PARKWAY

Linking the two national parks is the Blue Ridge Parkway, begun in 1935 by men on relief during the Great Depression. It wasn't completed until 1987, with the last eight-mile segment across Grandfather Mountain in North Carolina held up for years by Grandfather's private owner, who demanded that engineers redesign it to mitigate the destruction of his mountainside. It was the first highway planned exclusively for leisure travel and scenic views. Outlooks are abundant on its 469 miles along the crest of the Blue Ridge.

With a total of eighty-seven thousand acres along its length, the Blue Ridge Parkway is the last Appalachian tract in federal ownership to approach the hundred-thousand-acre mark. Other federal parcels range from the eighty-six acres that inaugurated the Canaan Valley National Wildlife Refuge in 1994 to the more than sixty thousand acres in the New River Gorge National River, both in West Virginia. In addition to federal public lands, all Appalachian states operate their own systems of parks, forests, preserves, and wildlife management areas. These places are generally protected from the most destructive kinds of ecological disturbance. Occasionally, as in the case of Virginia's Goshen–Little North Mountain Wildlife Management Area, they link two otherwise separated expanses of public land. Rarely, though, do any of them exceed ten thousand acres in size.

The 150-mile segment of the Blue Ridge Parkway that passes through southwest Virginia and northwest North Carolina leaves the shelter of surrounding national forest and ventures across private lands. There, it forms the easternmost thread of the frayed fabric of Appalachian public lands. In its attenuated shape—an average of only eight hundred feet wide, bisected by a highway traveled by twenty million vehicles a year—the parkway embodies one of the most important issues for the incipient ecological state of Appalachia. What travel routes exist for plant seeds and animals that will otherwise become inbred, as obstacles posed by human development inexorably isolate small populations? In nature, as in society, connections are everything.

NEW OLD GROWTH

I BECAME CONSCIOUS OF THE POWER OF SUCCESSION AT THE OLD HOME-site Ralph and I bought in West Virginia. Within a few years, the trees on the slope below the ridge-top meadow grew tall enough to obscure the view. Within a decade, the knee-high maple seedlings on the grassy old cornfield grew up enough to shade out the grass. But it was what the briers gave way to that surprised me the most. I guess I had assumed that the hairball of brambles in a far corner would always be there, bristling and impenetrable, but saplings eventually began to poke through. Gradually, so that we didn't notice when we came to visit, the briers died back under the shade of young trees. One autumn day, when leaves cascaded in torrents of russet and gold, something in Day-Glo pink caught my eye. It was a 1950s station wagon. Eight or ten other models lay careened into position, glinting in the occasional shaft of sun that pierced the new forest canopy. Enough scattered body parts lay around to put together another dozen oldies. We owned an auto graveyard. Stunned into silliness, we struck bizarre poses among the wrecks and snapped photographs of each other.

Succession is the term for the stages a forest goes through as it ages, from open ground to thorny brush to mature trees. In any particular place, the sequence depends first on the kind of initial disturbance. A forest growing up in abandoned, formerly plowed soil will be much different in species and rate of growth from an established forest recovering from a lightning fire. Climate, soil, idiosyncrasies of plant species native to the area, and myriad local influences also shape succession. Ecologists used to believe in the permanence of climax vegetation—a particular community of trees in each type of forest that would predictably emerge as the final phase of succession. It was thought that climax vegetation would inevitably dominate the space and then remain, unchanging, until a significant disturbance started the cycle over again.

That was much too simple a model for a system as complex as a forest. "The secondary forest not only may tell nothing about the nature of the original cover," wrote Lucy Braun in her 1950 book about eastern forests, "but also it may even be very misleading in its implications." Current ecological thinking acknowledges that forests are flexible. There are so many factors influencing succession that predicting exactly how the forest will respond to a disturbance—say, a timber cut—is extremely difficult. Sometimes trees don't grow back at all, because the soil erodes too deeply, or rhododendrons shade them out, or some unknown factor that was previously inconsequential acquires a new significance. The only dependable constants are change and time.

Given time and left alone, even a recovering forest will grow old. In the moistest, richest Appalachian coves, a stand of trees may begin to develop the structural complexities of old growth in 100 years, although the appropriate amount of dead and downed wood will be seriously deficient for perhaps another century. Forests on dry, exposed ridges and thin-soiled slopes need several centuries to mature, and even then they may not necessarily develop all the intricacies of old growth. Most of the trees on public lands in Appalachia lie somewhere around the midpoint on the continuum of forest maturity, having grown up after the holocaustic logging in the late nineteenth and early twentieth centuries. They represent the old growth that could be, the potential for a new Great Forest. Only on public lands is it politically and socially feasible to secure the long-term protection needed to realize that potential.

As studies in the ecology of old growth expanded in both the western and the eastern United States, researchers focused on birds to measure how well forests were functioning. Being mobile, birds can leave deteriorating habitats to search for better conditions. A decline in birds that live in mature forests can signal a decline in suitable habitat. The spotted owl in the Pacific Northwest, dependent on economically valuable old-growth Douglas fir forests, became a symbol of the conflict between the timber industry and environmental science, one that reduced the issue to the simplistic level of a bumper sticker. "Save a logger, eat an owl," read one.

In the East, attention focused on birds that return from parts south every spring to nest in the woods. Called Neotropical migrants, these include birds of many different feathers—thrushes, warblers, vireos, swifts, tanagers, flycatchers, orioles, swallows—that fly together twice a year in migration. Otherwise they have little in common, each group using the forest in a different way. Neotropical migrants outnumber the year-round resident birds by a factor of two or three and consume incalculable numbers of insects. They are the jewels of the forest canopy, flashing their vivid plumage through tree leaves like tiny, animate gems. Their names incorporate descriptions such as rose-breasted, black-throated, golden-winged, ruby-crowned, yellow-rumped, gray-cheeked, red-eyed, scarlet, cerulean, and hooded. Their varied songs are a trilling, buzzing, warbling, clucking, chirping matrix of melodies.

With one notable exception: the ceaseless shriek of the nocturnal whippoorwill. Every May and June, Ralph and I lie awake nights cursing the fact that something about our house attracts them. We've tried everything to shoo them away, from guns to a plastic parrot with a recorder that repeats what's said to it. Instead of spooking the whippoorwill, the parrot seemed to challenge him to sing even faster, louder, and longer.

For several decades now, the populations of many species of Neotropical migrants have been declining precipitously. At first, deforestation of their winter habitat in Central and South America was blamed and was well documented. Then evidence also began to implicate nesting failures caused by fragmentation of forests across the East.

Jane Holt has helped to gather that evidence. She was born in Corinth, Mississippi, in the 1930s. At four years old she found a dead goldfinch in the driveway and thought it the most beautiful thing she had ever seen. She could hardly bear to bury it underground, as her parents instructed her to do. Her father was the son of a Presbyterian minister and had taken up his father's vocation. When Jane was eight, he took her on a family trip to a conference at a Presbyterian mountain retreat, aptly named Montreat, near Asheville, North Carolina. It was the first time she had seen mountains, and she loved them.

A few years later, her father died unexpectedly from a heart attack, and her mother decided to move to Montreat. There was a girls' high school and college there, which Jane attended. Lacking binoculars in those days, she craned her neck for hours trying to search out all the birds she heard in Montreat's forest. She left to go to graduate school and spent a couple of decades teaching biology in Presbyterian colleges too small to support courses dedicated to birds. Then she accepted a part-time position teaching ornithology at the University of North Carolina at Asheville and moved back to the house in Montreat.

It was one of the earliest houses built there, before bulldozers came into use. It nestled into a steep slope and had what seemed even to me to be an endless flight of steps up to the first floor. They helped keep Jane vigorous. "I just wish I had had the time to hike around Montreat doing bird surveys, as I have at Highlands," she said over breakfast tea steaming in pretty china cups. We were lingering in her glass-enclosed dining room before setting out for a conference in Asheville. The house was furnished with solid family pieces of a style to match the pine floors and claw-foot bathtubs. In contrast to my jeans and T-shirt, Jane was dressed in a skirt and blouse. She wore pants only for fieldwork. Shy and unassuming, she had an air of gracious southern formality. For many summers, she had hiked circuits of several miles each through different study plots near the Highlands Biological Station, a research facility of the University of North Carolina. The pioneering ecologist Eugene Odum had censused the forests there in the 1940s, providing one of the earliest inventories of what proved to be the greatest diversity of songbirds in the Southeast.

Jane's work showed how the birds were responding to changes since Odum's time. The woods around Highlands are mostly second-growth hemlock and hardwood forests with a few stands of older trees. Highlands is the only place in Appalachia that rivals the Smoky Mountains for wetness, and succession progressed quickly after the Forest Service purchased some of the land. In one plot, Odum had found 227 pairs of Neotropical migrants per hundred acres in 1947. Jane found 258 in 1960, probably reflecting the increasing attraction that the maturing stand had for birds of the deep forest. But in 1972, she found only 186 pairs per hundred acres. In 1994, her most recent survey, the number was down to 139. Fifteen species showed a decline over those years, and in the last survey, there were no ovenbirds or Blackburnian warblers at all. Her study plots remained undisturbed in their continuing development toward old growth, but they had become islands of woodlots in a sea of change.

Shopping malls, housing developments, and golf courses on surrounding private land, and clear-cutting on adjacent national forest, had sliced up the landscape. For birds adapted to the habitats of the forest interior, the smaller the plot of forest, the more dangerous it becomes. Many studies have documented the disappearance of warblers and vireos from woods smaller than about ten acres. Forests of such small sizes tend to be overwhelmed by a set of ecological phenomena known as edge effect. Sunlight and wind from the perimeter penetrate to the very center of the woods, rendering it too dry for plants of the inner forest. The successional sequence remains arrested at an early stage.

The real danger for birds, though, comes from animals. The edge between two different kinds of habitats offers access to twice the variety of food sources found in any one habitat, so edges attract an array of wildlife, from browsers like deer to predators like bobcats. For this reason, timber managers often extol the benefits of creating edges through logging, pointing out that the total number of wildlife species is higher along edges than in the deep forest. They imply that biodiversity would be best served by cutting lots of edges. The problem with this argument is that, unlike deep forest habitat, edges are already abundant in a landscape interrupted by human uses. So are the species that utilize edge habitats.

"We love our generalists, our rufous-sided towhees and song sparrows and robins that can survive in a variety of habitats," Jane said, "but it's our forest interior specialists, mostly the warblers, that are suffering. Each of them gleans insects from a very specific structural element of the forest, like the leaves at a certain canopy level, or tips of branches, or the base of trees." The only warbler that likes disturbed areas is the chestnut-sided. "John James Audubon saw a chestnut-sided warbler just once," Jane said, referring to the American ornithologist whose paintings of birds in the mid-1800s have become collector's items. "For him, the chestnut-sided was a rare bird."

It is much more common today, whereas other warblers suffer from the very diversity that edges encourage. In a small woods, edge-loving predators like raccoons, opossums, blue jays, crows, and domestic cats roam throughout the stand, easily finding the open-cup, low-to-the-ground nests characteristic of many birds of the forest interior. Even in large, unfragmented woods, squirrels and chipmunks may eat forty percent or more of the young of some bird species; in small forests with a lot of edge, the rate of loss can go up steeply. Some of the most voracious nest predators, raccoons and opossums, apparently weren't abundant in the past, during the days of the great logging boom, which may help explain why many species of Neotropical migrants didn't go extinct then.

Where forests are fragmented near agricultural areas, brown-headed cowbirds move in. Cowbirds are native to the American grasslands, where they followed bison herds to eat the insects stirred up by grazing hoofs and the undigested seeds in bison dung. Bison were nomadic, and cowbirds didn't remain in any area long enough to tend a nest, so they developed a strategy of brood parasitism. They lay their eggs in the nests of other birds, which nurture them as their own. Young cowbirds are bigger than the young of many songbirds and devour the majority of food brought by the adults. The other nestlings starve. In some places, cowbirds and predators combined may kill all the young of certain birds. Such places are called population sinks. Only if there are larger forests where nesting success is higher, producing young birds in search of new territories, can population sinks continue to host birds.

Historical records are sparse, and it's unclear how widespread cowbirds were in the Appalachians before European settlers arrived with their land clearing and livestock. Travelers a century ago occasionally noted cowbirds in mid-Atlantic and southeastern states. The first record of a cowbird egg in the Virginia mountains seems to be 1959, at the Mountain Lake Biological Research Station. Studies on nests there date back to 1913. The absence of cowbirds during the logging of earlier decades might be another reason why some Neotropical migrants didn't go extinct then. Cowbirds have also benefited from the modern era of bird feeders, as people like me set out dependable sources of food across the countryside. Every spring I am chagrined by the whistling song and the sleek, shining feathers of the males. They are probably attracted to the opening we created in the forest, one of the many changes resulting from our occupancy.

The cumulation of many studies shows that bigger is better when it comes to forests. The larger the forest, the more species of birds that are likely to succeed there. One researcher estimated that a minimum size of seven thousand acres was necessary to retain all species of forest-breeding birds in the mid-Atlantic states. A few species of birds, for example the scarlet tanager, will colonize mature forests as small as fifteen acres. What seems to make the difference is landscape context, the way the woods lie in relation to other forests in the region. A connection to a larger forest, by a forested strip along a river or even a tree-lined fencerow that links otherwise isolated forests, offers a travel way through hostile habitats such as crop fields and shopping centers. In theory, birds can soar above it all, but in practice, they need to feed, rest, and take cover from hawks as they travel.

Natural corridors allow migration not only of birds but also of many other travelers that can't navigate through human ecosystems of asphalt and lawn. Without an influx of new genes, populations of both animals and plants are vulnerable to the debilitation that comes with inbreeding. Although corridors can also provide routes for unwelcome invaders, such as diseases or nonnative species, they represent genetic salvation in a landscape broken into pieces.

Jane recognized an opportunity to put some of the pieces together. Montreat is contiguous with the Pisgah National Forest and the protected watershed of the city of Asheville and is close to the Blue Ridge Parkway and Mount Mitchell State Park. To this conjunction of public lands, Montreat could contribute a cove extending from 2,500 feet in elevation to the 5,360-foot summit of Gray Beard Mountain. The forest of mixed hardwoods has the diversity typical of southern Appalachia, including several species of plants found only in the locale.

Before we left for Asheville, Jane gave me a tour of the place. It was founded in 1897 by northerners looking for a place where outdoor recreation and educational programs could be combined with spiritual enrichment. Early conferences were held in tents, but there is now a substantial infrastructure. In her mild, quiet way, Jane had led a campaign to set aside nearly three thousand of Montreat's four thousand acres from any further development. Once the management council made the official decision, she wrote the conservation plan. "Wilderness values shall take precedence over all other considerations," the plan states.

Montreat's private wilderness begins a few hundred feet up the hill behind Jane's house. The trees on the mountainside were dripping in morning fog as we left, each soft plop sounding a testimony to a union of the scientific and the spiritual. "We are stewards of what we've been given," Jane said. "We want future generations to feel the connection with the Creator that can only be found in the Creation. We need to think a hundred years into the future. The best thing we can do to protect biodiversity is to encourage large, connected old-growth forests across the landscape."

Their beauty and their ability to fly make songbirds highly popular with people. Long associated with the clammy clutter in the pockets of small boys, salamanders are hard to glamorize. They do, after all, live under rocks. They have names like "slimy" and "shovelnose" for reasons entirely deserved. Even scientific interest has been prejudiced. Writing about the class Amphibia, to which salamanders belong, the great taxonomist Carolus Linnaeus in his 1758 *Systema Naturae* called them "foul and loathsome animals . . . abhorrent because of their cold body . . . fierce aspect . . . and squalid habitation."

It's true that amphibians, having evolved from freshwater fish into the first land vertebrates some 350 million years ago, still associate intimately with wet or at least damp places. Still, typical salamander habitat in limpid mountain creeks or hidden springs, under draping moss curtains near streambanks, and beneath the punky mass of decayed trees on silent slopes hardly rates as squalid. As for a cold body, salamanders, like other amphibians, simply reflect the soil or water temperature in which they reside. Admittedly, salamander diets are foul and loathsome if snails, slugs, spiders, ants, beetles, mites, millipedes, and the like are not to your taste. And it's true that salamanders are surprisingly fierce for such small and slow-moving creatures, some of them being among the few known cannibalistic animals. But the aesthetic balance tips sharply in their favor when you throw in their exquisitely delicate toes; their subtle colors and designs; their scaleless, shining skin; and their elegant tails, which serve as a treasure chest for body fats.

A few of the world's approximately 350 salamander species live in Asia and Europe, but most inhabit the New World. In North America, the greatest abundance and variety of salamanders occur in the central and southern Appalachians. Some fifty species creep through crevices of rock and soil in the mountains, especially in the higher elevations of national forests and parks. No one is sure why salamander evolution burgeoned here, but the moist conditions obviously suited the animals, and the lack of glaciation gave them uninterrupted eons to develop.

Appalachian salamander genes are concentrated in the family Plethodontidae. These are the lungless salamanders, the only four-footed animals to evolve away their lungs. They respire principally by passing dissolved oxygen and carbon dioxide through a moist membrane over a thin skin. Many are completely terrestrial; the larval aquatic phase occurs within the egg, and the young hatch out as miniature adults. Woodland salamanders spend their lives in leaf litter or underground. They depend on soil moisture trapped in deep humus by a closed canopy and on a forest floor littered with decaying logs.

These features signal the onset of old growth. For traditional foresters, they warn of an "overmature" woods where trees have stopped the rapid growth of early succession. Instead of using energy to add woody mass to their trunks for future harvest by humans, they channel it into maintaining their large crowns. Economic efficiency demands that trees be cut as soon as they reach maturity, just as they begin to exhibit qualities of good salamander habitat.

Unlike the similarly shaped reptilian lizards and skinks, salamanders do not skitter. They proceed with cautious deliberation slowly around a territory of a few square yards of forest floor. If those square yards are clear-cut, the forest floor dries out and the salamanders die. Whole populations of some species exist only along a few mountainsides. Logging, the most frequent disturbance in salamander country, can therefore wipe out an entire species or leave unbridgeable distances between remnant populations.

New species of salamanders are still being discovered in the Appalachians. Some species may have been driven extinct by industrial logging before anyone ever recorded them. One species, named the Cow Knob salamander after a mountain a few miles west of my house, was identified in 1972. I once spent a day with a couple of Forest Service wildlife biologists, two examples of a growing breed of national forest personnel who do not pay homage to timber production. They hoped to prevent logging from eradicating the Cow Knob salamander by gathering information on its range, so that timber sales would not be planned there. For salamandering, you need stout walking boots, a quick eye for snakes, and a ready sprint against yellow jackets. A metal walking stick with a crook on the end for lifting rocks is nice for the squeamish, but bare hands serve just as well. Beneath mountain boulders small enough to pry up, I saw white rootlets, black tunnels, pieces of snail shells, acorns, insect parts, ant nests, spiders, and matted spider webs. Sometimes, a salamander.

In parts of the Appalachians, salamanders are so abundant that they outweigh all the birds and mammals in the area combined. They are the top predators of the leaf litter community, concentrating proteins in their tissues. In turn, salamanders are food for larger animals such as wild turkeys, snakes, shrews, crows, blue jays, raccoons, opossums, and skunks. But the role of salamanders in forest life remains unappreciated, except by amphibian aficionados like me. A study estimated that clear-cutting in western North Carolina killed nearly fourteen million salamanders a year, and that fifty to seventy years were required for local populations to rebuild. Chronic losses of salamanders over a regional landscape were estimated at a quarter of a billion individuals. Where are the animal rights people when you need them?

The best place to search for songbirds and salamanders on the hundred acres where I live is Mushroom Flat. This is where South Creek flows through an unusually wide bottomland, at the border of our property and the George Washington National Forest. Mushroom Flat is a flare of decent soil along the slender, braided flow of the creek, a tiny cove of a few acres. The trees here are no older than the surrounding trees—seventy to ninety years—but they're larger because of the soil and because of the protected aspect, down between two steep slopes. They're big enough to attract serious attention from pileated woodpeckers, as many oval holes attest. The undergrowth is subtly different from that of other areas. There's a lot of deadwood, including a lightning-split tree I use for a bench. Mushroom Flat is the nearest thing to old growth on this side of Cross Mountain, a green shadow of the Great Forest. Here, I'm as close to the past as I can stand to get, and as near to the future as I can ever hope to be.

I think I've heard a wood thrush singing from hereabouts, but I've never found a nest. It's probably up the creek, across the border into the national forest. Private owners have cut several large patches around the foot of the mountain in the years we've lived here, but so far, the Forest Service has made only two small clear-cuts on the mountain itself. I'm on the district mailing list, and I keep a close eye on the notices the district ranger is required to send announcing the latest Forest Service plans.

If a new Great Forest is going to emerge, it will be through the Forest Service planning process, with its requirement for public input. Recognition of that possibility prompted a handful of people to form the Southern Appalachian Forest Coalition in 1994. All of them had master's degrees or doctorates. All had spent years working for one kind of social improvement or another, from elimination of poverty to revisionist views of Native American history. They knew how to go about getting grants. All were dyed-in-the-wool environmentalists, and although none had been born in the mountains, they now called them home. Most had been active in Appalachian national forest issues for years. They saw a chance for concerted action when the comprehensive forest plans, created in the 1980s, began to come due for the first round of revisions.

The coalition set itself up in Asheville, on the second floor of a house of approximately the same vintage as Jane Holt's home. In the heat of July, the true mark of southern graciousness was a shady parking space in back. Two high-ceilinged, connected rooms wallowed waist deep in stacks of paper, from which old wooden desks poked up like islands, topped with computers instead of palm trees. Computer-generated maps of the mountains lined the walls. These were both substance and symbol of the coalition's goal: to preserve native biodiversity on public lands through scientific knowledge and public participation in national forest planning.

In the hip municipality of Asheville, we had our choice of ethnic restaurants for lunch. Susan Andrew, the coalition's ecologist, steered us toward her favorite East Indian cuisine. Her long, lean frame was accentuated by very long hair. Birds were one of her specialties, and she had done fieldwork in Papua New Guinea and Costa Rica. Her role at the coalition was to expand knowledge of the specific locations where biodiversity was greatest. This would help set priorities for core areas. Places needed to be identified, cataloged, and electronically mapped. "Using science-based data, we want to prod the Forest Service to come up with a coordinated set of plans that will ensure habitat for all native species," she said. "Basically, that means a connected series of mature forests."

The rest of the conversation was about strategies to achieve that. First was to build membership. Three environmental heavyweights had helped to found the coalition and joined immediately: the Southern Environmental Law Center, a nonprofit organization of lawyers dedicated to environmental protection; the Sierra Club, which has several levels of local organization throughout the region; and the Wilderness Society, whose southeastern office had for years been producing detailed biological and economic analyses of southern Appalachia.

The coalition further enlisted a dozen of the smaller grassroots groups—that is, people who lived in or near the Appalachian national forests and had organized to challenge the Forest Service. Taylor Barnhill was in charge of grassroot contacts. He was in his late forties and had, like me, moved to Appalachia to get back to the land. He had married a mountain woman, a "seventh-generation Appalachian," as he called her, in part because she was a professional folksinger and he was fascinated by the music. She had refused to move to land he had purchased because it lay in a part of the county where family enemies lived. Taylor still lived out in the county, though he was now single. "When I meet people at workshops and conferences, I make an unconscious if not a conscious tally of native mountaineers versus nonnatives," he said. "And most are nonnative, no question about it."

The coalition acted as a clearinghouse, using newsletters and endless phone calls to keep all its members informed of what the others were doing, so that each could build on the others' knowledge and experience. Coalition staff alerted members to Forest Service actions and articulated responses to Forest Service proposals. One of their greatest successes was persuading a bipartisan group of politicians to support a moratorium on the building of new roads into roadless areas. Generally defined in Appalachian national forests as no more than a half mile of road per thousand acres, roadless areas total about 750,000 acres with only nominal protection against intrusions. The coalition drove van loads of people to Washington, D.C., to join western activists lobbying for the idea. President Bill Clinton agreed, and although the moratorium was hedged with exceptions, the coalition hoped it would be an important prod in a new direction.

There were signs that the Forest Service might be slowly getting the hint. In 1996, it produced a publication entitled *The Southern Appalachian Assessment*. The assessment comprised five volumes of data on all aspects of Appalachian life. It was not the first overview of Appalachia from the perspective of the forests—witness the 1902 report to Congress that documented the carnage of industrial logging. But it was a first for the Forest Service. The notion of the assessment grew out of the Southern Appalachian Man and the Biosphere program, inaugurated in 1988 as part of an international scientific effort to conserve biodiversity. Many sources contributed to the assessment to make it one of the greatest masses of information about Appalachia ever compiled. It provided an invaluable resource, despite what coalition members thought were some misleading calculations and projections.

Unfortunately, the assessment lacked geographical comprehensiveness: it included the Talladega National Forest at the southernmost tip of the Appalachians in Alabama, but excluded the Monongahela in West Virginia and the Daniel Boone in Kentucky. The Monongahela was left out because it lies in Region 9 of the Forest Service hierarchy, rather than in Region 8, like all the other Appalachian national forests. The Daniel Boone in Kentucky was left out because it was considered part of the Cumberland Plateau, which was not included in the land classification system the Forest Service used. There have been many different delineations of Appalachia, but few of them have been so constrained as to leave out West Virginia and eastern Kentucky.

Nevertheless, the assessment described a landscape perspective, which was an approach contradicted by actual Forest Service operations. Timber sales continued, despite the overwhelming evidence being assembled against them. It seemed to me that one simple policy change was the obvious solution: no commercial logging. The Sierra Club made headlines when it adopted this "no cut" position toward all public lands across the country. It's an idea particularly well suited to the national forests of Appalachia, where timber supports a smaller segment of the economy than does tourism. The coalition couldn't take a position on "no cut" because of its nature; each member group had its own view. "We have a spectrum of opinions, but we're all pulling in the same direction," Hugh Irwin said.

Hugh was the conservation planner and the mapper. During his studies in forest ecology, he had learned how to use the electronic database known as the Geographical Information System and had applied it to numerous volunteer jobs for the Sierra Club. For the coalition, he took the information Susan collected and overlaid it with the computer data compiled by the assessment, which are freely accessible and in the public domain. The resulting multilayered map makes possible many different views of Appalachia. You can identify all the stream segments that support native trout, the whereabouts of plant and animal species, various grades of roads, all trees of a certain age, waterways and watersheds, and human demographics down to the level of where the duplexes are.

Whenever I see a map of Appalachia, I always look for where I live, to find what its colors are. It won't be the dark green of old growth for many years yet, but in Mushroom Flat I see promise. I gave up on finding the wood thrush nest that I was looking for there and started walking down the creek, stepping on big rocks and picking up little ones, hunting for salamanders. At the pools, water striders skated quickly to one side at my approach, then ignored me. Long, entangling arms of roots hugged the stream bank. I peered in all the dark, spider-webby holes, imagining the salamanders or frogs, mice or voles, chipmunks or Little People that might live there. Time disappeared. Nothing moved but the stream sliding by, nothing existed beyond what I touched. When I got back to the house, I was astonished to see how many hours had passed. After a while, I realized what had happened. I had reentered a long-forgotten state of mind, a childish reverie of wonder. I was playing.

PLAYGROUND OF THE EAST

HALFWAY DOWN THE STEEP, WOODED SLOPE, JACK'S BIKE BUCKED HIM like a horse, and he tumbled head over heels almost down to the stream. "Keep an eye on Jack," our mountain biking guide had warned our small group, as we arrived in West Virginia by ones and twos from points throughout the East. "He had a heart attack less than a year ago." But Jack jumped up grinning, living proof that the sport of mountain biking can accommodate the weak of heart if not the faint of spirit.

To my relief, I was neither the oldest nor the most timid among those assembled for a weekend-long mountain biking clinic at Elk River Touring Center, near the tiny town of Slatyfork. Jack was approaching retirement age, and Linda, though decades younger, hung back and walked her bike as much as she rode it. That was fine; we weren't there to compete but to improve our individual skills. Fat-tire, lightweight bicycles suited to the roughest backcountry started out as toys of speed-crazed young men in California in the 1970s. It took years to convince hikers that mountain bikers could be responsible trail users, but middle-aged riders like me are now lending respectability. And although the West remains a mecca for mountain bikers, readers of *Mountain Bike Magazine* have rated West Virginia among their top four favorite destinations in the world.

No wonder. West Virginia is God's own mountain biking country. Slatyfork is nearly surrounded by Monongahela National Forest. Two hundred miles of trails were immediately accessible from the door of the old farmhouse where we stayed, which Elk River Center had remodeled into a lodge. Another eight hundred miles were available within a short drive.

And what trails! Singletrack—biker jargon for the most demanding kind of track, so narrow that travelers can traverse it only in single file—is the glory of West Virginia biking. Trails wind up and down the slopes of four-thousand-foot-high mountains, through some of the most beautiful hardwood forests on earth. Deep green canopies of oaks, maples, and hickories create a cool and shadowy world where bears and bobcats thrive. Banks of ferns and moss-covered boulders edge the many splashing creeks. Occasional sunny glades offer glimpses of massive views, mountains piled one atop the other seemingly to the edge of the planet.

The Mon also has miles of old logging roads, cut in the early twentieth century during the great timber boom. Decades of leaf-fall have softened them into wide, quiet lanes. The railroads that were laid around the same time have long since had their steel tracks and crossties pulled up, or the crossties have rotted, offering easy, gradual grades (the eighty-mile, nearly flat Greenbrier River Trail is one of the best known). In the ultimate recreational turnaround, strip mines that were gouged out along the contours of the mountains, and that are incapable of supporting much vegetative growth, provide spacious, finely graveled bike routes with scenic outlooks.

Mountain biking can turn even the worst scars of Appalachian history to good use. Gil Willis saw its potential in the 1980s, after he had established a bed-and-breakfast and cross-country ski center at Elk River. The old farm that his father had bought years earlier, as both a tax and a summer haven from the family's residence near Washington, D.C., lent itself well to a small-scale tourist service. Gil's ace in the hole was his location at the base of Snowshoe Ski Resort, where he could count on substantial numbers of people passing by.

Snowshoe is a typical example of the large ski and lake resorts that proliferated across Appalachia in the 1960s and 1970s. When demand for recreation began to rise dramatically after World War II, big resorts were assumed to be the precursors of an economic boom. It didn't exactly work out that way. Just as with timber and coal, outside investors generally took most of the profits. Jobs for locals tended to be seasonal and paid minimum wage. Costs of providing services to second home owners attracted by the resorts sometimes amounted to more than the taxes the new people paid. The income from recreation was concentrated rather than distributed through the region. In hot spots, land prices inflated, taxes went up, and landownership continued to pass from native mountaineers to nonresidents.

Many of the twentieth-century resorts like Snowshoe were built to capitalize on the public lands, but big hotels were an Appalachian tradition long before the federal government moved into the region. Thermal springs and mineral waters attracted tourists from the first days of exploration. In an era when doctors couldn't offer much else, the restorative, even curative powers of hot baths and medicinal waters were much favored for a wide variety of ailments. Springs are present in the Appalachians from New York to Alabama, but spas tended to congregate in the mountains of Virginia and West Virginia. The waters there issue forth where Oriskany sandstone and Helderbert limestone, laid 350 million years ago, are cut off by broad upward folds of rock strata called anticlines. Some springs carry salts of calcium, magnesium, or sodium; others have hydrogen sulfide or iron.

Some are hot, like the stream that bubbled up through the drain of a big old bathtub and rolled over the old-fashioned curled edge in a clear, liquid sheet, to splash onto a tile floor at the Homestead Hotel, in Hot Springs, Virginia. With an inn built in 1766, the Homestead was one of the first and definitely one of the toniest of all the spas on the popular summer mountain resort circuit that developed in the mid-1800s. At each hotel, the wives of prosperous southern planters made social life a classy and class-conscious affair. I found one little legacy of those days a bit awkward: I'm not used to having an attendant pat me dry after a bath.

Development of summer homes followed in the wake of the resorts. Decades before the Civil War, wealthy people in lowland cities such as Charleston, South Carolina, and Atlanta, Georgia, established the tradition of fleeing the malarial, cholera-ridden summers of the fetid lowlands for the uplands. The healthiness of mountain air and cleanliness of mountain water were widely admired. By the early twentieth century, hotels and summer homes had become integral to the lives of a number of Appalachian communities.

Hikers and naturalists have also been attracted to the Appalachians since at least 1791, when William Bartram published his *Travels.* His father, John Bartram, was appointed botanist to His Majesty George III of England in 1765 and founded the first botanical garden in America, in Philadelphia. William surpassed even his father in knowledge and appreciation of New World plants. His ecstatic descriptions of the diverse beauties of the Southeast, although criticized by some reviewers at the time as "rather too luxuriant and florid," were particularly popular in Europe. Poets such as William Wordsworth and Samuel Coleridge used Bartram's romantic images in their own portrayals of nature.

Small but steady numbers of hikers entered the Appalachians in search of scientific knowledge and aesthetic experience. By necessity if not by choice, these travelers made do with more rustic accommodations than those offered by the handful of big resorts. The Northeast, in particular, seemed to be a nucleus of hiking activity. The Appalachian Mountain Club was organized in 1876 by well-heeled New Englanders and soon boasted over a thousand members. Its mission was not only the preservation of Appalachian forests but also the building of paths and camps to enhance the enjoyment of them.

The persistent demand for walking routes in the mountains eventually culminated in the development of one of the longest marked hiking paths in the world. There were men before Benton MacKaye who suggested networks of trails through the Appalachians, especially in the New England states, but the idea for the Appalachian Trail was MacKaye's own. He was a Harvard graduate and a forester from Massachusetts. In 1921, he published an article entitled "An Appalachian Trail, a Project in Regional Planning," in the *Journal of the American Institute of Architects.* He proposed to link natural areas suitable for recreation by a trail accessible to city dwellers along the Atlantic seaboard.

Many volunteers responded to his article. MacKaye organized groups that not only plotted routes but also felled trees. Marking the path was a challenge, because whole sections of the mountains, especially the crests in the southern half of the Appalachians, were not well known. The national forests, still in their first decade, couldn't possibly host the entire trail, so private landowners had to be approached for sale or rights-of-way. Such was the enthusiasm and dedication of hiking groups that the trail was completed in less than two decades. It runs for 2,155 miles from

Mount Katahdin in Maine to Springer Mountain in Georgia and is protected for ninety-seven percent of its course by federal or state ownership of the land or by rights-of-way.

U.S. Forest Service, George Washington National Forest, Bridgewater, VA

CCCers taking a break from building the Appalachian Trail through Shenandoah National Park, probably summer 1933.

About four million people a year use some part of the Appalachian Trail. In places it is worn into a hip-deep trench. Between one thousand

and two thousand people a year set out to hike the whole thing, which takes five or six months. About two hundred make it. The trail has become a pilgrimage from civilization to nature, despite occasional all-too-human problems such as theft, contagious diseases, and even murder. Blind people have hiked it; so have people with laptop computers by which they post regular updates on the Internet. Everyone takes self-liberating trail names like "Beorn" and "Bloodroot" and "Screaming Coyote," signing them in cabin logbooks along the way. I've trod on the trail in segments from Maine to southwest Virginia, but generally I avoid it because of the crowds. And because I haven't come up with a good trail name.

U.S. Forest Service, George Washington National Forest, Bridgewater, VA

CCCer using mule to remove rocks during the building of the Appalachian Trail through Shenandoah National Park, probably summer 1933.

Trails are nice, but roads are essential. Bad roads have always been an obstacle to the development of all aspects of the Appalachian economy. Building better ones was a primary focus of the Appalachian Regional Commission, inaugurated by President Lyndon Johnson during his War on Poverty in the 1960s. The commission has spent billions of dollars creating a network of interstate and secondary highways. When I drove through Pikeville in Kentucky, the decent mountain two-lane I was on metamorphosed abruptly into an eerily empty urban freeway. I was dazed by the amount of stone and cement around me, and by its verticality. An aerial view of the Pikeville Cut is featured on local postcards. Two mountains have been sculpted into pyramid shapes, with the Levisa Fork of the Big Sandy River channeled between them like a gutter. "They moved a mountain for you," reads the caption.

Better roads made it possible to disperse tourism more widely. The era of big resorts was followed by a gradual trend toward smaller facilities, a trend that meshed with the national shift from a manufacturing to a service economy. By the end of the twentieth century, outdoor recreation on federal lands accounted for at least ten percent of the jobs in a dozen Appalachian counties. In some fifty additional counties, between one and ten percent of all jobs came to depend on nature-based tourism.

Recreationists have increased not only in number but also in kind. Old favorite pastimes such as scenic driving and picnicking, hunting and fishing, swimming and boating, and downhill skiing at the big resorts continue to be popular, but so are white-watering, backpacking, rock climbing, cross-country skiing, caving, and nature study. Not to mention mountain biking, which in West Virginia may be the fastest growing activity of all.

With corporate acuity for the bottom line, Snowshoe Resort developed into a four-season facility with something for everyone, including mountain bikers. It serves at least ten thousand of them a year, through a season that runs from early May to early November. The Elk River Center accommodates two thousand to three thousand riders, allowing Gil Willis to offer more customized service. Plus his wife, Mary, runs the restaurant. People come down from Snowshoe's lodges for her sophisticated and inventive menu. It was over Saturday night's dinner of spinach-mint soup and fresh local trout that the bruises I knew would come started to make themselves felt.

We had covered nearly twenty miles, some of it "technical," biker jargon for roots and rocks. Mud splattered on shins as we swished through puddles, and I noticed deer and raccoon tracks imprinted on the wet dirt alongside. Sometimes a meadow would open up before us in a blaze of light; other times we moved through tunnels of green. On the downhills, birdsong streaked behind me in a blur of sound. Spiderwebs stuck across my face, but I couldn't release the handlebars to wipe them away. Life was simple: I had to clear my mind of everything but the next rock, the next curve of trail, or I would fall off. When I got it right, it was like dancing down the mountain with my bike.

Local residents have so far been unimpressed by the charms of mountain biking or mountain bikers. Some years ago, as Gil's clientele grew noticeable on paved roads cycling to and from national forest trails, people passing in cars would occasionally throw beer bottles at them. Shots were fired once or twice. No one was hurt, Gil hastened to assure me, and such incidents have mostly ceased. One or two of his sons' schoolmates were now learning to bike.

Mountaineers preferred motors. Off-highway vehicles became popular very quickly in Appalachia. We learned this not from Gil but from evidence on our West Virginia land when we arrived for a visit years ago. A new road greeted us, a narrow track up a vertical slope, with the forest floor churned into powder. Rain would soon turn it into a gully. We knew right off it was OHVs. We raced up the new road, cursing, yelling ideas back and forth about how to fell logs across the road and stud them with case-hardened nails. We felt righteous with ownership, passionate with protectiveness. The road continued up to the barbed wire fence that marked our boundary. The wire had been cut, and the track crossed our border to join an old path along the ridge. We had explored that path and then forgotten it, forgotten that our property was linked into a generations-old network of trails.

As I planned how to cunningly angle the nails, we heard the chugging of motors. A caravan of four OHVs came into view just below, moving toward us up the hill. Ralph raised his arms and walked toward them down the middle of the new track, palms out, fingers spread, like an evangelist at a camp meeting. For a few seconds I thought that the vehicles might swerve clean around him and keep going. But they stopped. Ralph stood beside the first one while I walked up and straddled the front wheel, leaned into it, put one hand on the handlebars. I hadn't studied mountain manners all these years for nothing. There was going to be no doubt about who had rights here.

The lead vehicle was decked out like an Amish buggy: a square of thick black vinyl stretched over a pipe frame welded to the body of the OHV, with plastic windows zippered into the front and sides. Later we heard that the driver had black lung from a lifetime spent mining coal and couldn't tolerate wind in his face. From his creases and the texture of his skin, I guessed that he was in his sixties. His hair was still dark, and his eyes were the darkest, most solid brown I've ever seen. They were shaped like almonds, slightly tilted.

"I own this property," Ralph began, "and I'm just real surprised to find this road here." His voice was calm and twangy with the mountain drawl we had picked up and slipped into years earlier, at first unconsciously, for protective coloration.

"We're just going to our hunting place to put this stuff out for the deer," the man in the first OHV said. Near his feet, apples bulged round and red through plastic mesh bags. "It's legal," he added quickly. "Baiting's all legal except for bear." I had been looking for guns without even realizing it, scanning the rears of the OHVs and glancing at shoulders for rifles slung there as carelessly as sacks of apples. We almost always brought a gun with us when we camped here. Mainly we used it to answer when shots sounded too close for comfort—a rural dialogue to announce our presence. Now, I realized that this was one of the few times when we could expect not to see guns: hunters, accustoming their prey to being fed in certain places, were too easily accused of poaching if guns were in sight. It was a reassuring thought.

"Well, I don't know who put this road in, but it's eroding on that steep place there and I don't much like that," Ralph said. "And whoever put it in cut my fence."

"We never cut no fence," the man said. "We started riding through here after we saw the road. I thought the preacher owned it yet. If I'd of knowed how to get in touch with you, I'd of asked you."

Well, now, no one could demand more than that. Grateful to him for the face-saving he was offering, we eased a bit. "He used to," Ralph said, meaning the preacher. "We bought it fifteen years ago, and this is the most people we've seen in all these years." I was pleased that the man seemed surprised. I kept looking for a power fulcrum, a way to show that we weren't total strangers here, people from the city who didn't know spotlighting from a Sunday drive.

The three young men who were driving the other OHVs got off. We all stood around for some time, kicking our toes into clumps of grass and shielding our eyes from the sun as we talked in brief spurts between bouts of silence. The state did not provide a registration procedure for

OHVs, they explained, and it was illegal to run unregistered vehicles on state roads. So they had to stay off-road or get a stiff fine. We walked around looking for a better place on our slope to put a road, but there wasn't any. In the meantime, three more OHVs and then two motorbikes drove up and stopped at a distance, waiting for the crowd to clear out. A regular wilderness road had developed across our place.

"Tell you what," the man said. "You give me and my boys permission to come through here to hunt, and we'll build you gates. We'll put one down below where we come on, and one up there where we go off. We'll do it and mail you the keys."

It was an honorable solution, and without a doubt the best we could hope for under the circumstances. Ralph got out some paper and wrote Jesse Hoover's name down, followed by six sons. "I knew you wasn't a hard kind of feller," Jesse said, slapping his knee. Who could blame him for using the road, once he had noticed it? With locked gates, we could at least limit the damage to the forest. And by giving Jesse proprietary rights, we would make an ally of him and give him incentive to look out for our interests. Maybe this would prove to be the tie to the larger community we had been trying for years to make. Maybe it wasn't, as it seemed at first, the end of a dream, our outdated vision of serenity and isolation. We all shook hands, and a month later, two keys arrived in the mail. Jesse and his caravan pulled away, and Ralph walked down to the next group.

"I don't know who put this road in," he began again, "but it's tearing up . . ."

"You know Jesse Hoover?" one of the drivers interrupted him. "He put it in."

The campaign to secure places from the intrusion of machines could be called the last battle of the wilderness. To have places where people can go to escape industrial life, if only for a day or two, is the ultimate in outdoor recreation. To have places where natural processes are allowed to rule without interference is also a milestone in human humility.

Under the influence of Aldo Leopold, one of the most beloved conservationists in American history, the Forest Service took the lead in setting aside land to remain untouched. Beginning in 1924 with the Gila wilderness in New Mexico, where Leopold was then working for the Forest Service, some nine million acres in western national forests were designated as "primitive" areas. There was no management policy, and depending on the Forest Service staff in charge, each area received various degrees of protection from road building, logging, and mining. When Bob Marshall, a friend of Leopold's, became head of the Forest Service Division of Recreation in 1937, categories of "wilderness" and "wild area" were established according to the size of the tract, and regulations were codified for full protection. Marshall's own definition of wilderness was an area in which "a person may spend a week or two of travel . . . without crossing his own tracks."

But the Forest Service was fundamentally hostile to the loss of large acreages from the timber base. It acted very slowly to reclassify primitive areas to wilderness or wild status. A movement to protect such places by law instead of by administrative decision began after World War II and intensified throughout the 1950s. It took environmentalists years of fighting heavy opposition from timber and mining industries, and from professional foresters in and out of the Forest Service, to get the Wilderness Act passed in 1964.

The act established a mechanism by which citizens could propose to Congress individual, carefully delineated places to be included in a system of legally designated wilderness areas. Prior to congressional action, each area had to be the subject of public hearings, where testimony from government officials and private citizens would be noted. If Congress agreed, any place officially designated as wilderness would be protected from all motorized vehicles and equipment, permanent buildings, lumbering, and mining (with some exceptions, due to the power of the minerals lobby). Hunting, fishing, and in some cases grazing continued to be allowed. The language was fairly specific but not tight enough to prevent plenty of later controversies about what should and shouldn't be allowed in individual wildernesses. The 1964 act defined wilderness as a place "where the earth and its community of life are untrammeled by man, where man himself is a visitor who does not remain." It was aimed at western national forests and included only three areas in the East: Great Gulf in New Hampshire and Shining Rock and Linville Gorge in the Pisgah National Forest of North Carolina. The Forest Service resisted any additional wilderness areas in the East, claiming that no place could meet the criteria. Numerous easterners disagreed, especially Ernest Dickerman, a thin bachelor near retirement age who was then living in Knoxville, Tennessee. Ernie is known as the grandfather of eastern wilderness. From the day that he discovered the Great Smoky Mountains, Ernie committed his life to the preservation of the wild. "I knew," he said, "as soon as I entered the Smokies that I had found what I was looking for."

He was standing in his yard when I turned in the driveway of his retirement home in Buffalo Gap, Virginia. Wearing shorts and a plaid shirt, he had dressed up for our interview in a bolo tie made from an unusual shell he had found on a Florida beach. The skin of his arms was mottled with age, but his face was clear, almost translucent. Ernie had been born in Illinois in 1910 but spent his childhood years first in the Adirondacks, then in Roanoke, Virginia, in sight of mountains. His parents enjoyed the outdoors, but they weren't seriously interested in it. Ernie's love of nature came from within himself, "simply a matter of my own temperament, of liking best of all to be prowling around outdoors," as he put it.

After graduating from Oberlin College in Ohio, he was among the early employees hired by the newly formed Tennessee Valley Authority (TVA). It brought him to Knoxville in 1933, where he met his mountain mentor, Harvey Broome. Broome was eight years older and had been born in Knoxville when it was still a provincial valley town, with rutted lanes for streets. The pale blue band of mountains forty miles distant filtered slowly into Broome's early consciousness. His parents took him there, by train, on occasional picnics. A two-week camping trip into the Smokies in 1917, when Broome was fifteen, fixed the mountains forever in his heart and his life. With teenage labor at a premium during World War I, Broome worked at an apple orchard near Mount LeConte and seized the opportunity to backpack to its summit. It was the beginning of innumerable treks. Broome wrote in later life that he found "something beautiful, different, and intensely desirable" in the wild Smokies.

Even while he earned a degree from Harvard Law School, he returned to Knoxville in the summers to get into the mountains. He grew skilled in woodcraft, hiking through deep snow and through rains so soaking that pockets of moisture in his firewood exploded, dousing the flames. He hiked "far past the last rough homestead where visitors were so rare that it was the prudent custom to pause outside the fence and call before approaching for fear of being shot."

It wasn't long before Broome saw places he loved being destroyed by careless logging and fires. He became an ardent conservationist. He was the driving spirit behind the Smoky Mountains Hiking Club, organized in 1924 to help promote the formation of a national park. A few years later, he led the mapping project for the Appalachian Trail through mazes of remote Smokies ridges. It was through the hiking club that Ernie met Harvey Broome, within a month of moving to Knoxville.

"It was customary in those days to work Saturday mornings," Ernie said. "We'd leave in the afternoon and head out over fifty miles of mostly dirt, winding roads that got worse as you got closer to the Smokies." On one of those outings, though without Ernie, somewhere between Newfound Gap and Clingman's Dome, Harvey Broome, Bob Marshall, and several others founded the Wilderness Society. A private, nonprofit organization, its goal was and remains the saving of whatever wild places are left on public lands in America, for the sake of letting each wild place operate on its own unique ecological terms. Ernie joined as a charter member. He left TVA to work for a plastics molding firm but remained in Knoxville. He couldn't get enough of the Smokies. With his friends in the Wilderness Society, he pioneered a new vision of Appalachian forests. Their efforts culminated in the Wilderness Act of 1964.

Two years later, Ernie retired from thirty years in the plastics factory and took a job with the Wilderness Society. His position description could be summed up in one phrase: to apply the Wilderness Act to the East. For four years he covered the Southeast out of Knoxville, traveling widely to awaken citizens to the opportunities that the act offered. He mobilized people to act within the political system and taught them how to legally protect the places they loved. First he would tramp around with people who knew the area, assessing individual wilderness possibilities. Under his direction, they composed and mailed out brochures and talked to community groups. With his advice, they visited their legislators to feel out which one might be willing to sponsor a bill. Ernie spoke at meetings of every kind, spontaneously, volubly, and with a quiet passion that moved many people. He gained a reputation for being able to deal with many different persuasions, even his adversaries, without alienating them.

In 1969, he moved to the Washington, D.C., headquarters of the Wilderness Society to concentrate on lobbying for eastern wilderness. He convinced congressmen and senators and, perhaps more important, their staffs about the benefits of wilderness: the possibility of gaining critical scientific knowledge by the study of natural processes, the maintenance of wildlife habitat for popular game as well as nongame animals, the protection of watersheds for pure supplies of drinking water, the chance for the most challenging kind of outdoor recreation. He also pointed out that eastern wilderness areas would compose such a small percentage of the national forests that they could hardly threaten any extractive industries.

His major opponent in Washington was the Forest Service, but as Ernie constantly reminded the congressional staffers, citizens vote; the Forest Service doesn't. His work grew increasingly intense in 1973 and 1974. In 1975, President Gerald Ford signed the Eastern Wilderness Act. It acknowledged that eastern forests could recover from previous human abuse to regain a natural appearance. Included in the act were sixteen wildernesses totaling nearly 207,000 acres, with seventeen more to be evaluated for inclusion. Eight of these thirty-three areas were in Appalachia.

In 1976, Ernie retired from the Wilderness Society to his nephew's summer home in Buffalo Gap, Virginia, cradled between Big North and Little North Mountains. The next year, the Forest Service began a roadless area review and evaluation for wilderness designation. Almost immediately, Ernie was asked to lead a small group working for wilderness in Virginia. I met Ernie when I joined that group some years later. He was both the inspiration and the steadying hand behind a campaign that resulted in the 1984 designation of eleven wilderness and four wilderness study areas in the Virginia mountains. The study areas became wilderness in 1988. Ernie also helped wilderness advocates in other states plot their strategies. By the late 1990s, when a conservative political climate had brought wilderness campaigns nearly to a standstill, there were forty-five wilderness areas from the George Washington National Forest in Virginia to the Chattahoochee National Forest in Georgia.

Together, they comprise a little more than half a million acres, less than ten percent of the federal lands, which are themselves less than twenty percent of Appalachia. Some four hundred thousand acres proposed for wilderness (by Ernie, naturally) in Great Smoky Mountains National Park would nearly double the total, but congressional approval has been stymied for decades by a right-wing senator from North Carolina who was slightly younger than Ernie. Ernie was hoping to bury him. A new generation, having learned from Ernie, bides its time for a swing in the political pendulum that will be favorable to wilderness designation.

Many mountain people reacted strongly against local efforts to designate wilderness areas. They saw that wilderness meant a ban on logging, although Appalachian wilderness areas are typically only six thousand to eight thousand acres at high elevations and don't have very good timber. They saw that wilderness designation brought in recreationists from outside. Mountaineers who owned inholdings in proposed wildernesses feared restrictions on the use of their own land. There was a false but unshakable belief that once a wilderness was established, the next step would be to outlaw hunting. Most of all, the exclusion of motorized vehicles enraged mountaineers. "You put it in wilderness," threatened a homemade plywood sign in the late 1970s in the Chattahoochee National Forest, "and we'll put it in ashes."

Ernie recognized that mountaineers had none of the motives that drove urban dwellers to support wilderness. Patiently, clearly, he explained what wilderness designation really meant. He never got rattled, even at meetings so heated that his friends worried they would all get beaten up. Over the years, Ernie never seemed to lose his energy, hiking up mountains and sending out letters to galvanize action. He still mowed his own lawn.

He showed me around his yard, pointing to trees he had transplanted over the years. His house was as spare as he was: the living room had a couch, a woodstove, a desk, and a few chairs, with drapes strung across the end of the room to wall off a downstairs bedroom. He hated television and got his news by phone from his many contacts, as well as from the *Wall Street Journal*. He subscribed in order to see what the opposition was up to. He had never married because he always knew what he wanted to do and feared that it would cause too much conflict with a spouse's desires. On his refrigerator was a sign: Age and treachery will overcome youth and skill.

As we sat on his front porch talking, a thunderstorm blew up. The day turned darker, as if night were approaching, though it was still afternoon. I said, "Ernie, I'm sure you're like me, you watch the forest and see the cycle of birth, death, and rebirth, and it helps you consider your own death."

"Sure, absolutely," he said.

"So do you have anything in mind for your tombstone?"

Ernie chuckled, something he did often. He had decided years ago to be cremated, he said, and at first wanted his ashes scattered in the Smokies, as he had scattered those of his friend Harvey Broome years ago.

"But I've lived here near Buffalo Gap for so long now, more than twenty years," he said, "that I've changed my mind." Ernie had rarely elaborated on the spiritual benefits of wilderness, in the way he spoke at length of its other advantages. He saw no merit in organized religions. Nonetheless, it was the spiritual power he felt in nature that gave meaning to his life. The wind strengthened, flipping up the undersides of leaves, which gave off a strange bright glow in the stormy gloom. Rain began to spatter on the roof, and from the earth rose the tangy smell of dust slaked. In the simple, direct, yet profoundly eloquent way that characterized him, Ernie reduced all the palaver about wilderness to a few basic concepts. "If you can't get beyond yourself, you're pretty narrow," he said. "There is obviously a greater force beyond our comprehension, and we respect it by preserving the creation in which this force is manifested."

Before I left, I asked Ernie if he had ever read a novel called *Trail of the Lonesome Pine.* It was not an irrelevant question. "Oh, hello!" Ernie said. "It was one of the first books I ever read. I thought it was wonderful that the hero wanted to be in the woods. I read it two or three times, probably while I was still in Roanoke." That city, where Ernie spent part of his childhood, is not far from Big Stone Gap, near Virginia's border with Kentucky. In Big Stone Gap lived John Fox, Jr., the author of *Trail* and one of the two most influential popular writers about Appalachia.

Fox was part of the "local-color" school of writing that developed after the Civil War. At the end of the nineteenth century, rapid industrialization was transforming an agrarian society into an urban one. The early twentieth century brought a flood of dark-complexioned immigrants from eastern Europe. The changes seemed like threats to many in mainstream society. Writers for magazines and newspapers went looking for authentic America. They thought they had found it in the quaint, ferocious lifeways of Appalachia. It didn't hurt that mountaineers were demonstrably of "pure" Anglo-Saxon stock. In what has been called another type of exploitation, local-color writers used mountaineers to entertain their readers with strange and peculiar ways. In so doing, they established a prevailing image of Appalachia that continues to shape cultural tourism.

John Fox, Jr., came to the mountains in the 1880s, when he was already in his twenties and a Harvard graduate. His affluent family from Kentucky's bluegrass country was speculating in coal and timber, and he helped his brother manage the business. Big Stone Gap was expected to become the Pittsburgh of the South. It didn't, and to make money when the bubble burst, Fox began to write short stories and books based on real mountaineers he had met and real events in their lives. *The Little Shepherd of Kingdom Come,* published in 1903, is believed to be the first American novel to sell a million copies. But it was *The Trail of the Lonesome Pine* in 1908 that established his most enduring fame. It became the basis for an outdoor musical in Fox's adopted hometown that seemed like a must on any tour of Appalachia.

Big Stone Gap is a modern small town, complete with a downtown park with a statue of a coal miner and a bench on which an elderly man dozed. I was puzzled by a mosaic on the park walkway that enshrined the word "Drugs," until I learned that a pharmacy had once stood there. The Victorian mansions of the coal and timber barons covered a knoll named Poplar Hill. One of the finest, the home of onetime Virginia attorney general Rufus Ayers, has become the Southwest Virginia Museum. The displays, as elegant as the house, highlighted local pride in coal mining. In the more modest residential section below, the Fox house, which is open to the public, is country architecture, a low-ceilinged cabin of cedar shakes and beadboard that started with four rooms and ended with twenty-two.

Fox worked off and on in New York and around the world as a correspondent for *Harper's* and *Scribner's* magazines. His house was filled with small statues, brass candlesticks, Oriental rugs, and fancy bookends holding row after row of books. Despite being dark and rich with the requisite red velvet couch, it felt simple and uncluttered. Fox married a Viennese opera singer whom he met in New York. She sang scales on the screened porch off their bedroom upstairs. She couldn't perform professionally in Big Stone Gap, and Fox couldn't write well in New York City, so their marriage failed after five years. Fox died of pneumonia on the screened porch in 1919, at the age of fifty-six. He was a small, suave man of frail health and weak eyes, vigorous in his youth but later enjoying the wealth his writing brought. He did what might be called slumming. Fascinated by mountaineers, he came to admire them. After all, he chose to live among them, as does the eastern geologist hero of *Trail*.

Like Fox himself, the hero, Jack Hale, is looking for mineral wealth in the mountains. He falls in love with a dewy mountain girl, June Tolliver, whom he educates to be a singer. In his fiction, Fox had his protagonist do what he could not manage with his own wife: reconcile two different worlds. After many troubles, the hero and heroine of *Trail* marry and plan to spend at least part of every year in Lonesome Cove, June's mountain homeplace. Jack promises to "plant young poplars to cover the sight of every bit of uptorn earth" that had resulted from the logging and mining he helped to instigate. The once crystal creek was now black as soot, with sawdust whirling in eddies, but June told herself that the ugly spot was such a little one after all, and the creek was still clear above the mine opening.

The outdoor drama was held in the yard next to the Tolliver house, where the girl on which June's character was based is said to have stayed when she came to town for schooling. The play, financed by donations and grants, was performed by professional gospel singers and community theater actors. The calling of tree frogs in the falling dusk almost drowned out the actors' voices. The Appalachian Strings, a family group on guitars and banjo, performed a rousing warm-up to some foot-stomping and yee-hawing from an audience of around three hundred. We sat on wooden pews. The foreground of the four-foot-high stage was a flower garden terraced by railroad ties. The soft splash of a tiny waterfall on one side mingled with a sound track of deer snorting and birds singing. There was a painted backdrop with trees, mountains, and clouds in an impressionist style. A central tree above a rock was, I assumed, the lonesome pine of the title. It's said that there was once a real pine, but the owner got so tired of people looking for it that he cut it down.

Within the first few minutes of the play, two men have pulled a gun and a knife on each other. The story has all the Appalachian archetypes: clans, incest, feuds, moonshine, hostility to strangers, and a rough code of honor. As an outsider making a profit from the mountains, Fox was predisposed to see mountaineers as needing the services of civilization. But he also portrayed their intelligence, kindness, and loyalty. The applause was warm, before we turned toward the exit and the long, black line of mountain that loomed over the summer night. Several of Fox's books are still in print, and there's no question of his continuing appeal, not least of all to the descendants of his mountaineers.

The next day, the search for Sunday dinner in Big Stone Gap prompted me to ruminate on the work of Horace Kephart, the second writer who fixed vivid images of Appalachia in the American mind. Kephart may have been the first twentieth-century hippie. He dropped out from a prestigious professional life as a librarian at Yale and other lofty institutions and left his wife and six children. Alcohol was his drug of choice. While recovering from a breakdown of some kind at his father's house in Ohio, Kephart searched the map for the nearest wild land and a place to start afresh. His forebears had been pioneers, and from an early age he was drawn to woodcraft and the practice of survival skills. In 1904, he arrived in the Smokies.

He obtained permission to use an abandoned cabin near an old copper mine by Hazel Creek, which is now within Great Smoky Mountains National Park. There, and later in the nearby town of Bryson City, North Carolina, Kephart lived a simple, mostly solitary life. He had come with the intention of supporting himself by writing about his experiences and sold numerous articles about camping, hunting, and fishing to *Sports Afield, Forest and Stream,* and *Outing Magazine.* In the 1920s, he began writing in support of the movement for a national park in the Smokies. Four days before he was killed in a car accident in 1931, he learned that the last of the big timber companies that was holding out had agreed to sell. Several features in the park are named after him.

Like John Fox, Jr., Kephart undertook to portray the mountaineers. Unlike Fox, Kephart wrote nonfiction, but his characterizations are similar. Kephart was particularly interested in moonshining and described many adventures centered on stills. He also tackled aspects of mountain life important to potential tourists. "The chief drawback to travel in this region, aside from the roads," he wrote in his most famous book, *Our Southern Highlanders* (1913), "is not the character of the people, but the quality of bed and board. . . . Many of the village inns are dirty, and their tables a shock and a despair to the hungry pilgrim." Execrable food and filthy lodgings have been the twin complaints of travelers in Appalachia since the eighteenth century. Has this historically abysmal reputation, I asked myself as I wandered hungrily through Big Stone Gap, suffered any improvements?

Yes, when it comes to locally owned, nonfranchise motels like the Country Inn, where I was staying. These are a great bargain, costing on average half or less of the going rate at hotel chains in the larger valley towns. For that price you get a room that is reasonably and sometimes spotlessly clean, a television that may or may not come equipped with remote control, and a phone if, as a lady in a front office once said to me, "they ain't tore it out yet." Most of the time the hot water works. The beds are usually all right, although once in Robbinsville, North Carolina, we did have to pull a thin mattress off of senile springs and sleep on the floor. The window curtains, sometimes homemade, may have cigarette burns or missing hardware. The rooms invariably smell musty but have individual venting systems, which quickly clear the air. The lighting is quirky. Ice and drink machines are always available, often there is a little flower garden, and some motels have swimming pools. Beyond that, there are few frills. It's becoming increasingly common for motels to be run by East Indians.

In contrast, a good restaurant can be hard to find in Appalachia. The traditional, tasty staples of pork and cornmeal have been almost obliterated by burgers and white bread. I've learned that I can depend on fast-food chains in even the smallest Appalachian village, but other options may be limited. Occasionally, family restaurants such as Stringer's in Big Stone Gap look inviting, although I found it closed on a Sunday afternoon after the church crowd had left. Breakfasts are often the best meal, with puffy biscuits and a soup bowl of gravy. Here and there you come across really good homemade cole slaw or pie. I couldn't find either in Big Stone Gap and ended up at the Dairy Queen.

Grass Roots

Morning mist was blowing across the top of Potts Mountain as I drove into West Virginia from Roanoke. Although it was the end of July, I turned on the car heater. Fog lay along the sixty-mile length of Peters Mountain, too, and I could hardly see the valley below. At the top of the mountain was a realtor's For Sale sign. What I glimpsed of the valley looked prosperous, with large farms and quite a few modern houses. The road was paved but narrow, and sure enough, here came the inevitable pickup truck speeding around a curve, hogging the one lane. But I was hugging the shoulder, ready for him. Nothing was going to push me off the trail of a native-born Appalachian forest activist.

They were proving to be a small and scattered species. Whenever I met local leaders in forest conservation, I asked about the mountain-born component of their constituency. The standard response was a short, rueful snort accompanied by a sidelong glance. Expression of environmental concern is not an Appalachian tradition, in a culture where land is valued for its immediate utility and individualism is esteemed at the expense of collective action. In any culture where education is minimal and economic oppression is the rule, passivity is common. Resistance to degradation of the mountains didn't gain strength until the late 1960s, after the nationwide movements for civil rights, women's equality, and environmental protection provided models for dissent and contacts for resources.

Strip mining, which began on a large scale in the early 1950s, galvanized the first burst of community organizing. The worst abuses were in eastern Kentucky, and that's where the most intense opposition centered. Some people lay down in the path of bulldozers; others blew the bulldozers up. In 1972, a group of women shut down a strip mine in Knott County. It was a heady, empowering victory, especially in a culture where women were expected to be docile, and it contributed eventually to restrictive new legislation on mining. It also spurred communities in other places to form groups to protest instances of environmental destruction—a dam here, a highway there. The story of the pollution of Yellow Creek in Bell County, Kentucky, quickly became a favorite topic for academic theses on environmental injustice—and the case is hardly over yet.

The Middlesboro Tanning Company had been periodically turning Yellow Creek black and stinking since the late 1800s. For most of that time, the tannery was the single largest employer in the area, providing up to 450 jobs. In the 1960s, the factory changed from plant-based methods to chromium, a toxic metal. The condition of the creek worsened. More than a thousand people lived along the fourteen miles of Yellow Creek, and they happened to be some of the poorest people in the nation. They experienced blinding fumes and nosebleeds. Some wells became so contaminated that bathroom showers caused rashes. Leukemia, kidney disorders, stillbirths, miscarriages, and birth defects proliferated. Fish in the creek died in huge numbers, and farm animals and pets died after drinking the water.

Individuals on Yellow Creek had been complaining about the pollution almost since the tannery opened. This was coal country, and the small, isolated communities in the valley were the remnants of old coal camps. For years, the camps had been manipulated by coal companies to compete with one another, in baseball and other sports, instead of cooperating in ways that might, for example, lead to union organizing. The hostility among communities that sometimes broke out in fistfights did not dissipate until rural schools were consolidated and friendships among teenagers began to span community boundaries. When asked why residents of Yellow Creek waited until 1980 to organize, the founder of Yellow Creek Concerned Citizens, Larry Wilson, paused for a long moment and then replied, "It just didn't occur to anyone as a possibility."

Wilson had worked outside the valley and brought back knowledge about how to use the system. The group began with three married couples who met over a picnic table in a park. They agreed to phone some trusted friends, who did the same, until they felt strong enough to go public. They feared reprisals, with good reason. Wilson was shot at, his dog was poisoned, and his children were harassed by teachers at school. Other group members were denied credit at local banks. "The Clique," as Wilson's group called the local elite with political power, seemed less concerned about the money involved in a cleanup than about losing their power to run the show.

For the first two years, the group appealed to the Middlesboro city government to enforce the ordinance already on the books that would restrict tannery waste. Shouting matches between group members and the mayor were common, and once several members took over city hall. Officials at the state department of natural resources were not responsive at first, nor was the federal Environmental Protection Agency, although it later became a key force in improving conditions. In 1983, the group filed a $31 million class action suit against the city and the tannery. This elevated the fight from the backwoods to the national media. The suit against the city was settled out of court in 1985 by an agreement that set limits for waste discharges and established deadlines for compliance. The suit against the tannery went on and on, with tannery owners deploying various tactics to evade a judgment. A decision in favor of Yellow Creek Concerned Citizens finally came in 1995, but settlement was still subject to impending appeals by the owners.

Single-issue community groups like Wilson's sprang up among mountaineers, but few of them focused on preservation of forests. I made it my business to search out some that did, which was why I was creeping down the fog-filled curves of Peters Mountain. I turned left at Sweet Springs. Amy South was waiting for me at the Zenith General Store, which was just about the only building in town. It was a cavernous space with two pool tables, a small refrigerator case of sandwich meats, a drink machine, and some shelves of dry goods. It served as a community gathering place, and everyone who came in knew Amy. We sat in the slightly remodeled chairs of two antique school desks to talk.

Amy was not quite thirty years old. She had bangs and long, brown hair with golden tints, and eyes much the same. She was tall and thin, with large, capable hands. She wore petite diamond-chip earrings, a T-shirt that read "Almost Heaven, West Virginia," and jeans. "We get married and buried in blue jeans," she said. Her family had settled in this long, rich valley at least as far back as her great-great-grandfather on her father's side; her mother's people also came from Peters Mountain. Her parents moved to Cleveland, Ohio, to work, but her mother came back when Amy was one because she missed country life so badly. Her father followed shortly afterward. Her family bought back some property that had been sold off years ago, making a four-hundred-acre farm that they all worked together. They raised sheep, beef cattle, and four acres of burley tobacco. "I don't smoke or chew, and I know some people are against it," Amy said, "but it's important income for us."

She had five siblings, and all lived on or within sight of Peters Mountain. Her husband and her brother ran a small timber operation. They didn't cut on the Jefferson National Forest, which owned large parts of Peters Mountain, but on private lands. "We don't clear-cut; we don't believe in that, it's a horrible devastation," she said. "We selective cut and don't take trees below so many inches." She brought in some income as a self-employed florist, arranging fresh flowers with moss and ferns she found in the woods. "Would you like a tour?" she asked. "I can take you up the road past my new flower shop."

The shop was a log cabin that Amy intended would also serve as an arts and crafts shop for local people's quilts, paintings, and wood carvings. Family members had bought the structure, dated in the early 1800s, at a place miles away, and eight of them had moved it. "We like to work where we live," Amy said. "We've got a good life, and we love it. The mountain is like a part of our family. We have something endangered and we have worked together to protect it."

Half a dozen years earlier, the American Electric Power Company (formerly Appalachian Power Company) had held a public meeting in the Monroe County Courthouse. The company was requesting a two-hundred-foot right-of-way from the national forest to cross Peters Mountain, for one of the biggest power lines in the world. It would carry 765,000 volts, stand twelve stories tall, glow on rainy nights, and light up unconnected fluorescent bulbs sixty feet away. It would carry electricity from Wyoming County, West Virginia, for 115 miles to Cloverdale, Virginia, allowing the company to boost its sales to other utilities. The syndrome famous in environmental circles as the NIMBY response—Not In My Back Yard—applied almost literally in Amy's case. The line would have filled her view at close range.

"But it's not the view," Amy said. "It's more the water. They would use chemical sprays to keep the growth down along the line. Peters Mountain is full of springs, and there's water bottling plants in several towns around here. And I wouldn't be able to sit on my porch and listen to the mountain. The hum of the lines would drown out the creek." It would also muffle a unique feature of Peters Mountain, a meteorological phenomenon reported to occur in only one other place on earth, the Pennine Mountains in England. Every so often, the wind rushes at the mountain in a way that produces a mighty roar. Amy had heard it. She liked to listen for it. "The power line would ruin our way of life mentally and physically," she said.

Amy began to meet regularly with neighbors at the Zenith Country Store. They organized themselves as the Border Conservancy. They held pie suppers and dances, and one lady made a quilt for raffle, a great big one of red, white, and blue with "No Power Tower" on it, and embroidered with deer, bears, turkeys, and other wildlife that the line would affect. Something like two thousand people in the county gave them support in one way or another. A community down the valley started holding bake sales. By these means, they raised money for a lawyer. Amy's sister went to Washington, D.C., to testify before the Senate. Shortly before I visited, the Jefferson National Forest had announced that it would deny permission for the right-of-way, but Amy was wary. "We're not ready to celebrate," she said. "There still might be a snake in the grass."

Driving back to the store, we passed the lane that led first to her house and then to her parents'. At the turnoff, there was a colorful, hand-painted sign with a scene of trees and a creek and several verses of a poem that a local person had written about Peters Mountain. Amy pulled over so that I could read it. "I'm never leaving the mountain," she said. She once had a job in a florist shop, where she learned the trade, but she quit because she couldn't stand to be away from home.

"How far away was the job?" I asked.

"Ten miles," she said.

Buzz Williams could be called a single-issue Appalachian activist, but the preservation of the Chattooga River was one whopper of a cause. He could also be accused of the NIMBY response, but the 180,000 acres of the Chattooga watershed made one whopper of a backyard. Everything from the microclimate of mosses in old growth to the care and feeding of celebrity river runners lay within his purview as director of the Chattooga River Watershed Coalition. He was equal to the job. The shelves in his storefront office in Clayton, Georgia, held *Sun Tzu's Aphorisms, The Honest Herbal, Laurel's Kitchen,* and *The Tragedies of William Shakespeare,* along with standard tomes such as *Manual of the Vascular Flora of the Carolinas.*

Buzz was in his mid-forties, as tall, lean, and creased in the face as the Scots-Irish were supposed to be. "I'm of Scots-Irish and Welsh stock," he said, "stubborn and contentious." He was born and raised in the town of Pendleton, fifty miles away in South Carolina, and his accent rang true to place. His hair, a dark shade of sandy brown, was fashionably cut to lie lightly on his neck. When he put his bifocals on, he looked scholarly.

His grandfather had owned a two-hundred-acre farm, and all Buzz had wanted to do was inherit it and farm until he died. But he could see the Blue Ridge, a mysterious, beckoning presence, from the pasture. As soon as he was old enough to thumb a ride, he went there. He tramped around the national forests—the Sumter, Nantahala, and Chattahoochee—that come together at the borders of South Carolina, North Carolina, and Georgia. He attributed his inclination toward nature to his mother and grandmother. "The first time I ever got my butt kicked badly was when I broke some bird eggs," he remembered.

His first experience with white water was at age twelve, when he tried to canoe from a lake to the ocean in an aluminum craft loaded with everything. "I almost made it through the first set of rapids," he said, "and they were respectable white water." When he was eighteen, he started running the Chattooga, years before its 1974 designation by Congress as a Wild and Scenic River.

An interstate highway was built very close to his grandfather's farm, and Buzz took off on various travels, "looking," he said, "for pristine places." Along the way, he picked up a degree in forestry and a tattoo of a peregrine falcon on his left inside forearm. Buzz had traced the design from a book about the prehistoric Native American culture called the Southeastern Ceremonial Complex and given it to a tattoo artist. "He wasn't too drunk," Buzz said, "so he got most of the lines straight." Buzz was moved to do this through a spiritual experience. On Cumberland Island, off the coast of Georgia, he encountered one of the endangered falcons eye to eye, then watched the bird fly faster than seemed physically possible—a consummate work of evolution, brought to the edge of extinction by human stupidity. Buzz received it as a personal message about the power and fragility of nature.

When he came back to the mountains in the mid-1970s, it dawned on him that the best thing he could do was to stay home and preserve whatever pristine nature was there. For a dozen years, he made a living as a white-water guide on the Chattooga, learning every pothole. During low water, he photographed the rocks for lengthy study. He couldn't get enough of the river, and every time he went down it he learned something new. He took up again the hikes of his youth, getting to know every corner of the watershed and its contribution to the character of the river. When writer James Dickey returned to the Chattooga, the river he fictionalized in *Deliverance,* his novel (and movie) about homosexual rape, Buzz was his guide. "Local people hated Dickey and his novel," Buzz said. "There were some death threats."

For a while, he worked seasonally for the Forest Service, in recreation and law enforcement. As use of the wild and scenic river corridor increased, the Forest Service recruited him to manage it. When Buzz first met the Chattooga in the late 1960s, he estimated that about six hundred people a year canoed or rafted down it. Twenty-five years later, he calculated that the three licensed river guides served a minimum of forty thousand clients, not counting clinics and private boaters. These probably brought the total to one hundred thousand people a year just on the river, not to mention picnickers and hikers in the woods.

With his years of experience, Buzz was the obvious choice for manager, but things soon got tense on the job. "The Forest Service wants to cut every tree over a hundred years old," he said. He had been hearing about an in-house group, the Association of Forest Service Employees for Environmental Ethics, organized in the Pacific Northwest in opposition to Forest Service cutting practices there. Buzz established the first chapter in the East. Eventually, he said, the Forest Service discontinued his position.

This freed him to pursue an idea that had originated in the mind of Bob Zahner, the grand old man of old growth in the Chattooga's headwaters at Highlands, North Carolina. The Chattooga River, suggested Bob, would make an excellent model for the new philosophy of "ecosystem management" that the Forest Service began to proclaim in the early 1990s. The definition of an ecosystem is problematic. It can apply to a drop of water with a community of microscopic life, as well as to thousands of square miles blanketed by a particular association of plants. Ecologists seek to understand the connections among living beings and their physical surroundings, so drawing lines that cut the connections is difficult. A watershed—all the land that drains into a specific stream—is one of the most practical definitions of an ecosystem, one that gives the human mind immediate purchase on the vast map of ecological intricacies. "We understand the entire [Chattooga] watershed to be a natural functioning landscape and must be treated as such for effective forest management," Buzz wrote in one of his earliest letters to the Forest Service.

The Chattooga was one of the wildest mountain streams remaining in the Southeast, with a watershed containing an enormous proportion of the biodiversity characteristic of the Appalachians, but its administration was fractured among three national forests that rarely communicated with one another. Forest Service headquarters in Washington, D.C., had funds available for demonstration projects, and agency administrators agreed to compile a body of information about the ecology of the Chattooga. More than $1 million later, a major study concluded that the river and its wild trout population were threatened by logging, poorly built roads, farming, and development.

The Forest Service showed little sign of actually utilizing what it had learned. The various district rangers continued to cut timber across the watershed, sometimes right up to the boundary of the wild and scenic river designation, one-quarter mile from the river's bank. It was obvious that the Forest Service wasn't going to treat the Chattooga watershed as an ecosystem, weighing each management action against the impact on the whole, unless someone made them do it. Buzz was without a doubt the single best person to try.

He put together an association with membership that included national-level environmental organizations such as the Wilderness Society and the Sierra Club. A gregarious good old boy, he also drew on a network of contacts made during years on the river to get endorsements from all kinds of people, from river runners to birders to sawmill owners. Thirty percent of the Chattooga watershed is privately owned, and Buzz took care to involve key local people.

Buzz's wife, Nicole, wrote the first grant awarded to the Chattooga River Watershed Coalition (by the Mary Reynolds Babcock Foundation). Nicole had come south to the Chattooga during summers while in college up north, where she lived. A leggy, long-haired brunette, she came to have fun but also to work. She still worked part-time as a photographer, taking Polaroids of river runners that they could buy as soon as they got out of the water. Nicole was the first paid employee of the coalition, with what she referred to as a "do everything" job description. She was ten years younger than Buzz, an edge she needed to keep up with him.

In 1994, when several more grants came through, the coalition's board hired Buzz as full-time director. With Nicole, and with the occasional help of interns and experts, they published a quarterly journal on every aspect of Chattooga natural and cultural history. They taught youth groups how to test water quality and rallied attendance at Forest Service planning meetings. They hosted meetings at local cafés. "Buzz has a Southern Baptist upbringing," Nicole said, "and he knows how to preach." They purchased software for the computerized Geographical Information System. They published a twenty-five-page conservation plan for the Chattooga watershed. They offered consultation services to private landowners who wanted to cut timber and held a workshop on horse logging that was covered by the international broadcasting company CNN. Without a doubt, the most dramatic thing they did was to hold a month-long vigil at Rabun Bald.

The Forest Service planned to build nine miles of road through a fourteen-thousand-acre roadless tract and sell eight hundred acres of timber near the top of the bald. It was a locally popular scenic area, as well as one of the only concentrations of old growth in the watershed. Buzz organized some thirty volunteers to camp, at least two a night, on the bald. He had a secret camp ready in case the Forest Service forced him off the summit. He was there most of the month, talking to the hikers who made the six-mile round-trip trek to see the September view from the observation tower. A few newspaper reporters even made it up to the top. The *Atlanta Journal* ran an editorial opposing the Forest Service. The result of the combined pressure didn't force the Forest Service to completely abandon the sale, but Buzz was able to negotiate a compromise that kept the road out of the roadless area.

"This piecemeal approach is not the answer," he said, the tattoo on his left arm resting facedown on the rattling windowsill of his old pickup truck. For some reason or other, it hadn't worked out to run the river while I was there, so Buzz just drove me around. "In a way," he said, "environmentalists have cut off their noses because we've challenged the Forest Service on its procedures and made them get the paperwork right. It was only a delaying action. It allowed us time to mobilize more people, but in the long run it hasn't really been successful. In each of four cases, the trees we were trying to protect were eventually cut. We need to forge a new conservation ethic based on a wider view, and involving the people in the area." He supported the Sierra Club's "no cut" policy on public lands, as long as it was applied slowly to phase timbering out and wean loggers off public lands.

I saw a red fox run through a clear-cut. On the other side of the road, the river was obscured by trees. You know you're in tourist country when you can get black-bean burgers and tabouli for lunch at a restaurant on a country road. In what I took as a mark of honor, Buzz decided to show me the fifty-five acres he and Nicole owned. The road in was very long and clearly a major cause of the truck's battered condition. Hot, still air made for a lowlands intensity of heat, in which butterflies shimmered instead of flitted. This was piney woods, fragrant with resin. We parked in a ragged little opening, just big enough for the timber-frame sawmill shed Buzz was building. He showed me how a broadax works, how it's designed to square a log without abrading your hand. He had planted Ocoee bells, an endangered wildflower that grew only in the local area, and was having good luck.

He and Nicole lived in a tent. They called it a yurt, a kind of large, amorphous dwelling made of heavy fabrics that is native to the Mongolian steppes. Flowered rugs covered the dirt floor. Mosquito netting hung over the bed. They cooked on a two-burner propane stove as well as over an open fire. Tools and utensils lay strewn about; there was no way to secure them, and they didn't worry about it. The shower was, of course, solar powered—not simply a crude, black, fifty-five-gallon drum mounted head-high, but fed by spring water piped into tubes that coursed across a glass panel before reaching the barrel. They had lived there two years, although the previous winter they had gratefully accepted a friend's offer to stay in an empty cabin. Buzz wanted to build a timber-frame house but figured he'd need a decade to do it; in the meantime, he was hoping to finish the sawmill shed in time to move in for the winter. Last night they had turned the Coleman lantern off and watched lightning bugs flicker against the tent ceiling and counted themselves the luckiest two people on earth.

We met Nicole for dinner at a restaurant on the outskirts of Clayton. One of the waitresses, a middle-aged lady with a bouffant hairdo, recognized Buzz and brought him a notebook of her poems. She opened it to one called "The Henchmen." It was about the Forest Service and was as uncomplimentary as its title implied. It was, she told us, inspired by her experience at the Rabun Bald vigil. Over salad, Buzz said, "It's very powerful when you can get local people to say to the Forest Service, 'I'm not against logging, but what you're doing here is wrong.' We've preached to the choir long enough. Now we need to reach the people who can vote conservation-minded politicians into Congress."

At dusk we went for a swim at Bull Sluice on the river. The water boiled over huge boulders into furious standing waves that looked like death traps to me. I got in gingerly. It was not nearly as cold as I expected. A group of young people, having not yet reached the age when mortality acquires a personal aspect, were taking turns riding a rapid on a boogie board. Buzz swam over to two jutting rocks and wedged himself between them. "There's an air pocket under here where you can breathe," he said, and disappeared into the shadowed water. I decided to take his word for it.

Eighteen people sat around two tables pushed together lengthwise in a brick conference room at Davis and Elkins College in Elkins, West

Virginia. Several faces were familiar from other meetings over the years, in other hot, bland rooms. I recognized them as the radical fringe. These were the people that the Forest Service and mainstream society considered environmental extremists, who didn't so much want to work within the system as change it altogether. They were meeting on a drizzly day in April for a project with a scope far grander than a backyard or even a watershed. Leading them, at the head of the table, was Than Hitt, a native West Virginian.

Even from my seat at the bottom of the table, Than's eyes were captivating—wide-set, clear, dark blue. He had been born in Morgantown, and judging by his smooth, young face, it couldn't have been much more than two decades ago. His sandy brown hair was longish and curly, and he wore sideburns. His father came from the coal camps around Bluefield, in the southern part of the state; his mother came from northern West Virginia. She was involved with issues of social justice and was studying to be a minister. His father had often taken Than (short for Nathaniel) hiking and backpacking in the mountains. When Than was sixteen, he decided that he wanted to do a solo hike. His mother said no, his dad said yes. Only a few friends understood why he wanted to do it; he couldn't entirely explain it himself. His girlfriend asked him how he would use the bathroom. Than rolled his eyes. "That relationship didn't last long," he said. He walked ninety miles that autumn, following the Cheat River. "It was," he said, "a life-changing experience." He thought about life on the fast track and knew that it wasn't for him.

A recent graduate in environmental science from the College of Wooster in Ohio, Than had frequented the nearby Mohican Memorial State Forest during his student years. His first experience with activism came when the state planned to log it. Than helped mobilize hundreds of people in protest and spoke before a state senate subcommittee. He felt driven and empowered. He moved to Athens, Ohio, to work for the Buckeye Forest Council, a nonprofit state-level group associated with a larger preservation organization called Heartwood. When Heartwood inaugurated its Appalachian Restoration Campaign in the summer of 1995, Than jumped at the chance to earn meager pay and spend long hours directing it. A grant from a coalition of outfitting companies got him started.

The Central Appalachian Assessment was the first step in Than's campaign. It would utilize the computer-based Geographic Information System, which Than had access to in Ohio University's cartographic labs. Modeled to some degree on the *Southern Appalachian Assessment* recently published by the Forest Service, the Central Appalachian Assessment would compile a wide array of data about central Appalachia. This area was defined as running from the Cumberland Plateau east to the Blue Ridge, and from the northern border of Pennsylvania to the southern borders of Virginia and Kentucky, which form a continuous east-west line. The goal of the campaign was to plan the means by which that landscape could recover and nurture all the species of life that had lived there when Europeans first arrived—those that had not already gone extinct. The principles of conservation biology would guide the methodology.

A branch of science that developed in the 1980s, conservation biology brings together information from many disciplines, including molecular genetics, biochemistry, ecology, geography, and systems analysis. It applies this information to the actual, functioning natural world, to find the most effective ways to preserve the world's shrinking array of living creatures within the constraints imposed by human societies. It was conservation biologists who determined that large sizes and connections were necessary to make forest preserves work. The land planning models that some conservation biologists propose are continental in scale and have core areas representing every type of native ecosystem. In those core areas, human intrusion would be minimal or nonexistent. Surrounding the cores are buffer areas, including connections between and among the cores, in which some human activities would be allowed. Only outside the buffers, after the rest of creation had been provided for, would humanity have its own way. "Conservation biology is not value free," Than said. "The largest extinction in sixty-five million years is not to be taken lightly."

Like Buzz Williams, Than felt that the brushfire approach of challenging individual timber sales on Forest Service lands wasn't enough. He wanted to go beyond the watershed approach, toward a regional land-use plan. To create it, he hoped to activate three broad streams of society: public agencies, private citizens, and academic scientists. "We need to pull all kinds of things together," he said. "It's a major failing in so many of our conservation efforts, leaving things disconnected."

The main item on Than's agenda for today's meeting was to carry out a vision mapping exercise. "Veesion," he said, mocking his own local dialect. He had brought along the materials to demonstrate how a new map of the world might be drawn, one that perceived not just lifeless physical terrain but the contours of biodiversity. He passed out transparencies, colored marking pens, and photocopies of two maps of Ohio—one with ecological regions, and the other with dots identifying the locations of rare, threatened, and endangered species. Although only the Appalachian part of the state was the focus of the restoration campaign, it would serve as a useful demonstration of how conservation biology worked.

We traced the ecological boundaries of the state in blue on a transparency. We added blurbs and bubbles in red where rare species were clustered, the hot spots of biodiversity. Finally, we drew green latitude lines at one-degree intervals, for use as a grid. Within every swath of latitude, some part of every ecosystem present there should be represented in a system of protected enclaves.

We put a clean transparency on top. In black, we circled what we thought should be core areas and linked them with corridors, preferably along rivers. It was not as easy as it sounds. "Keep in mind that riparian strips—the edges of rivers and streams—are ten times more valuable than other kinds of terrain," Than said. "At this stage, we're not taking into account whether land is in private or public ownership. And remember, north-south and east-west connections are necessary to allow movement in response to climate change."

Global climate change looms over the future of all conservation strategies. Of the nearly two dozen computer models set up by various researchers to massage meteorological data, most predict a warming trend of 1.5 to 4.5 degrees Celsius over a fifty- to one-hundred year period. Models are only as good as the assumptions and data on which they are built, and the world's weather is one of the most complex of all systems, so there is some debate about their validity. There's no question, though, that the greenhouse gases that trap sunlight and heat on the earth's surface (mainly carbon dioxide released by the burning of fossil fuels) have increased substantially over the last century. Most arguments in the scientific community focus not on whether global warming is happening but on how it will affect particular locales and at what rate those effects will become noticeable. There is speculation that the climate zones that determine forest types could change by more than a mile a year, much faster than forests have been known to move by natural reproduction. And that's only one small aspect of the potential changes.

With so many factors to keep in mind, everyone sketched a slightly different map. The last step in the exercise, one we wouldn't take that day, would be to evaluate the core areas as home ranges for cerulean warblers and cougars. Because both of these animals need large parcels of forest, Than would use them as umbrella species to protect the habitats of others.

Than was looking for volunteers to do this kind of vision mapping across the entire central Appalachian area. There was some discussion about where all the data would come from. Than had already received a lot of it from the Nature Conservancy, a private nonprofit group that purchases and studies rare ecological sites around the country. He had also contacted state natural resource agencies and the director of the federal Environmental Protection Agency's project, the Mid-Atlantic Highlands Assessment.

There seemed to be plenty of assessments going on, but there were still big information gaps. For example, little was known about how to design effective corridors in eastern deciduous forests. How wide did they need to be to accommodate songbirds and other species? What kind of vegetation was most appropriate? One fellow suggested that Than get an intern to review the scientific literature. Another recommended fuzzy set theory as a general approach. "The procedures by which different researchers do their studies are all different," Than pointed out, "which makes it difficult to integrate the findings in the real world."

After the Central Appalachian Assessment was completed, Than would identify existing protected areas on public and private lands and calculate the degree to which they served the goal of preserving ecosystems and species. Then he would locate the best opportunities on private and public lands for restoration of natural ecological conditions. He would document the land policy reforms necessary to secure such places on public lands. He planned to outline economic incentives for private landowners to leave their land in a natural state, and to develop programs enabling private landowners to leave their properties to non-profit land trusts that would oversee permanent conservation. "It won't pay off in this generation," he said. "It's easier for someone to say, 'I'll will my property' if they're thinking about preserving it."

To facilitate all this, he would have an outreach strategy to educate the media and to involve conservation groups, natural resource professionals, and nontraditional environmentalists. "We have right on our side," Than said, "so we have nothing to hide." Already he had received a couple of letters calling him a Communist and accusing him of planning to seize land from rightful owners. Inevitably, discussion slipped into the deep, dark pit of social change.

"That's the biggest can of worms," said someone at the far end of the table. "It'll take generations."

"People think we value salamanders more than humans," a young woman on my right said.

"So what's the problem?" asked one of the men.

Than ran the meeting in a calm way that nonetheless advanced the day's agenda. He respectfully invited anyone with a comment to make it but did not hesitate to say that we were drifting when conversation got off course. He concluded the meeting by calling our attention to the schedule he had chalked on the portable blackboard. There were tasks scheduled for completion in every month through the rest of the year. For January 2, he had noted, "World Saved!"

The entity known as Appalachia-Science in the Public Interest (ASPI) in eastern Kentucky takes yet another approach to saving the world, one that in a way reverts to a single issue. But this issue is a single pair of hands and what they alone can accomplish to restore one's own backyard.

The hands of Paul Kalisz, director of the sustainable forestry program at ASPI, were working their way into forest duff, feeling for earthworms. Kalisz is a Slavic name; his family came from eastern Europe to the coalfields of western Pennsylvania in the first few decades of the twentieth century. Paul was of medium height, thin, with heavy dark eyebrows over dark eyes. He wore a hearing aid in one ear from his Navy days, when he worked with airplanes and lost his high-frequency range. He still couldn't pick out certain warbler songs. A cowlick fell over his high forehead. His beard was graying. He had small, slender hands, the hands of a musician or a surgeon. He had been a professor in the University of

Kentucky's Department of Forestry since 1982, spending half his time teaching courses on soils and geomorphology and the other half doing research on soil invertebrates. His work on the invasion of nonnative earthworms in Appalachia was, so to speak, groundbreaking.

He peeled back last year's leaves to show the tunnels that voles, mice, shrews, ants, snails, and beetle and fly larvae make through the first few inches of soil. Paul's observations had led him to overturn the common image of earthworms as the major soil mixers and builders. "It's a misconception, at least in the forests of this region," he said, brushing moist, crumbling flakes of decomposing leaves off his fingers. "Earthworms have a role, but it's not to drive the decomposition process. In addition to small animals, especially shrews, wild turkeys and smaller ground-foraging birds are more important for stirring the soil up." I remembered how vigorously the white-throated sparrows, rufous-sided towhees, and juncos scratched in the bushes where I threw them seed.

Paul had fifty permanent study plots in the best forest areas across Kentucky. He described the battle to preserve twelve thousand acres of Robinson Forest, the university's own research site, which happened to have the largest block of unmined coal in the eastern part of the state. "Some of the university board members were crying at one point, they wanted to mine it so badly," Paul said. He helped push the state into protecting the forest but expected that protection to be rescinded within a few years. A local Hardee's fast-food restaurant hung a needlepoint sampler that said, "We want jobs not earthworms."

Kentucky's forests had a hundred species of worms, but Paul had found sizable populations on only twenty-five percent of the land he sampled. Only on ten percent of it were they dominant, and that was in the richest coves. "Are coves rich because of worms, or are worms attracted to the richest soil?" he asked. I took this as a rhetorical question and answered with an indeterminate nod.

Paul was sure that he was finding new earthworm species, but he didn't want to take the time to collect and dissect enough specimens to scientifically name them. He was finding patches of introduced worms along roads, trails, and old homesites, but not in undisturbed forests. Of the thirty-five most common introduced species of worms, all had been traced back to ports, carried in such things as potted plants. Ships used to use soil as ballast, which they dumped wherever convenient. Along fishing creeks and lakes, bait worms that were thrown away now thrive in colonies.

Four of Paul's fifty plots were at ASPI. The center owns 32 acres and has access to an adjoining 150 acres held in a land trust, across the road from the Rockcastle River near Livingston. Both tracts border the Daniel Boone National Forest, where Paul had found a remnant old-growth stand. It was fertile ground for earthworms and for ideas about how to live humbly in earthworm country. I spent a couple of days at ASPI, sleeping on the worn couch in the library, to see how Appalachian traditions were being recast for a new millennium.

ASPI is a complex of small, mostly solar-powered buildings joined together by steps and decks, interspersed with flower beds. One building, a round one, was made of cordwood—one-foot lengths of small to medium-sized tree trunks—cemented in place to form walls. It was designed to show how inexpensive, locally available materials could be used to build a sturdy home. Al Fritsch, ASPI's founder, had lived there until recently, when he moved to Mount Vernon, a small town nearby, to make room for another staff member. There was a small kitchen and a bathroom with a composting toilet, an odor-free, low-cost, fertilizer-producing feature that exemplified ASPI's endeavors. Maps of the world and of Appalachia decorated the walls, along with bundles of dried herbs and Indian corn. The living room was full of file cabinets, a couple of computers, another worn couch, and some battered chairs. Several dogs were eager to be friends, and there was an amiable gray cat.

It was a comfortable place to spend a good part of an afternoon talking with Al. He was a thick-set man with thick white hair accentuated by black-rimmed glasses. He had been born in Mason County in northeastern Kentucky, and his mother came from the mountains. His father worked as a farmer, carpenter, blacksmith, whatever was needed. "He took old farms," Al said, "and made them nice places." He remembered his parents as very ethical people. Al entered the Catholic Society of Jesuits in 1956, after completing a master's degree in science. In 1964, he graduated from Fordham University with a Ph.D. in chemistry. After postdoctoral research at the University of Texas, he worked as a chemical consultant to Ralph Nader, the man who initiated a massive social movement to protect consumers from corporate manipulation and greed.

By the 1970s, Al was working full-time on public-interest issues. He helped Nader establish the Center for Science in the Public Interest in Washington, D.C., to influence policy makers. "I was trying to sell a simple lifestyle inside the Beltway," he said, "and I didn't get very far." As priests, Jesuits are not tied to parishes, and in 1977 Al left Washington in frustration and came back to Kentucky to establish ASPI. "When a parent has cancer, you come home," he said, "and I saw that the land had cancer and needed tending."

He envisioned ASPI as a model to demonstrate how science and technology could fashion a low-impact lifestyle. He particularly wanted to make appropriate technology accessible to low-income people, but he wasn't going to force knowledge on anyone, because he knew that wouldn't work in Appalachia. "Build it and they will come" could have been his credo.

"We Appalachians are an individualistic people," he said. "It's our strength and our weakness. You can easily set us against each other, which is what various economic interests have historically done." On his own staff, he had to be careful not to pair two of the men who worked for him. They used to get along but fell out over something and refused to speak to each other. "There's always the underlying threat of violence among mountain people," Al said.

To maintain itself, ASPI has eight to ten employees at any given time, most of them local people with hard-luck stories—disabled husbands, sick children, extra dependents. Operating funds come principally from monetary donations of all sizes, and many ASPI programs depend largely on voluntary services and in-kind donations. Al earns money as a resource auditor, visiting institutions, mostly religious communities such as convents, to analyze energy efficiency and environmental impact and recommend plans for improvement. Additional dollars are brought in by the sale of printed materials such as leaflets in ASPI's technical series and the annual "Simple Lifestyle Calendar," with black-and-white photographs of people doing old-fashioned things with food.

Al also writes books and essays. His subjects range from *Special Topics in Heterocyclic Chemistry* to *Christianity and the Environmental Ethos.* He is recognized as an influential thinker on the connection between environmentalism and religion and is invited to teach in philosophy departments at various universities around the country. One of his primary concerns as a writer is to show how the most common routines of everyday life can serve to express a spiritual appreciation of nature. The book that caught my eye on the ASPI rack was entitled *Down to Earth Spirituality* (Sheed and Ward, 1992). The format was a few paragraphs of reflection about life, then practical suggestions for action. Page one suggested that building a compost pile was a way to appreciate the microorganisms of the soil. On page five, the reader was asked to identify and give up one luxury this year. I thought uneasily about the expensive, flavored, decaffeinated coffee beans I sometimes splurged on, which I was sure were grown in rain-forest-destroying tropical plantations and drenched in pesticides and herbicides.

Organic gardening was a major element in Al's program. He had a big garden across the road next to the river. "On one-twentieth of an acre," he said, "you can grow a thousand pounds of food a year, what one person needs to live. Without machinery." Al felt that the tractor had gone a long way toward destroying Appalachian self-sufficiency by requiring bigger farms that could earn hard cash for gas and oil. Smaller-scale pieces of equipment such as tillers were less enslaving and more suitable. More than anything else, Al wanted to convey to people around him that gardening was honorable work for men. "My mother always did the garden," he said. "Dad broke up ground with the horse but never touched it otherwise. It's a very entrenched gender role." He thought that he might be having some success, because he saw people growing vegetables that they hadn't before, but he couldn't be sure.

"Fidelity to what you believe is more important than success," he said. "There are enormous amounts of dishonesty in the environmental movement. A person sitting in total bliss under a tree while the forest disintegrates, that's a deceptive bliss."

"What about Buddhist and Zen monks, and the old Christian mystics, who lived as hermits while searching for inner enlightenment?" I asked.

"I can't make a judgment on the purely contemplative," Al said. "But those who seek connections with the earth without doing something to repair the damage, that is a false spirituality. Spirituality is just what the old prophets said: repair the ills in our society. In our times, overconsumption of material things is a great evil. Spirituality is the ability to see the damage we've done, and act to redeem it. I see myself as the contemplative in action. The highest calling in Christianity is to act for good."

Al's latest act had been to can pickles from the excess cucumbers in his garden. There was some joking among the several volunteers and staff present, who had prior experience with Al's culinary skill, as to whether Al's pickles were for anyone's good. It had taken him hours and had thrown him off schedule. Normally he got up at three o'clock every morning for a prayer session. Then he jogged seven or eight miles. He was running late today and had a lot of business to catch up on. He had a long discussion about the Internet with Janet Powell, an ASPI volunteer and a University of Kentucky student who was working on the ASPI page for the World Wide Web. He caught up on correspondence from the mountains of Peru, where ASPI was sponsoring an experiment with high-efficiency woodstoves that reduced the need for fuel to one-seventh the usual amount. He made notes for his weekly TV show, called *Earth Healing.* He listened to a report from the staff member who supervised an outreach program on the Rockcastle River in local schools.

Toward the end of the day, Al gathered up the pages of a petition with a thousand local signatures in support of an alternative to the land-use plan being proposed by the Daniel Boone National Forest. The Forest Service was holding a public meeting the next day, and Al planned to deliver the petition then. He had been part of the group that wrote the two-hundred-page alternative plan, with chapters on wilderness, roads, biodiversity, timbering, and other aspects of the forest.

Al also needed to prepare for a trip to the southern end of the state, to protest plans for a new chip mill. More than one hundred of these huge, highly automated factories had popped up across Appalachia and the South in just a few years. Most were owned by corporate giants such as Willamette Industries, Inc., of Portland, Oregon. Chip mills could shred hardwood trees as small as three inches in diameter to produce hundreds of thousands of tons of chips a year for paper pulp. Every year, thousands of acres of forest within hauling radius of the mills—sixty miles or more, depending on roads—were being clear-cut. It was happening so fast that monthly monitoring flights by an environmental flying service in eastern Tennessee could hardly track the cutting. Al and other environmentalists feared that landowners in Kentucky would also be seduced into clear-cutting their forests to maximize short-term profits. Once again, they feared, there would be transient mills to cut out and get out, robbing Appalachian forests of their promise.

Small landowners like me don't often have a chance to earn money for the low-quality trees that are characteristic of private woodlots. A market for such trees could be useful, if it was sustained over the long term instead of coming in an urgent rush, and if a land ethic was in place that emphasized long-term values. Being able to sell skinny saplings thinned out from a crowded stand, deformed or deficient trees no good for lumber, and trees dying from pests or diseases could be an incentive to improve the management of woodlots in a nondestructive way. More and better wood from private land could relieve pressure on public lands to produce lumber. But the mills were enormous, and the land ethic tenuous. Al planned to argue that tourism was a larger source of income than timber and would be hurt by the loss of scenic wooded views. The mill wouldn't necessarily provide a lot of good, permanent jobs, either, and would take out most profits instead of investing locally.

Al was well aware that ASPI was situated very near the epicenter of Lucy Braun's mixed mesophytic area, with its high rate of biodiversity. It pained him that most mountain people had no idea of the treasure around them; the fact wasn't mentioned in the schools because even schoolteachers didn't know it. Al had met Paul Kalisz among the environmental activists opposed to timbering on the Daniel Boone National Forest. He recognized in Paul a similar kind of quiet but devout spirituality, and asked him to demonstrate how sustainable forestry could work at ASPI. Paul had years ago worked out for himself a religious logic in which not only life-forms themselves but also the evolutionary processes that produced them were sacred. It was humanity's highest obligation, Paul felt, to safeguard those processes. At ASPI, he explored hands-on ways of doing that.

"The foundation of ecoforestry," he said, "is to mimic nature." We were on a forest trail rising behind ASPI. After studying the surrounding forest, Paul began implementing a strategy for harvesting it in a way that would retain its biodiversity. We stopped at a patch cut he had done for firewood to help heat the center's buildings. He had taken out eight or nine white oaks in an area about the length of one of those trees. This adhered to the principle that when a tree falls in the forest, whether or not there is anyone around to hear, it takes down a swath the length of itself. In the suddenly sunny opening, I saw poplar and red maple seedlings. Paul cut only when leaves were down, making controlled tree felling easier. He rendered treetops and branches down so that they would decay quickly and minimize fire danger.

"Of course," he said, "I wouldn't take out a really nice tree, a vigorous grower whose genes should stay in the forest. Or a cavity tree useful to animals." Paying attention to individual trees was a basic tenet of Paul's approach. He identified those that by species and form were likely to make good lumber, and tended them. This involved cutting nearby trees whose canopies touched the selected tree, which could be tricky, because you didn't want to introduce enough sun to stimulate branch growth on the lower trunk of the tree. Pruning of the first eighteen feet was done as necessary, to minimize the number of potential knots. Both in patch cuts and in individual tree selection, Paul occasionally dropped a log and left it. ASPI's forest had a dearth of deadwood, and Paul wanted at least one large downed log per acre. He also valued standing dead snags and the pits and mounds left by huge trees that fell over. "These features," he said, "are the biological legacy of old growth. They account for a high degree of biodiversity, because around a quarter of all forest species require deadwood at some stage of their life cycle."

Selected lumber trees had to reach a certain size before he would cut them. If a tree died before it reached the limit, he would leave it to forest processes. If it reached the limit, he wouldn't immediately cut it but would assess its health every year. Not until it began to fail would he take it. "That would allow it to reach its full potential and seed itself for many years," he said. "You'd be removing it not at the minimum but at the maximum level. I call it 'go-with-the-flow forestry,' where you take what you can get from within natural boundaries."

Chances were good, Paul felt, that this method would produce some big, sound trees. Nobody could say how marketing would go or what value such trees might have in the future. And in the meantime, there would certainly be a sacrifice period while the trees were growing. "We need to adjust economic values to suit ecological realities," Paul said. "We've done it the other way for too long."

I followed Paul over the ridge and across the line into the national forest. Just downslope was the pocket of old growth he had discovered. It was on a moist north slope, and there were some big northern red oaks.

There were also white basswood, yellow buckeye, white oak, white ash, beech, poplar, red maple, and sugar maple. A broad-winged hawk whistled very low overhead and swept its shadow over us like a blessing. Moss-covered logs could have served as green pews without the high, straight backs. In the understory there was bloodroot, wood lettuce, violet, black cohosh, trillium, wild ginger, wild yam, Christmas fern, false Solomon's seal, Allegheny spurge, yellow mandarin, bellwort, maidenhair fern, spicebush, greenbrier, bedstraw, yellow lady's slipper, and twinleaf. And that was just within convenient kneeling distance.

Back at ASPI's library that night, after everyone but the dogs and the cat had gone home, the sky was still so bright at nine o'clock that I could read by window light. I had my choice of seven thousand titles on small-scale applied technology, but the raucous chorus of tree frogs distracted me. Lightning bugs were rising. A catbird complained about the cat prowling down the walk. The night was filled with rustlings and buzzings. I left early in the morning. The sun was rising pale and clean over the rumpled bedspread of a landscape. The morning was fresh, washed, shining, and the road ahead was empty and beckoning. I felt buoyed by an aura of hope. Restoration, redemption, resurrection: these could be the three Rs of the Appalachian future.

THE FUTURE FOREST

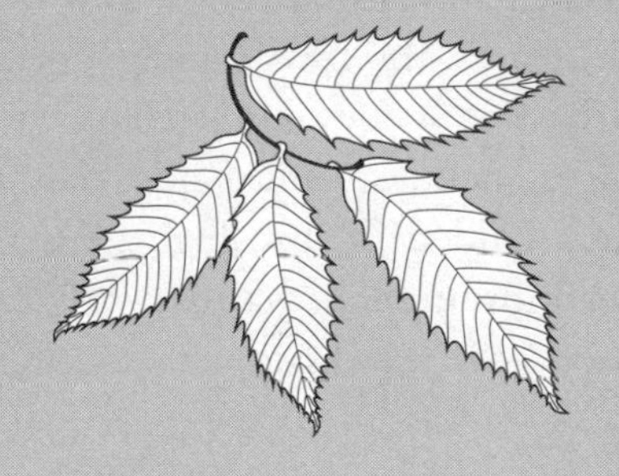

Chestnuts and the Plant Kingdom

If you knew exactly where to look off Interstate 81 at the Meadowview exit in southwest Virginia, you could glimpse the great green hope of Appalachian restoration. It lives in an orchard. In the shape and set of their leaves, the rows look like peach trees, but they're not. They're part of the largest chestnut breeding operation in the world, which also happens to include some world-class groundhog holes—gaping ankle-breakers hidden in shin-high grass. We stepped around them and over a dead groundhog that one of Dr. Fred Hebard's two dogs had killed. "Good boy!" Fred said with equal fervor to both as they bounded around us.

Groundhogs eat young chestnut trees. So do deer and cattle, but Fred had put up good fences to prevent that. These trees represented not only the future of Appalachia but his entire career. He began working on the pathology of chestnut blight as an undergraduate, after a walk in the woods with a farmer who mourned the loss of the trees. It was a loss beyond calculation, almost beyond comprehension. Chestnut trees once covered two hundred million acres from Maine to Georgia and west to the Mississippi River. They dominated the forests of central and southern Appalachia, constituting one out of every two trees in some places and one out of four over much of the region. They grew on average about a hundred feet tall and had wide, spreading crowns that made for an archetypal tree shape. Their girth was remarkable. They quite commonly reached five to eight feet in diameter. The stoutest chestnut tree measured, in western North Carolina, had a diameter of seventeen feet.

THE AMERICAN CHESTNUT FOUNDATION, BENNINGTON, VT

American chestnut trees in the Great Smoky Mountains, western North Carolina, 1890.

Chestnut wood resisted weather and decay because of its exceptionally high tannic acid content. The straight, coarse grain of chestnut wood was easy to work, and settlers made cabins, barns, and furniture out of it, from cradles to coffins. Most of all, they made fences, splitting miles and miles of chestnut rails and stacking them in various configurations. They used it for firewood, and because it burned hot, long, and without much smoke to signal its presence, it became a favorite of moonshiners. Money could be made by selling chestnut bark and wood to tanneries and logs to lumber buyers for fence posts, telegraph and telephone poles, ship masts, and railroad ties. But it was the nuts that elevated the chestnut to what some mountain people called a gift of God.

Chestnuts flower in early summer, in clusters of long, white, arching catkins. Looking down on a canopy of chestnuts in bloom must have been a sight. Unlike oaks, hickories, and other nut-producing trees, which bloom earlier so that frost often blasts their flowers, chestnuts produced a dependable crop every year. Mountain families, especially children, gathered the nuts every fall by the bushel. Over the winter, everyone ate the nuts raw, boiled, or roasted. They hauled them by wagon to markets in valley towns for cash to buy shoes, toys, bullets,

The American Chestnut Foundation, Bennington, VT

Cutting chestnut trees, western North Carolina, ca. 1900.

whatever they needed. In the fall, they turned their pigs loose in the woods to gorge. The sweet, rich nuts fed practically every wild animal in the forest, either directly or indirectly. The fabulous amount of game—deer, squirrels, wild turkeys, grouse, bears—described by early explorers reflects the sustenance provided by chestnuts. Elderly hunters say that back when there were chestnuts, bears got so fat they could hardly run.

In 1904, someone noticed that the chestnut trees in the New York Zoological Park were dying. A nonnative species of fungus, later named *Cryphonectria parasitica,* had arrived with Chinese chestnut trees imported from Asia for nursery stock. The fungus entered trees through small cracks

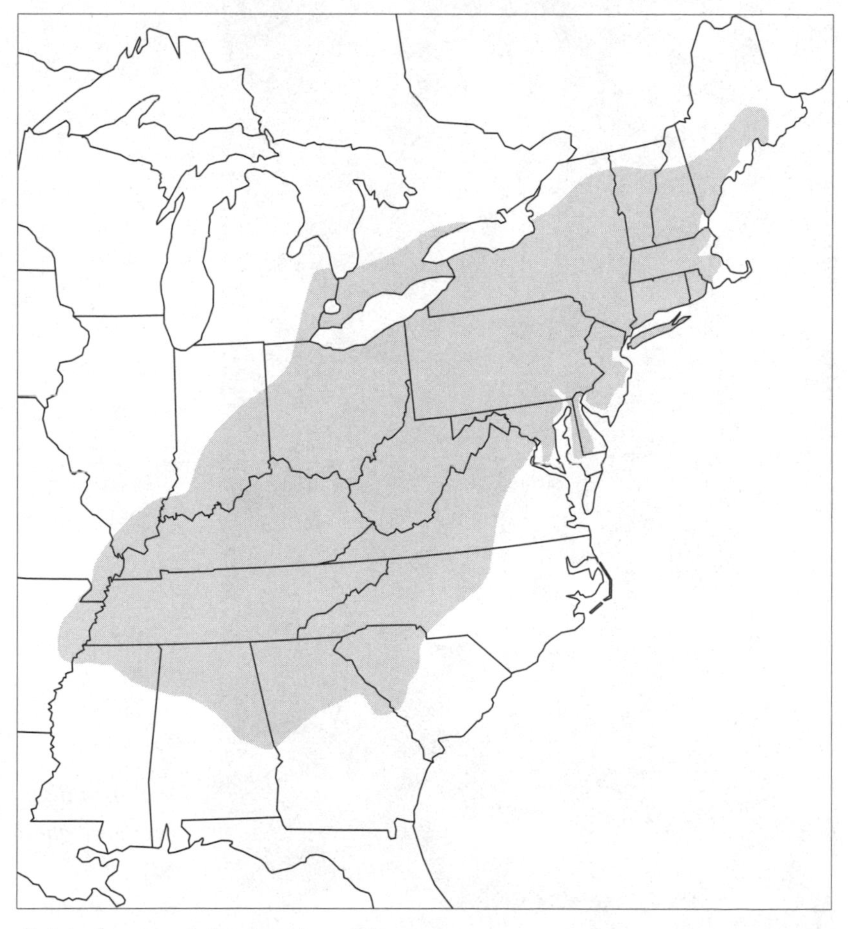

Original range of the American Chestnut.

and wounds in the bark and sent filaments deep into the inner bark. These girdled the tree and killed the cells that transported nutrients. The tree starved to death. The Chinese chestnut, a species otherwise not nearly as vigorous or statuesque as the American, had evolved with the fungus and developed a resistance to it.

Microscopic fungal spores were carried on the wind, on the feet of birds and insects, and on the shoes and axes of loggers. By 1910, American chestnut trees across Pennsylvania were dying, and the blight was moving south at the rate of fifty miles a year. Every attempt to stop it, including a mile-wide quarantine swath cut through Pennsylvania,

THE AMERICAN CHESTNUT FOUNDATION, BENNINGTON, VT

Dead chestnut trees, called ghost trees, western North Carolina, ca. 1940s.

failed utterly. Through the 1920s and 1930s, whole mountainsides were studded with ghostly gray skeletons. By 1950, the American chestnut had ceased to exist as an ecological factor in Appalachian forests. Little research had been done to document what exactly its role was, but at least one species of moth depended on it and went extinct. Nuts for vendors to roast and sell on city streets in winter were imported from Italy.

The U.S. Department of Agriculture had been experimenting with cross-breeding of Asian, European, and American chestnuts since the late 1800s. After the blight hit, government staff aimed at breeding Chinese resistance into American genes, but the projects were not carried out in accordance with the principles of genetic theory. In the 1970s, Dr. Charles Burnham, a plant geneticist at the University of Minnesota, noticed the error. He communicated with the handful of other scientists working on chestnuts and proposed a new method. And he followed up many leads to obtain pollen from the rare American chestnut trees that still flowered. Although 99.9 percent of chestnut stems died in the East, the roots frequently were not affected. Even today, sprouts continue to shoot up from some of the stumps. I find them on rambles through the woods, and it's pitiful to see them, knowing that they will soon sicken and die. Very occasionally, one matures enough to flower and produce pollen. Also, a few surviving groves had been planted far out of chestnut (and blight) range in the Midwest and West by westering pioneers. These several sources made propagation of the American chestnut feasible.

In 1984, Dr. Burnham and a small group of like-minded scientists founded the nonprofit American Chestnut Foundation. They knew that government funding was too variable and short-term to accommodate their purposes. Instead, the foundation's first president, Dr. Phil Rutter, devoted much energy to building a membership of two to three thousand people, a few of whom were substantial donors. He also obtained a couple of large private grants. The foundation's sole purpose was to breed a tree that would be an American chestnut in every respect except resistance to blight, which would be incorporated into it from the Chinese chestnut. In 1989, the foundation secured a long-term lease on a twenty-acre farm in Meadowview and began looking for a research scientist–cum–field hand.

Fred Hebard was doing postdoctoral work on chestnut blight at the University of Kentucky when he heard about the job. The salary was

$12,000 a year, and Fred had a wife and two babies. Moving to tiny, rural Meadowview would terminate the career of his wife, who also had a Ph.D. in plant pathology, but she couldn't work for the foundation because its budget was already stretched to the breaking point. They packed up anyway. "Dearly beloved," said foundation president Phil Rutter at the dedication of the farm, "we are gathered here today, in the sight of the rain and the wind, the mountains and the trees, to join with one another and with this land in a bond of holy determination. Let us plant!"

In less than a decade, Fred and helpers planted some eight thousand trees. The breeding strategy was based on classic genetic backcrossing theory: start with half-and-half hybrids produced by a mating between a Chinese and an American parent, pollinate these with American trees, and repeat that procedure with their progeny for two more generations. The third backcross would produce trees that were fifteen-sixteenths American. As each generation reached four years old, Fred inoculated it with two different strains of the blight. Within a few months, the blight cankers appeared on the bark like open sores. Over the next year or two, until the trees began to flower, Fred observed them closely to identify those that showed the greatest blight resistance. These were the trees he used to produce the next generation.

Fred fertilized his trees, and the two-year-olds were already head-high. He wanted to protect them against the area's tendency toward drought and was piecing together an irrigation system from parts he had picked up here and there. White bags were clipped over flower clusters on some of the largest trees to safeguard pollination. As we walked down the rows, Fred pinched branch tips from four different trees and pointed out variations in twig color, leaf hairiness, and other features between Chinese and American species. His hands showed the nicks and grime of constant tinkering with the farm's three tractors. He kept track of the changes in physical traits among the trees to correlate them with blight resistance. They served as visible markers of unseen events.

Fred was looking on the molecular level as well, working with other scientists to take advantage of insight offered by new technologies. He planned to map the genes of the Chinese chestnut to locate blight resistance, which could then theoretically be snipped out and added to an American tree.

Members of the foundation's New York chapter were taking a more offbeat approach. They wanted to introduce genes from snails into an American chestnut. Snail skin is a moist environment perfect for fungus growth, but no fungus grows there. Experiments showed that snails produced small proteins that killed fungus spores, including chestnut blight. Both the mapping and the snail trials will take many years and will cost lots of money. "And who knows what else snail genes would carry into chestnuts?" Fred said.

He planned to have nuts from third-backcross trees available for off-farm planting in the early years of the twenty-first century. We walked to the end of the orchard to see one of his favorite trees, the nicest one for size, though it did tend to get its branches frosted back in spring. "It's not a tree from the mountains," he said. "Mountain chestnuts tend not to break their buds open before frost. We'll probably have to breed for local adaptations." That can be done only in local places. How, I wondered, would the foundation distribute the several thousand nuts that would be produced each year? Most importantly, would members (like me) have first chance at them?

The foundation's board of directors hadn't yet finalized a strategy, and Fred was diplomatically vague. Cooperating institutions will almost certainly have priority over individuals, at least at first, because of the need for assurance that land on which the trees are planted will remain undeveloped for decades to come. "It could take fifty years to find out if three backcrosses are enough to make chestnuts competitive with other forest trees in the wild," Fred said. "It will take three hundred years before American chestnuts can begin to regain their stature as a major force in the forest." I hope Fred's children inherit his resistance to the allure of instant gratification.

Chestnut blight is itself merely the most dramatic symptom of an epidemic in Appalachian forests, one that came in with the twentieth century but has hardly run its course. The globalization of the world's economy is being accompanied by a less beneficial globalization of its ecology. International trade has opened the door to some very undesirable immigrants. Brought in purposely for one reason or another, or unintentionally on lumber, furniture, exotic plants, and sundry other imports, more than a dozen introduced pests and diseases now assail Appalachia. They are arguably more disastrous than industrial logging, because they may be even more relentlessly impoverishing than massive erosion of soil.

Separated by oceans, the plants and animals on one continent had no reason to evolve genetic resistance to pests on others. Nor did ecosystems that lacked particular pests develop the checks and balances that ecosystems with them evolved as control measures. Some aliens are so insidious that forest experts didn't even detect them until damage was irreparable. Gypsy moths, though, rank second only to chestnut blight for traumatic effect.

After the eggs hatch in early spring, the caterpillars crawl up trees to feed. As they eat, they chew off pieces of leaves, which drop. In July, we scuffed through dead leaves on the trails as if it were late autumn. Caterpillar feces fell like rain. The caterpillars will eat five hundred species of plants, but they prefer oaks above all. Oaks multiplied in Appalachian forests after the chestnuts died, because they are adapted to take advantage of sunny openings left by dead trees. It was as if the chestnut blight primed the pump for gypsy moths.

Native to Europe, moths were brought to Massachusetts in 1869 for experiments in silk production. Some escaped into the woods. In 1889, in the first moth population explosion, most fruit and shade trees in a 360-square-mile area near Medford were defoliated by gypsy moth caterpillars. Decade by decade, a gypsy moth frontier moved south and west. Behind the front, the moths settled in as permanent residents in the forests. They went through cycles of high and low populations, reflected in the acreage of trees defoliated, although no cycle was ever quite as bad as the first one, when the moths were new to an area. Millions of acres were defoliated every year across the East.

The moths reached northern Virginia in the late 1980s. There were public meetings where distraught home owners feared the loss of shade trees. Foresters warned of the impending death of all valuable lumber trees. Government-subsidized programs to spray insecticides from the air were demanded and supplied, despite the fact that every entomologist consulted stated unequivocally that the moths could never be eradicated. Expensive spray programs would have to continue forever, because as soon as they stopped, the moth population would rebound. In the meantime, the sprays would kill beneficial insects as well. The Forest Service used the threat of gypsy moths to conduct "salvage" sales, sometimes in areas where very few of the moths could actually be found. Salvage cutting first became popular in western national forests, where a series of record wildfires in the 1980s and 1990s gave the Forest Service an excuse to cut the forest to save it. Salvage sales are exempt from many of the environmental regulations governing other timber cuts.

We decided simply to suffer through the moth invasion. Many of our largest oaks died from the stress of defoliation. Across the valley, along the flank of Little North Mountain, I can see a concentrated forty-acre strip of dead trees. Even larger areas were reported to have lost virtually every sizable tree. It's not pretty, but it's hardly the demise of the forest. Trees will grow up in the openings made by gypsy moths just as they did in the gaps made by chestnut blight. The difference is that the new trees are less likely to be oaks. In the Northeast, where the moths have been present for a century, the net impact seems to be that the number of oaks has declined.

Over the next century, if gypsy moths continue their recurrent pattern of eating all the oaks they can find, other species of trees will take over the dominance of the forest. That will mean fewer acorns, which now serve as the main substitute for chestnuts as wildlife food. The number of wild animals that Appalachian forests can support will take another sharp dip.

But something unexpected has happened to challenge that prediction. In 1989, a fungus *(Entomophaga maimaiga)* that killed gypsy moth caterpillars was observed in New England. A native of Japan, where it attacks only gypsy moths, the fungus was probably brought to America during an early research effort against the moth, but its origin isn't definitely known. Shortly after its discovery, the fungus was cultured and spread by researchers from the U.S. Department of Agriculture. The total number of defoliated acres plummeted to less than 200,000 annually by the mid 1990s. Virginia showed the most amazing decline, from 850,000 defoliated acres to 0 from one year to the next.

So I look at the oaks with hope, but sometimes I try not to look at the dogwoods at all. That's hard, because there are a lot of them, and they're usually in my immediate view. They compose most of the forest's midlevel canopy. In April, their blossoms spangle white across the tender green of unfurling spring. Early in the fall, the bright red berries attract birds. Migrating Neotropical and resident songbirds alike prefer them to most other food. In addition, in their personal chemistry, dogwoods accumulate calcium. This makes other minerals more available to roots; it also attracts some kinds of soil-building invertebrates. The dirt under dogwoods tends to be the most fertile in the forest.

A fungus known as dogwood anthracnose was reported to be killing dogwoods from Massachusetts to Alabama to the Pacific Northwest in the 1980s. No one is certain where or when it originated. In the higher, wetter places in the Appalachians, the kind of habitat fungi love, dogwoods have died out completely since then. Some research suggests that the fungus is aided by acid rain, which is also a confounding factor in many other diseases. I see dark spots on dogwood leaves around here that I think are anthracnose. The best hope is drought to keep the spores at bay.

The list of infamous fungi goes on. One of unknown origin has almost exterminated the butternut, once prized for its white walnuts. The American elm, a magnificent riverside shade tree, is being attacked through most of its range in the East by a fungus from Asia that enters the bark where a beetle from Europe has chomped. Native fungi are killing beech trees by the grove through holes made by a species of tiny scale insects from Europe.

There is also a least-wanted list of insects. Ranked even higher than gypsy moths for rapid invasive impact are two tiny sap suckers called adelgids. The hemlock woolly adelgid came from Asia in the 1950s and seems capable of killing most eastern hemlocks, whose dense, dark stands are a refuge for many kinds of wildlife and host several species of plants known to exist only in such stands. The balsam woolly adelgid came from Europe and has infested virtually all the older Fraser firs in the rare spruce-fir forests on the highest peaks of the Appalachians. The trees usually die within two to seven years.

It's easy to understand why "forest health" has become a buzzword among foresters. Some of the most ecologically important of the estimated 2,250 species of vascular plants in the central and southern Appalachians are suffering serious threats to their existence. The most clearly identified problems are imported ones, but the syndrome known as oak decline is believed to be homegrown. The main symptom is the death of twigs and branches from the crown downward. Crown dieback doesn't necessarily progress to death within a few years; some oaks may recover, and not all species of oaks are susceptible. Oak decline seems to be caused by unfathomably complex interactions among such factors as the aging of the tree, drought, spring frosts, poor soil, insects, fungi, and any other possible source of tree stress. Because oak decline has been associated with periods of drought since the early twentieth century, some biologists believe it is a naturally recurring cycle. Nearly four million acres of upland oak forests in the Appalachians exhibit some sign of crown dieback. Private lands generally show less oak decline than national forests, which tend to have older oaks. Although affected oaks don't sprout well from stumps, the Forest Service sometimes uses oak decline as a justification for clear-cutting to reinvigorate oak stands.

Except for the fungus that attacks gypsy moths, Forest Service and academic research on problems of forest health has so far turned up few solutions that are practical for application to large acreages of general forest. Some of the afflicted species of trees are raised in nurseries and sold as ornamentals, to live a life suffused as necessary with sprays, so that they might not technically go extinct. Cold comfort.

No overview of the Appalachian plant kingdom would be complete without mention of ginseng. It is one of the world's most valuable herbs, and it financed much of Appalachian settlement. Related to carrots and parsnips, ginseng is valued not for its aboveground parts, which are shy and inconspicuous, but for its roots. Ginseng grows in the understory of hardwood forests throughout eastern North America. Just as important to its history here is the fact that it grows in China.

Human use of ginseng roots dates back at least five thousand years in the mountains of Manchuria. Ginseng was recorded in a book of Chinese pharmacology in A.D. 500. Emperors sent ginseng hunters out by the thousands. Marco Polo, who traveled to China in 1274, wrote that the root was "powdered, cooked, and used as a tea, syrup, or food condiment and even burned as incense in the sickroom." Ginseng was traded all over Asia. Roots could weigh up to half a pound each and when dried were worth their weight in gold.

The root has a shape that suggests the human body—the more it does so, the more valuable the root. It was believed to be capable of prolonging life, inducing wellness, and bringing bodily systems into equilibrium. Western scientists have made some effort to investigate these claims, and although research tends to support its medicinal qualities, so far nothing conclusive has emerged. Ginseng's active ingredient is thought to be a complex carbohydrate, perhaps a sugar combined with either alcohol or a phenol. It has been shown to stimulate protein metabolism in vitro. It may increase strength and stamina of both body and mind. It may lower cholesterol, retard formation of plaque in arteries, and stimulate the immune system. There is speculation that it counteracts some aspects of the aging process.

Ginseng has been documented at ninety years old (you can count the root scars), but the older it gets, the less robust its root. The best roots are five to ten years old. Ginseng doesn't start producing berries until it is at least three years old, and plants can be propagated by planting these berries. Careless harvesting, before plants are mature in age or in season, reduces their number. Few wild plants grow today across Asia. Cultivation of ginseng started in the sixteenth century in Korea and grew into an industry that produces five million pounds a year for half a billion dollars. And at that, cultivated ginseng is less valued than wild-grown.

In 1709, Father Jartoux, a Jesuit missionary among the Chinese, wrote a letter describing ginseng to a fellow French priest that was published by the Royal Academy of Science in Paris. A copy came into the hands of Father Lafitau, a priest among the Iroquois Indians in Quebec. Having reason to believe that such a plant might grow in Canadian forests, the good father made diligent inquiry and untiring search for it. After a year, he was successful. It's not clear whether North American Indians valued ginseng to any great extent before white settlement; it doesn't appear to have been an intertribal trade item.

Lafitau had his Indians gather and dry the roots, and he packed them off to China. They were so popular that a business sprang up immediately. Roots purchased from collectors at 35 cents a pound sold in China for ten times that amount. The Indians dug all they could find, and fur traders included ginseng in their business. Trade had reached the $100,000 mark in 1752, an enormous amount in those times, when the market crashed. In that year, in their rush to make money, Canadians dug a lot of ginseng out of season and dried it improperly, so that upon its arrival in China, it was deemed unacceptable. Only $6,500 worth was purchased the next year, and after that, trade ceased entirely. It was more than a century before the stigma attached to Canadian ginseng faded.

Word had traveled south to the new United States about the trade in ginseng. States from New England to the Mississippi took advantage of Canada's vacancy from the market. Ginseng gatherers were known locally as cheng, chang, shang, or—in Appalachia—seng hunters. Daniel Boone was one of the first. He is believed to have gathered and purchased tons of it for resale. By the 1850s, more than 350,000 pounds a year were being exported. Roots sold for around 50 cents a pound. The plant was getting hard to find; the quantity of roots exported decreased after that, and the price went up. In 1897, the price per pound reached nearly $5. A century later, the price for wild-dug ginseng ranged from $100 to more than $300 a pound. Cultivated roots brought a third of that.

Wild ginseng has become so uncommon that it is regulated by both federal and state agencies, which require permits, seasonal harvesting to allow the seeds to ripen, and proper planting of the seeds. Cases of poaching on public lands are well documented. The feeling among botanists is that the plant is becoming very scarce. The atmosphere of secrecy about ginseng locations doesn't help in assessing its population status. Seng hunters never give away where they find it, for fear that someone else will steal the roots. Biologists keep quiet for the same reason.

There's enough money even in cultivated ginseng that quite a few people have made plantations of it. Growing ginseng has been an agricultural enterprise in America since the late 1800s, and state and federal agencies have published a number of how-to manuals. You can grow ginseng in beds with artificial shade, but I prefer the method of naturalizing it in the forest. Growing ginseng this way requires a well-drained but moist area of forest floor under a canopy of hardwoods. The main problem with this method, besides the constant threat of fungus, is that someone else might find the plants. Ralph planted a few ginseng some years ago, but I won't even say whether they're on our West Virginia or Virginia property. If they don't make us rich, at least they'll keep us in a healthy state of paranoia.

Black Bears and the Animal Kingdom

Bear hunting can be boring. You spend the day creeping slowly along a mountain ridge, holding interminable strategy sessions by CB with your bushwhacking cohorts about how to approach the rendezvous ravine. You sit for hours, waiting for the pack of dogs your companions set loose on the other side of the mountain to strike a trail and drive a bear into your waiting rifles. Sometimes you hear the dogs baying deep and urgent in the distance, the sound wavering on the breeze; you hardly breathe as you listen, trying to tell whether they're running toward you. Most of the time you hear nothing but an occasional woodpecker and the far-off drone of traffic that can hardly be escaped anywhere in the Appalachians. You get hungry but are reluctant to eat, in case you have to move quickly. And at the end of the day you have nothing to show but ruddy skin and scuffed shoes.

That was OK with me. I was after style on this hunt, not substance. Bear hunting is a cornerstone of Appalachian culture. Whenever I talk with people about Appalachia, they bring up bear hunting without any instigation from me. Bear hunters are widely perceived as a distinct group, and one with an unsavory reputation. I decided to see what bear hunting was all about. I called the president and founder of the Back Creek Sportsmen, a bear hunting club in Virginia's Blue Ridge, and asked if I could go along.

"Sure," Jesse Bridge said. Early one morning, with a full moon setting through the fringe of trees along the mountaintops, I pulled into his driveway. I ate the ham biscuits and coffee he had ready for me, while Jesse's nephew Doug adjusted the CB, trying to raise Paul Eddy. Doug had taken a week's vacation from work to hunt bears. Jesse was gleeful. "I got it made now I'm retired," he said. "You ready?"

"We're always ready," Boyd answered. Boyd had blue eyes, a white beard, and a red shirt. He could have been on his way to a job as a department store Santa on that December day. We went out, and it was light enough to see the guns, slung over shoulders and cradled in arms—12-gauge shotguns, 30-30s, 30-06s, a 357 Magnum in a long, narrow holster. We drove up the mountain behind Jesse's place in a caravan of four trucks with one or two men in each and a dog caged in back, picking up more trucks and men and dogs at several stops until there were more than a dozen men, with almost as many dogs. They represented about a third of the club's membership.

Most early settlers had dogs that they used for chasing game as well as for maintaining security around the house. Bears can usually be driven into trees by dogs, where they are easily shot. In the days when bears were abundant, even hunters without dogs killed many. Hunting in frontier days tended to be a solitary business, though. It's not clear when bear hunting with shared packs of dogs emerged as a group ritual, particularly in the mountains of Virginia, West Virginia, North Carolina, and Tennessee, but it seems to have been in the latter part of the nineteenth century.

Bears were becoming scarce by then. Most states paid bounties on bears from the early 1700s until well into the twentieth century, just as they did for wolves, cougars, and other varmints. Throughout the Appalachians, as farming and logging drove bears out and as hunters continually harassed them without any legal restrictions, bears survived only in the highest, most laurel-choked mountain slopes. One man, even with several good dogs, was unlikely to find and tree a bear successfully by himself. In the Smoky Mountains, for example, much of the land was cleared up to four thousand feet, and bears were rare to nonexistent at lower elevations by the 1920s. Large parties of local hunters would spend two weeks working the mountaintops and kill as many as eight bears during a hunt. It was considered good luck to dream about quarreling

GREAT SMOKY MOUNTAINS NATIONAL PARK

Hunters with black bear in what became Great Smoky Mountains National Park, ca. 1900.

with a woman the night before, because it meant that you would kill a she-bear the next day.

Mountaineers generally disliked bears, in part because they feared them, although bears usually avoid humans, and attacks have always been rare. In the 1920s, children of families in what is now Shenandoah National Park had been taught to fear bears more than anything else, despite the fact that the animals had been virtually extirpated from the area by then. There was more justification for the animosity that some mountaineers felt toward bears as raiders of livestock, orchards, and crop fields. In the 1930s, the editor of the *Pocahontas Times* in Pocahontas County, West Virginia, wrote, "The bear is no fitten companion either of man or beast. He is a barbarian and cannot be civilized. . . . The man who has to live in the same community with bears hates him with a cruel and lasting hatred and with good and sufficient cause." Without the timely advent of the national parks and forests to protect bear habitat, and the passage of laws defining hunting seasons and bag limits to restrain hunters, there's not much question that bears would have been entirely eliminated from Appalachia, as they were from the surrounding countryside.

As Jesse drove, a streaky sunrise turned the mountains from homespun brown to Civil War blue and gray. "We killed fifteen bear last year,"

Jesse told me as we drove along. That's about one bear every three days through the six weeks of bear season in western Virginia, from late November to early January. In the early 1980s, Virginia hunters began to set new records almost every year for the number of bears killed. Something similar happened in other Appalachian states with huntable bear populations. In Virginia, the number of bears killed climbed to six, seven, then eight hundred.

I began to wonder how many bears there could be. When I asked the Virginia Department of Game and Inland Fisheries, the only answer was a redundancy: the number of bears killed was figured to be approximately twenty percent of the total bear population. Therefore, the more bears that were killed each year, the more the population was growing. This logic made me uneasy. I thought I'd see what that was all about, too. But first, the hunt.

Jesse was headed toward Big Levels in the George Washington National Forest, just south of Shenandoah National Park. It's one of the best places in Virginia to hunt bears. Industrial and residential developments are crowding the borders of the park, making it difficult for park bears to move into other territories. Young bears looking for their own domain, old bears that have been displaced by younger ones, and bears of all ages searching for food in years of drought or poor acorn production spill out of the park into ten encircling counties. They are met by hunters. Counties around the park usually boast the highest numbers of bears killed in Virginia in any given season.

Few game wardens are willing to guess how many additional bears are killed out of season, by illegal means, or on protected lands like the national park. Money as well as meanness provides an incentive for poaching. Bear gallbladders and paws sell for hundreds of dollars on the black market, because of tremendous demand for them in Asia. Traditional Oriental medicine ascribes great powers to bear parts. During a three-year undercover investigation in North Carolina and Tennessee in the mid-1980s, twenty-eight defendants were prosecuted for illegal bear hunting or sale of bear parts. A similar operation in Shenandoah National Park uncovered a poaching ring that stretched to Alaska. Several people around where I live have been apprehended recently for poaching bears and deer in the national forest. I once got an anonymous phone call about bear poaching along the Blue Ridge Parkway (I named my source Deep Bear), but it proved difficult to investigate the situation. I asked Jesse what he thought about it.

"It's bad further south, and it's been bad in Shenandoah National Park the last few years," he said. "I guess it still goes on, but I don't hear about it because everybody knows I don't like it."

While Jesse watched the road, I studied him. He had a kindly face framed in thinning, graying hair; he looked like anybody's grandfather. He was small and neatly dressed in a blue flannel shirt beneath brown overalls. We wore similar leather hiking boots. I remarked that his looked somehow fat and happy. "I used some grease they rendered from the last bear," he said.

"What's the meat like?" I asked.

"Can't stand it," Jesse said. "I can't stand any kind of wild game. The only thing I'll eat is the white breast of a wild turkey." But someone takes the meat, he added quickly, and whoever makes the kill gets the bearskin.

Black bears are the biggest trophy animal in most of the eastern United States. I just heard about one, shot in Pennsylvania, that weighed over 800 pounds. Several bears killed in North Carolina in recent years weighed over 600 pounds. Just last season, a group of eleven men put nine shots into a 440-pounder on Massanutten Mountain nearby. Average weights run considerably less, with adult males usually 250 to 350 pounds and females 120 to 180. In the West, where black bears still roam in healthy numbers, weights are generally less, because the arid climate is relatively unproductive of plant foods. Home ranges for western bears often encompass fifty square miles, whereas home ranges in the most productive Appalachian areas may be as small as five square miles for females.

Black bears ranged throughout most of North America before European settlement. Afterward, bear populations were drastically reduced all across the East, although they recovered somewhat in the Northeast and the Lake States as farms were abandoned in the nineteenth and twentieth centuries and forests grew back. In Appalachia, bears survive on less than a tenth of their former range, mostly on public lands.

We drove past a meadow posted with "Llama Farm, No Hunting" signs about every ten feet. We passed a country store with a big sign invoking the name of Walton's Mountain; nearby was the place where Earl Hamner had grown up, to write the stories on which the TV family drama *The Waltons* was based. This is John Boy Walton country in a new age. Acres of prim landscaping guard new log cabins from unruly fourth-growth forest. A jogger in a natty blue sweat suit with racing stripes turned his head to avoid our exhaust. We crossed a creek whose moving water shone like new pennies; in the shadows of its banks hung icicles dull as lead. At the end of a gravel road that sliced up a narrow valley, the pickups gathered together and stopped, forming a forest of antennae. The men got out to talk strategy.

"A ridge goes this way, this way, and that way"—fingers pointed, hands waved, arms circled—"and we ought to have men on each of 'em."

"A bear crossed the upper end of that field Saturday. I reckon he's still around."

"Somebody ought to be in that there hollow, too."

"Hershel's coming soon as he takes his steer to market."

"You all take the dogs round yonder, we'll go up here."

"Don't shoot the man's goats. Goats ain't never in season."

Jesse and I began to walk up the road to our assigned place on the mountain. It was about 9:00 A.M. Several kittens, a dog, and a goose ambled toward us from a farmhouse a hundred yards away. Jesse got on his CB and guided his brother Hershel to us. Hershel was ten years older than Jesse, larger and heavier, with a thatch of white hair. The two men loaded their rifles and shouldered the corduroy CB pouches their sister had made for them. "We're going to hike up on top yonder, and take stands along the ridge, down to the gap over yonder," Jesse explained to Hershel. "It'll take the dogs an hour to come round." The goose waddled toward me, hissed, lunged, and bit me on the knee.

We walked up a road through an orchard, me walking backward to box with the goose stalking closely behind. Jesse had earlier secured permission from the landowner whose farm we were crossing. Deer tracks were frozen in the mud in the shadows, but in the sun, the road glistened with running water. When the road ended and we entered the woods, the goose turned back. The hillside was steep; it was like walking up the inside of a bowl, and we stopped often to catch our breath. Halfway up we began to find clipped stems and brush piles lying beside new paths. Someone had made the whole mountain accessible to an off-highway vehicle; we could see its tracks. Hershel said something about taking the huff and puff out of hunting. Jesse said to be sure and remember for next time that these trails were here.

Two hours later, all we had heard was the damned goose honking down in the valley and some shots behind us, with a dog yelping. "Not ours," Jesse had said, his head cocked toward the sounds. There are other bear hunting clubs up and down the Blue Ridge. Some men belong to more than one club. Jesse said that clubs don't formally outline their territories, and sometimes one club's dogs will chase a bear into another club's guns.

The sun was almost above the treetops. Small twigs at eye level gleamed like ice. On the east slope, the poplars were tall, gray, massive; on the west, laurel thickets were a twisted, cool green. "This is as pretty a woods as you'd want to see," Hershel said. He bent over a place where leaves had been scuffed up. "Turkey scratch," he said. "Looking for acorns. Deer go all in one direction, but this is a circle." He moved over to a bank from which the leaves had been kicked away. "Now this was deer coming down. We might see them if we keep our mouths shut." But Jesse yelled into the CB, "Doug, you copy?"

"I don't know nothing," Doug replied. "Blue and Buford took off and haven't come back yet."

"How 'bout you, Elmer Ray?" Jesse asked another group.

"Hey, there's four dogs come out down here at the road." Jesse passed the word on to Doug.

Noon. We climbed a knoll of green lichen-covered boulders, scarred trees, and blackened stumps from which we could see out all around. To the southwest, where a weak winter sun shone on them, the mountains hung in frozen billows of hazy gray smoke. In the other direction they were a clear, warm purple, sharply shadowing themselves in folds and rucks. The sky was a Wedgewood platter, its rim scalloped with white clouds. It was warm enough for bugs to fly around.

This was where we would take our stand. This meant that we found a log to sit on and settled into companionable silence. I ate some of Jesse's ham biscuits, packed from breakfast, and offered around some almonds and raisins I had brought to share. Hershel took some, but Jesse didn't. "I got to stay light," he murmured, "in case I got to run." A wren quietly poked around a brush pile not far away. Jesse's rifle leaned against a tree, and its shadow was long like a sundial, moving slowly down the bark.

"As soon as this bear thing is over," Hershel said, "I'm going back to Haiti." He was spending his retirement working for a Mennonite mission, drilling wells for poor people. He described the Haitians and shook his head at how little they had. He leaned back against a tree.

"I'd like to see a great, big, beautiful buck walk by," he said. His voice was lazy, dreamy. "So I could shoot it."

Somebody building houses in a development on a mountain across from us came on the CB, talking to his wife. Jesse was irritated. "I ought to tell 'em to get off," he said. "Nobody's supposed to be on channel 13 but bear hunters."

The mountain to the southwest, in the direction of the lowering sun, was brown and black and mottled with gold, drowsing like a calico cat. The only visible movement was sunlight swiveling along the strands of a million spider webs. I closed my eyes. A body could get sleepy, could forget what we came for.

Then we heard the dogs. The baying faded, then came closer, then faded as a breeze riffled up the hollow. "Listen!" Jesse whispered, his voice quivering. Jesse had told me that the reason he hunts is to hear the dogs run. In their insistent, rhythmic clamor he heard a beautiful music. "It's Fireball," Jesse said. He was standing now, alert and tense. "I don't know the other two." His tone was hopeful. "The bear might be five or ten minutes ahead of the dogs." There was a moment of furious CB conversation. "They jumped a track in a thicket!" Then quiet. The dogs had lost the trail.

"Well, we're just not having too much luck this year," Jesse said. The last bear the club got, he told me, was the week before, when some members shot a bear in his den. Jesse's kindly face was sad when he told me about it.

"It's all over when the bear's dead," he said. "Just think what they could have heard if they'd let the dogs run him!"

By 3:00 P.M. there was no more warmth in the sun. I buttoned my jacket. "If you don't do nothing by two o'clock you might as well quit," Hershel said, and went back. Jesse and I continued down the ridge. When we reached the gap, Jesse talked a long while with Doug about where the dogs had gone and who should do what. I waited on a stump and watched bars of sun and shadow slant through the woods. The mountains far away were a dusty pastel blue, as if they would rub off on your fingertips if you could reach out and touch them. "Come on down," Doug told Jesse. The hunt was over.

We skied straight down the mountainside on slick, dry leaves into the valley we had started from. In the dusk, the laurel leaves were deep jade and the forest floor a ruffled auburn. Fortunately, the goose was gone. Down on the road, we met up with several of the other hunters, who were counting dogs and coming up short. They regretted that the first and so far the only club member to own a radio transmitting collar for his dog wasn't hunting that day.

These collars are the same kind that revolutionized the study of wildlife in the 1970s. For the first time, researchers could track elusive, wide-ranging animals to understand their everyday habits and delineate their home ranges. Within a few years, collars became available for use on hunting dogs, too. Collared dogs are tracked with handheld receivers and antennae mounted on vehicles. Some receivers can tune in as many as two hundred dogs at one time. The distance over which they are effective ranges up to fifteen miles, depending on terrain and transmitting power.

According to the ethical standards of most sportsmen's associations, receivers are supposed to be used only after a hunt is over, to track lost dogs. But for animals like bears that tree when chased, being able to find the dog means being able to find the target. Collars can include activity and behavior signals that indicate whether a dog is running or keeping still and whether his head is pointing upward, as it would be when baying at a treed bear. The question of just how many hunters use collars to find bears rather than lost dogs is a ticklish one and impossible to answer. Even *Outdoor Life,* a staunchly pro-hunting magazine, admitted that "a few more bears are taken nowadays because tracking collars make hunters more efficient." Hunting efficiency skyrockets if hunters pick up signals from a collared bear. The radio frequencies set on collars used for wildlife research are different from those used for hunting dogs, but it can happen that hunters detect signals from a study animal. A collared bear was shot between the eyes while sleeping in a den in Pisgah National Forest Bear Sanctuary in North Carolina in 1986. A tip-off to the game warden forestalled the poaching of a second animal.

At several hundred dollars for a radio system, collars aren't cheap, but they're still cheaper than losing a dog. A thousand dollars is not an uncommon price for a redbone or a Walker hound, and values are sometimes much higher. One of the most prized hunting breeds is the Plott, which was developed in the Appalachians specifically to chase bears.

A few years after my hunt with the Back Creek Sportsmen, a survey by the Virginia game department showed that every bear hunter in Virginia had an electronic collar on his dog.

Starting with CBs, progressing to four-wheel-drives and off-highway vehicles, and culminating with radio collars on dogs, technology didn't so much change the old style of bear hunting as amplify every aspect of it. Already well organized, and now able to communicate instantaneously, move quickly over great distances, and pinpoint the bear's location exactly by radio-tracking the dogs, bear hunt clubs have evolved into highly efficient armies. Being organized into groups also facilitates their political influence on game departments, which is considerable. Clubs sometimes get together and hire lobbyists in state capitals to press their interests with state game agencies.

With radio collars just about to take over, my hunt was advantageously timed: it turned out that I caught what was probably the end of an unusual folkway. Boyd had a large conch shell tied around his neck. He lifted it and blew a deep, beautiful sound. He had trained his dogs to come to it, as had his father before him. But none of the other dogs had the benefit of this tradition, and two of them were missing. The men would have to drive all the back roads, searching. For miles down the highway, as Jesse and I drove home with the CB on, we heard the men talking to one another about the dogs.

I'm not terribly fond of dogs—I'm a cat person—so Jesse's passion didn't register with me. It wasn't until some years after I went on the hunt with him that I grasped what bear hunting was really all about. I was sitting in Hoyte Dillingham's café at the time. He also owned the adjacent D&D grocery and BP gas station that sat conveniently beside the road near Barnardsville, North Carolina. Videos, Nintendo games, and Marlboro cigarettes were advertised in the store windows. The clean, neat little restaurant served breakfast and lunch. Cement picnic tables were available outside, but it was summertime and too hot. We sat in a booth in the air-conditioned inside. There was a very large bear rug on the tile floor. "That was a record bear in North Carolina until a few years ago," Hoyte said. "It was 639 pounds." The rug had a full head with teeth showing and tongue hanging out.

Hoyte was a big, beefy man in a short-sleeved plaid shirt. His thinning white hair was swept back from his face. He wore glasses and a wide smile. He was articulate and friendly, a man with charm. His ancestor Absalom Dillingham had come to the Swannanoa valley in western Carolina in 1796, where he fell in love with Rebecca Foster. Her father objected, whereupon Absalom stole his bride from under the parental roof. They were all reconciled, and the father gave the couple land on Big Ivy Creek, where they raised a family. A grandson with the surname Barnard built and operated the first store in the community.

After he graduated from college, Hoyte managed a store for the Acme supermarket chain in the Washington, D.C., area. Thirty-odd years ago, he came home and started his own business. Back then, he knew everyone's name, from grandparents to grandkids. "Now we can have three hundred to five hundred people come through in a day," he said.

He used to do a lot of bear hunting in western Canada. "It was a hobby, not to see how much bear we could get, but to maintain sportsman standards." For years now, he had been hunting closer to home, in Big Ivy. He saw that the Great Smoky Mountains National Park, not far away, occasionally had to close campgrounds because of troublesome bears. "The bear population is ample for hunting," he said.

I had gotten Hoyte's name when I came to Big Ivy to do a magazine story on the old growth there. The Pisgah National Forest, which now owns most of the upper slopes of the Big Ivy watershed, had been selling timber there and was planning more sales. Old-growth stands of various types were scattered across the watershed. The Western North Carolina Alliance, an environmental group in Asheville, challenged the Forest Service's logging plans. To invite local support, alliance members left flyers at Hoyte's store.

That's how Hoyte heard about the plans for clear-cutting. He didn't join the alliance but went to some of the meetings. "They have some extreme ideas," he said. But he saw that what they said about Big Ivy was true. The old growth had too much rot to make good lumber and wasn't worth much except as a food supply for wildlife, for the large quantities of acorns that the big trees produced. He figured that the loggers would probably cut it and leave most of it lie. "Trees that old won't regenerate from stumps," he said. "The Forest Service tried to convince me that it would come back, but they had no proof. It certainly won't in my lifetime, and young trees won't support a bear population. I'm for selective cutting but not for clear-cutting. Waiting fifty to a hundred years for mast trees is too long for me."

I had heard the Back Creek Sportsmen with whom I had hunted in Virginia also blast Forest Service clear-cutting practices as a much greater threat to bears than hunting was. But Forest Service biologists pointed to research showing that bears will use clear-cuts for browsing and denning if they are not disturbed by hunters.

Over the years, Hoyte had watched his hunting area shrink. He was nearly surrounded by inaccessible lands: a large tract of posted company land, protected park lands around Mount Mitchell, and the off-limits Asheville city watershed. The only hunting area left open within easy reach was the Pisgah National Forest. "Cutting Big Ivy would deprive us of habitat for our game," he said. "Once bears leave the Pisgah National Forest, there's no way for us to get at them."

As we talked, he kept an eye on the comings and goings at the gas pumps. He waved through the window at people passing by, chatted with the woman who was mopping the floor, called hellos to customers entering the store. He was clearly a conduit of community opinion. It was through his influence that local people wrote letters to the Forest Service protesting the cutting of Big Ivy, which helped halt the cutting, at least for this round of Forest Service planning.

"Why don't local people become more active in environmental issues?" I asked.

"They don't get out and pull strings because they don't know what strings to pull and how, which outsiders do," he said. "Most activists are highly educated. Sometimes we need extremists to show us what's involved. It's good to a certain extent to have outsiders move in, but now we're getting too much anti, anti, anti. There should be some consideration for local people born and raised here."

Being born and raised there meant going hunting. "It's a heritage thing," he said, "having a family that knows what it is to bring a coon or possum home, and mom cooks it up and we eat it. And oh, my, there's women that can cook up bear meat. If I don't have some for the Dillingham family reunions, everyone's disappointed. You can't start hunting at age twenty-one." I thought about the bear hunters I see every winter when I go mountain biking on national forest roads around my house. They always have their sons along, little boys as young as five.

"It's not the bear itself," Hoyte said. "It's the group, being out in the forest, the socializing, turning a workday into a fun day, enjoying nature. It's eating a box of crackers and kneeling down at a spring for a drink of cold water. It's hearing old tales. Fifty years ago, killing a bear was big news in the community. Everybody came to help with the skinning so that they could have a little piece of meat and listen to the story of how the dogs did and how it all happened. We don't care about killing a bear; it's just part of the heritage we grew up with."

I murmured the word "bonding," and he said yes, that's what it was. "It's a bonding between you, the forest, the dogs, the people. As you get older, you start appreciating it all more. You realize that once the forest is gone, you'll never see it again. Young bucks can cut it all off and not worry about the next generation, because they've got other things on their minds, but once you've got home and family taken care of, you want to sit under a big tree and see squirrels. People over fifty in the community here are like that."

"So people here have an emotional or spiritual connection with the forest?" I asked.

"Nah," he said. "That comes in from outsiders, the old hippie thing."

Oh, dear. He had me pegged. I made a quick feint to the right and asked if there was any religious idea about stewardship. He shook his head.

But Hoyte Dillingham was wrong. It's not just aging hippies from the outside who feel mystical emanations from the forest. Jennifer Hensley is as true Blue Ridge Appalachian as anyone could be. Her ancestors were among the first settlers on the western flank of Virginia's Blue Ridge in the eighteenth century; so were her husband's. She met Thurman in high school at age fourteen and married him before she turned nineteen. Within a year, he had spent $1,000 on eighty acres of mountain land. Jennifer was dismayed, afraid that they would always be poor. Then Thurman taught her to hunt. She loved it, and she soon began to feel something more than simple sportsmanship. It was through hunting that she discovered her inner bear.

After high school, Jennifer went to beauty school but found that she couldn't stand working in a salon because of the constant frivolous chatter. She stayed home after the birth of her daughter, but when the child started school, Jennifer started searching. She tried making ceramics. She ran a gun shop. "I never felt like I fit in," she said. "I always felt like an impostor." She took college courses off and on and eventually worked as a technical writer for an electronics firm. She and Thurman bought more land, until they owned 250 acres that ran up to the border of Shenandoah National Park.

When they moved onto their property in 1979, Jennifer began to freelance for hunting magazines and to write a monthly column on hunting for a newspaper in a nearby town. She used her initials to avoid the gender hassle. She likes to recount stories of when some man she has met realizes that what he has been reading was written by a woman. "Listen here, little lady," one astonished fellow told her at a banquet for members of a wild turkey club, "you write just like a man!" She wasn't sure if she was being accused or congratulated.

She and Thurman moved into the basement of their house—they had built it themselves—one evening in June. That night, after Thurman left for the graveyard shift at his factory job, Jennifer saw hounds running through her yard. The chases continued all summer and through the rest of the year, then began again the next summer. Several times, she and Thurman found bear carcasses intact except for gallbladders and paws. Baiting is illegal in Virginia, but she found a rotten ham hanging from a tree. The worst was when she heard cubs screaming. "The hunters knock them out of trees for the dogs to chew on," she said. "They want the dogs to get the taste of bear's blood."

Thurman had grown up hunting bears with dogs, and his father was president of a local bear hunting club. But Thurman began to distance himself from bear hunting with hounds. Eventually, he repudiated it. Jennifer, who claims a full-blooded Cherokee for a great-grandmother, was reading about Native American ideas and felt that if you were going to hunt a bear, it should be you and the bear. "You should know something about the bear," she said. "If all you're going to do is raise hounds, you know the hounds but not the bear. That's not respectful."

Both Jennifer and Thurman remained otherwise avid hunters. Trophies lined the high walls of their family room: deer, elk, bears, pheasants, wild turkeys, ducks. A mountain goat, his entire body mounted, stood out against the dark paneling like snow. The largest elk was Jennifer's; she had also shot three bears, though she doubts that she will ever hunt bears again. She hunted for meat. "I believe in taking responsibility for what I eat," she said. "I don't even like to accept venison from other people because I'm not sure if they've properly honored the animal." As signs of honor, she draped hides from the deer she shot over her furniture and put a fanned wild turkey tail on a side table like a work of art.

After a couple years of experience with bear hunters on her property, Jennifer started writing about what she had learned. In 1983, a local newspaper ran a special edition of her writing on illegal bear hunting. The editor was threatened with having his office blown up. Then came anonymous phone calls to Jennifer about rape and pillage, until she finally had the line tapped, which stopped them. She and Thurman would run out when they heard hounds, he to grab the dogs or confront the hunters, she a little distance behind him dressed in black, so they wouldn't see her, and carrying a gun. "It's amazing," she said, "that nobody got killed."

Game wardens tried to help but were hampered by a law allowing hunters to retrieve their dogs even on posted land. The hunters were always just retrieving their dogs. At one point, Jennifer said, the game department wanted her to move with her daughter to an apartment in a nearby town. Her dog was poisoned. The lug nuts on Thurman's truck were loosened one day while he was hunting, but he avoided injury. The scariest time for Jennifer was one night when she drove up to two vehicles blocking the dirt road to her house. The license plates were taped over, and figures lurked in the dark. She had her daughter with her. "Do you have your seat belt on?" she asked, as she used her 1980 Blazer like a tank to nudge one of the vehicles aside and sped away.

This history did not give Jennifer much sway with bear hunters when she tried to start a new bear association in the early 1990s. I met her when she approached me at an outdoor writers' meeting, canvasing for support in her crusade against the new bear chase season. The Virginia game department was making it legal to chase bears with hounds in September, to train the dogs for the real season in December. Bears weren't allowed to be killed, just chased. Jennifer hoped to form a coalition of hunters with others in the community interested in bears. "We need an entity that will look out for the bear interests," she said, and no one else's." She wanted the new group to discuss the chase season and how it was bad for bears, stressing them when they needed to lay up fat for the winter, separating mothers and cubs, jeopardizing the reproductive success of females. Jennifer was attired in what I would learn was her usual extravagantly ursine fashion—bear earrings, several bear fetish necklaces, a bear claw ring that covered her finger to the knuckle, a sweatshirt patterned with bears. Naturally, I signed on to the club she was forming. At the first meeting, as the auditorium filled with men in flannel shirts and ball caps who spoke loudly among themselves in annoyed voices, it was clear what would happen. The bear hunters elected themselves as officers and the association expired.

"I think things have gotten better now to some extent," Jennifer said when I visited her one day several years later. "I would say forty percent of the people involved have changed their attitudes. We haven't had a chase go through here in a couple of years, though I worry that we've just pushed our problems over on other people. And not all bear hunters with dogs are like that." We were in her yard, and she was showing me the Bear Chi garden she had recently started. Chi is a Chinese concept of psychic energy. The strain of those years chasing bear hunters had taken their toll on Jennifer, and she had bouts of vague, difficult-to-diagnose illnesses. In the process of searching for relief, she discovered Tai Chi, a regimen of slow, relaxed, circular movements that can be used for self-defense or as an aid to meditation. She now taught it. She pointed out the worn spot in the lawn where she stood to do her exercises. A wildflower mix she had planted was in full bloom around a little artificial pool, where water tinkled.

One of the health problems she had was a chronic debilitating pain in a particular spot in her back. She tried everything, including acupuncture, but it persisted. After suffering with it for years, all of a sudden she remembered a bear that Thurman had shot while she was with him, not long before her back began to hurt. "I asked Thurman to touch my back where he had shot that bear and it was the exact same spot," she said. The pain is now slowly going away. Other seemingly odd coincidences, in which bears were central, continued to happen to her.

"Most people don't understand that there are definite connections between humans and other critters," she said. We meandered past a flagstone inscribed with a bear motif as we circled the garden. "It's hard to articulate. The root of my being is bear. My being has memory, and it has to do with bears. Sometimes I feel I'm being absorbed by the bears. I've tried to figure it out logically, but it doesn't work that way. I just feel I'm here for a reason, and that reason is related to black bears. I have work to do with them." Her shoulder-length hair, graying at the temples, was clipped back from her face. It was an overcast day, and her eyes were the exact shade of blue-gray as the sky, but clear and luminous.

The camera clicked as I posed with the bear in my arms. This was my trophy picture. I wasn't sure it was an altogether respectful thing to do, but it was irresistible. She was a small bear, sixty-five pounds, and had probably left her mother the spring before this one. She was most likely the bear that had been robbing the baits on the snare line we were running in Great Smoky Mountains National Park. It was all legal.

The bear's sides rose and fell with deep drafts of air. I was encouraged to pet her coarse hair and promptly found a tick. She was lean. She had big ears and big feet. The pad of her hind foot was like a human's, warm, tough, yet soft and yielding. I felt sorry for her poor limp body, drugged into abject vulnerability.

She had been snared in a routine that Michael Pelton, professor of wildlife science at the University of Tennessee, had perfected in the course of nearly thirty years of research on bears in the park. His were by far the longest-running studies of any large mammal in the Appalachians. In a discipline hobbled by the vagaries of unstable funding, most field research projects last fewer than five years, though in the case of bears, the study subjects may live for three decades. "If I had quit after five or even ten years," Mike said, "my conclusions about bear population dynamics would have been quite different. Short-term interpretations can be misleading."

He also studied otters, raccoons, and small mammals, but bears were his specialty. Sought internationally as a wildlife consultant, he had recently returned from a bear conference in Norway. Over the years, he has supervised nearly two thousand captures of nearly a thousand different bears. Last summer was a record year, with ninety-nine captures. This summer he had another good crop of graduate students who were running his snare lines as part of their research.

To set a leg snare, they picked a tree in a shady spot, cleared it of limbs so the bear couldn't impale herself, and removed obstacles. The trap was placed in a small hole, then covered with leaves and sprinkled with forest duff. Sardines were dropped in a trail leading toward the snare, with the last fish placed right on it. "I buy fifty cases of sardines at a time," Mike said. Logs were arranged to funnel the bear toward the snare, with sticks arranged around the snare to make only one place for the bear to put a foot. Bears won't step on sticks. An automobile hood spring added flex to the snare line, and a swivel kept the bear from winding tight.

Snares were set off the trail a ways, and we waited trailside while the students checked each one along their route. When they returned to say that this snare had caught a bear, we all approached the site quietly. At a distance of about eighty feet, to keep from agitating the bear any more than she already was, I watched the two students prepare to dart her. They spoke softly as they tipped a long pole with a needle full of drug and jabbed her in the haunch. She tried to climb the small tree under which the snare was set, but a branch broke under her, and she fell about eight feet. She bounced right back up and didn't appear hurt, but the students were appalled. This had not happened to them before.

The drug usually takes only a few minutes, but some individuals need longer. We walked away to wait. In less than ten minutes, the bear was down. One of the students clapped his hands close to her face to see if she responded. She didn't, and he put salve in her eyes and a bandanna across them to remedy the drug's drying effect. There was much concern over her fall, but they didn't think that she was hurt. Mike helped the students hoist the bear onto a scale to weigh her. They took the bear's rectal temperature and examined her teeth, holding her tongue to keep it from lolling out on the ground. They didn't extract a tooth, because she had already had one pulled last year; there was an ear tattoo to document the previous capture. They did take a blood sample, to be banked at the university veterinary school. They gave her an orange collar and ear tags, so she could be identified on videos being taped from tree mounts for another student's project. One student yanked a tuft of hair, leaving a small bald spot on the bear's belly.

"DNA analysis of hair samples might eliminate the need for some of this kind of handling," Mike said. He had been collecting hair since 1974. One of his projects was to trace the genealogy of bears that he caught, to try to determine how genetic health was related to population numbers. The current rule of thumb in conservation biology for long-term avoidance of inbreeding among mammals is about five hundred reproductively active animals in one population. Including animals too young or too old to reproduce, the total population could reach well over a thousand. This has implications for places such as Shenandoah National Park, where bear numbers don't add up to that many and can't be supplemented by outside bears because of human-built barriers.

The bear's foot twitched. "We need to hurry," Mike told the students. They gave the bear a counteracting shot of drug, and we all moved back in the bushes. "If the bear comes after you, you can't sue the University of Tennessee," said Tamra, Mike's wife.

The bear raised her head. She threw one foot forward but was still too wobbly to follow through. The orange wires stuck out like an alien's antennae from her big ears. She jumped a log and walked a little, then sat down and looked over at us. As we talked, she disappeared.

On our way out of the park, we stopped to chat with another snare line crew that had brought out a small female bear and was going to move her in an enclosed pickup truck to Big South Fork National Recreation Area. Mike was a consultant for the restoration program there, where bears had been eliminated decades ago. It was a tricky business, because no one knew the best method to introduce bears to a new area. They were concentrating on females, especially females with young, to make them stay put.

Young male bears must leave their birthplaces; their fathers won't tolerate them. Older males sometimes kill young males that don't light out for new territory or that wander through an elder's range while traveling. Females, in contrast, often settle near their mothers and are less inclined to roam. One of the newest lines of wildlife research is exploring how matriarchs pass on accumulated knowledge to their young, such as where to find emergency food when the usual sources fail.

Mike had thick, brown hair that turned silver at the temples and suddenly full white in his short beard. He had been born in Georgia, spent his childhood in Louisiana, then moved to Knoxville, his mother's home. He had always been interested in the natural world, although there was really no family background for it. He had lived for many years in a cedar-sided house tucked away in woods at the end of a gravel driveway in an upscale Knoxville suburb. Porches and decks overlooked terraced flower gardens. He had six mostly wooded acres that abutted a neighbor's six, to create twelve acres of tangled fourth-growth forest festooned with poison ivy. Through it he had established paths that he walked regularly. One of his hobbies was to find and record the box turtles on his paths. In the last ten years, he had marked 180 different turtles.

Counting was at the heart of Mike's work. His research on bears in the park focused on basic demographic questions: How many are there? What ages are they? How many are born and die each year? In trying to answer them, he also answered a lot of questions about how bears live. They are omnivorous eaters, dependent mostly on vegetable foods for survival. They are wary but curious, and quick to take advantage of any opportunity for a meal. In spring, bears eat the first leaves and stems to green up, insects they grub out of the ground, and especially squaw-root, a parasitic plant on oak tree roots. In summer, bears eat fruits of all kinds—serviceberries, blueberries, blackberries, pokeberries, huckle-berries, wild cherries, and grapes. Berries grow best in forest openings and along edges, a fact that the Forest Service uses to justify clear-cuts and roads.

Nearly half of the diet of the bears in Shenandoah National Park consists of apples, peaches, and pears from old, long-abandoned orchards. In both Appalachian parks, bears cross over the borders to raid cornfields and honeybee hives on private lands, to the aggravation of local farmers. The first summer our peach trees produced fruit, a bear found them. We saw the pits scattered on the ground, and one day Ralph saw the bear, to the startlement of them both. We don't have to make our living off peaches, so we didn't mind at all.

In the fall, bears begin an orgy of eating to store energy for denning. They do not enter true hibernation, defined as the suspension of meta-bolic processes, and they need fat reserves to maintain their body tem-perature for months of deep sleep. The high fat content of acorns, particularly white oak acorns, is essential to survive the winter. Acorn production is extremely variable. In years when the oaks in an area don't produce good mast, the bear population drops. Cubs are born in the den while the mother sleeps, but if the mother doesn't have enough fat, they are aborted or die, and the mother often dies with them. Even in years of bad mast, though, more bears die from encounters with humans, through hunting, poaching, and collision with vehicles on roads, than from natural causes.

Dens are in rock caves, in brush piles, and under logs. By far the most preferred den, especially by female bears, is a big standing tree with a hole fifty or more feet up. Such a tree offers insulation from cold and security from harassment.

As several million acres of oak-hickory woods on the recovering national parks and forests began to reach maturity around the 1970s, acorns became steadily more numerous. Mike believes that this increase in autumn food has been the driving force behind a marked upward trend in bear populations. He was documenting it in the park and deducing it from data in other areas of Appalachia. The state of Virginia was probably right: there *were* more bears out there to hunt. The increasing potential for old-growth forests led Mike to make a cautiously optimistic prediction for the future of bears on public lands. "Mature oaks are the single most important component of bear habitat," he said. "Since the Forest Service is moving, if grudgingly, toward an ecosystem approach, I think the amount of mature forest available to bears will remain relatively stable. If the gypsy moth does eventually kill a lot of oaks, that would change things. But the immediate problem is human population growth."

Because his study subjects roam widely without regard for political jurisdictions, Mike was an early proponent of an ecosystem approach. Wildlife management has a split personality: the federal government is responsible for animal habitat on the national forests and parks, but individual state governments are responsible for the actual bodies of the animals, dead or alive (except in the case of migratory species under federal authority, which bears are not). To a state game agency, management means regulation of hunting. Every Appalachian state sets its own bear seasons and has its own rules about such practices as baiting and changing the dogs during the hunt (that is, setting fresh dogs on a tired bear). Georgia, where hunting with hounds didn't become entrenched, is the only state in southern Appalachia to prohibit that custom (Pennsylvania discontinued it in the 1930s). Kentucky has hardly any bears to hunt, and South Carolina not many more.

Mike helped establish the Southern Appalachian Black Bear Study Group in 1974, composed of academic wildlife experts, national forest and park personnel, and state wildlife managers from Tennessee, North Carolina, and Georgia. They standardized their data collection methods and agreed to do sardine surveys to monitor selected bear populations on a regular basis.

The survey technique is to hang a partially opened can of sardines by nylon string at least ten feet high in small trees spaced at half-mile intervals on designated survey routes. Routes consist of roads, trails, and/or cross-country contours of topographically distinct features. After five nights, the baits are checked, and the percentage visitation by bears—that is, the number of cans torn open—is used to calculate a comparative index value. This is done at least every two years, to monitor trends in bear populations over time. This is the kind of information that state game agencies can use to make decisions about how many bears the population can afford to lose to hunters, and where they can be taken from.

The group's consolidated data and coordinated research made it possible to start assessing bear societies across the southern Appalachians. A picture of potential fragmentation emerged. Continuing urban and suburban growth was obliterating the possibilities for bears on most private lands, the group concluded. Although public lands represent a relatively stable land base, they are often fractured by private inholdings. The travel corridors that connect islands of habitats and clusters of bears are being cut by roads, and encroaching development sometimes takes over historic, low-elevation fall feeding sites. The bear study group identified roads as a major concern. Interstate 40 between Newport, Tennessee, and Asheville, North Carolina, slices Great Smoky Mountains National Park from Pisgah National Forest. It poses one of the greatest obstacles. Many bears are killed annually trying to cross it; many others are probably intimidated and deterred from trying. Although a few bears may succeed in getting across, the road effectively severs genetic flow.

Small roads through the woods are less of a barrier to bears but serve as a conduit into bear country for hunters and poachers. The bear study group consistently urges the Forest Service to reduce the amount of road mileage in national forests, even to close roads, to mitigate the efficiency of bear hunters.

Much of what has been learned about bears in the Smokies applies to bears in Virginia, but not all of it. Mike's and most other Appalachian studies have been conducted in the two national parks, where there is no hunting. Data about how a bear population is affected by heavy hunting pressure are scarce. For years, the only information gathered about Virginia's hunted bear populations was the number and gender of bears killed legally. Since it was agency policy to calculate the living bear population by extrapolating from the number killed, as harvests went up, the state gave an increasingly rosy assessment of the bear situation. More and better-equipped hunters, greater monetary incentives to poach, and more roads into formerly undisturbed bear habitat were never factored into the formula.

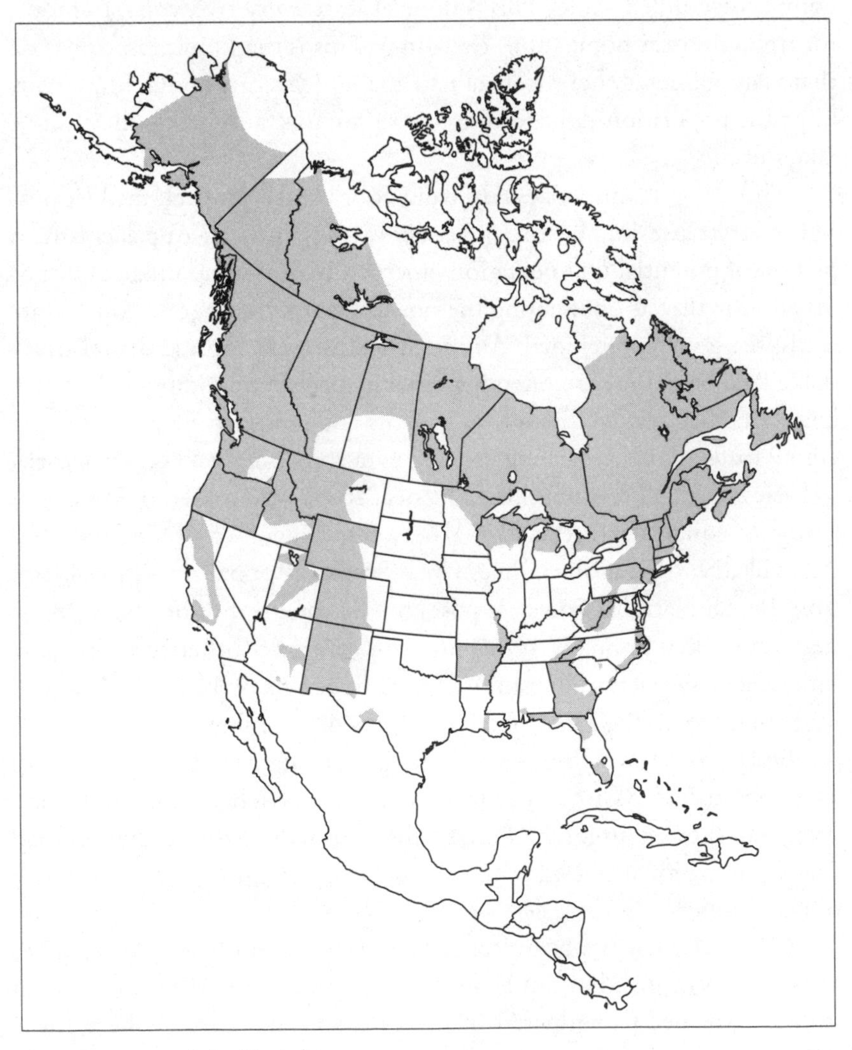

Current range of the black bear.

For a few years, the game department asked hunters to voluntarily turn in a tooth from each bear they killed. Bear teeth can be sectioned and the rings read for age, as in trees. Knowing the ages of the harvested bears gives important clues to the structure of the overall population. Few hunters responded. Finally, in the early 1990s, the state mandated that hunters relinquish a tooth. I had to make a Freedom of Information Act request to pry the first couple years' worth of data away from the state bear manager, and he sent it to me in the crudest computer form, just columns of numbers with no headings. But the relevant fact was easy enough to sift out: well over half the bears killed were two and a half years old or younger, still too young to reproduce.

It used to be one of the principles of wildlife management that a high percentage of very young animals in the hunting harvest meant that most of the old ones had already been taken, and the population was being exploited too heavily. Virginia's officials suggested that the high percentage reflected a large number of young bears that were dispersing and were therefore more likely to be caught by hunters. Many of these young bears would not find new territories anyway, they said, and would become nuisances on private lands, as was happening around Shenandoah National Park.

As in many other state game agencies, Virginia's wildlife managers are paid by hunting license fees and by federal allocations from taxes on firearms and ammunition. They don't depend on money from state coffers, and therefore they don't have to answer to anyone except hunters. And they do have to answer, quite literally, to bear hunters. Ralph and I attended one of the regular public meetings held by the Virginia game department to solicit citizen input on hunting regulations. We signed up to speak, as number twenty-something on the clipboard register on a table outside the meeting room.

We were going to ask the game department to consider an ecosystem bear management plan. It would involve mapping bear habitats across the state, examining corridors among them, joining the Southern Appalachian Black Bear Study Group, and doing sardine surveys. Once bear numbers and locations were better known, hunting limits could be set by district to ensure that no more than about a quarter of the bear population was killed every year. I had it all outlined on note cards.

One after another, the people who had signed up ahead of us got up and spoke. They stood at a microphone beside a table of game officials, in front of an audience of about 150 people. It seemed like every other speaker was a bear hunter. A gray-haired woman got up and said that she wanted to testify how she had recently gone bear hunting with her husband after many years of marriage and discovered it to be a heart-warming family communion. Mostly, it was men who got up to talk about how much they liked their particular kind of hunting and what they wanted the state people to do to maintain it.

The audience listened intently to every speaker and responded with cheers, whistles, clapping, and foot stomping. There were also angry murmurs and catcalls, as when a bear hunter got up to complain that bow hunters took too many female bears. Bear hunters don't like bow hunters, whose season starts much earlier, and the feeling is reciprocated. The evening was well along and the atmosphere quite lively by the time our number was called. Glancing furtively at each other, we both sank down in our seats until the next number was called. "I'll send a letter instead," I whispered.

Virginia has not yet even joined the regional bear study group, but it did initiate research on the hunted bear population in the George Washington National Forest. Fieldwork is planned for five years, and possibly ten, if funding continues to be available. In organization and technique, it is similar to Mike Pelton's work, and the goal is to get the same kind of fundamental information about the size, age, and birth and death rates of the population. At least they're counting live bears to estimate the living population, instead of dead ones. That seems like a step in the right direction.

As many people in the Virginia game department suspected, I did have an ulterior motive for prodding them toward ecosystem management of bears. However, it wasn't what they thought, which is that I was an antihunting fanatic plotting to overthrow the great American tradition on which their livelihood depends. My agenda was to use bears as an umbrella species; that is, to use the habitat needs of bears to cover those of other species about which less is known. There are an estimated 65 species of mammals, 80 species of amphibians and reptiles, and 175 species of terrestrial birds in central and southern Appalachia. The best guess for insect species is somewhere around 25,000. It will likely be some time before the habitat needs of all these animals are understood.

Bears require some of the largest and most varied ranges of all remaining Appalachian mammals. If currently occupied bear habitats were identified, protected, and connected, many other species besides bears would be likely to derive long-term benefits. Depending on the type of corridor, bobcats, foxes, weasels, deer, raccoons, skunks, opossums, chipmunks and other rodents, various kinds of birds, and possibly some amphibians and reptiles could utilize it. But it's bears that attract a lot of public sympathy for conservation, in a way that native species of wood rats, shrews, bats, and snakes don't, even if they are on the edge of extinction.

Each of these animals has a story as long and complicated as the bear's tale. Stories about Appalachia's animal kingdom can be classified into several types. The first, of course, is about loss. Elk, bison, wolves, cougars, and passenger pigeons are known to have been extirpated or driven extinct since European settlement, and there were probably other, smaller species whose loss went unrecorded. Scores of additional species have been reduced to dangerously small populations, especially in rivers and streams, where much of the detritus of civilization ends up.

The second category is stories of restoration. Since the 1920s, federal and state governments have cooperated to reestablish most of the popular game species, as well as red wolves, fishers, otters, peregrine falcons, several kinds of fish, and even a species of river snails. No such attempts have any guarantee of success, and several are problematic. Red wolves, for example (a smaller, less pack-oriented species than the gray wolf), have left the deep forests of Great Smoky Mountains National Park, where they were released, for the fields and edges of agricultural land, where small prey is more plentiful. Nearly two dozen claims for cattle kills have been paid out. The program may be discontinued if wolves don't stay in the park.

Overlapping the restoration efforts are stories of natural resurgence. When they and their habitats received some protection, bears rebounded on their own. Deer are overly abundant now in many regions. Many of the small mammals that would once have been prey to wolves and cougars are thriving in the absence of those two predators. Even these shiest, most elusive species may be coming back. It's uncertain where they're coming from, but a few cougars and wolves were documented in the 1990s in New England, where they have not been present for a long time. Maybe they will be able to travel south down the chain of mountains. Sightings of cougars have never completely ceased in the southern Appalachians, although few have been verified.

The category of exotic introduced species is amply represented by gypsy moths and the Russian wild pigs in the Smokies. In a category of their own are the coyotes. Indigenous to the West when European settlers arrived, coyotes began to emigrate in the late nineteenth century. It may be no coincidence that it was then that ranchers began a pogrom to poison, trap, shoot, or otherwise kill every single one of them. A few coyotes may have managed to cross the Mississippi River. By the 1930s, two streams of coyotes had ringed the Great Lakes, possibly interbreeding with the handful of gray wolves still resident in that area. By the 1970s, coyotes were being reported in every eastern state. By the 1980s, sheep farmers in the Virginia mountains began complaining of losses. I heard coyotes yipping unmistakably one night while I was camping on a friend's land near Seneca Rocks, West Virginia. At my own place, I have scatological reason to believe a coyote ate the Canada goose goslings at the pond this spring. But I could be wrong; it might have been the gray fox that I know lives here.

DROPPING ACID IN THE APPALACHIANS

THERE ARE, NO DOUBT, MANY INTERESTING STORIES TO BE TOLD about LSD in the mountains, but that's not the kind of acid I'm concerned with here. The kind that is falling from the sky provokes more frightening flash-forwards than any flashbacks from LSD.

The phenomenon called acid rain is caused by the burning of fossil fuels, particularly coal and oil and, to a lesser extent, natural gas. Electricity-generating utilities, many different kinds of factories, and vehicles are the major sources of emissions. Oxides of nitrogen and sulfur waft from smokestacks and exhaust pipes into the atmosphere, where they react with water vapor and a wide range of chemicals called volatile organic compounds. Some of these compounds are naturally present, given off by trees during normal processes of growth; others are emitted from vehicles and factories. The result of their interaction is the production of sulfuric and nitric acids and ground-level ozone. Fine sulfur particles are mostly responsible for the brown haze that has become infamous in both Appalachian national parks. The acids come down in rain, fog, sleet, and snow.

Acid rain is hardly new. It was recognized a couple centuries ago in London, where toxic smogs formed from sulfur discharged by burning coal in hundreds of thousands of household chimneys. In mid-nineteenth-century Germany, emissions from coal-burning factories were blamed for killing trees and other nearby vegetation. In America, declines in lake trout were noted in Big Moose Lake in the Adirondacks in the 1940s. By the late 1970s, a link between acidic deposition and acidification of lakes was established. Nearly half of forty high-elevation Adirondack lakes that were known to have fish in the 1930s have none now, due to the increasing acidity of the water.

Acid rain became a hot topic in the 1980s, as the federal government undertook a mammoth, decade-long survey, the National Acid Precipitation Assessment Program. The final reports were dense with information, but the interpretations drawn by the compilers were hedged with so many bets that few hard policy decisions could be wrung from them. There were allegations by some scientists that those participating in the survey had compromised the results to understate the true dimensions of the problem. Amendments in 1990 to the Clear Air Act of 1970 required the reduction of sulfur emissions from industrial sources, but nitrogen oxides and volatile organic compounds continue to increase.

Although the media virtually abandoned the subject of acid rain after the assessment, the rain kept falling. One of the facts to emerge from the welter of air pollution studies done on public lands as part of the assessment program was this: the central and southern Appalachians receive some of the most acidic rainfall recorded in the United States. The acidity of liquids is measured by the concentration of positively charged hydrogen ions, called the pH level. On a scale of 1 to 14, pure distilled water has a neutral pH of 7.0. Rising pH indicates alkalinity; declining pH indicates increasing acidity. Because of the chemical reactions between water vapor and atmospheric carbon dioxide, rainfall tends to be naturally slightly acidic, with a pH of 5.3 to 6.0. The pH of precipitation in Shenandoah National Park has been measured as low as 3.0, more acidic than vinegar.

Until the late 1980s, it was believed that mountain soils south of Pennsylvania were protected from the kind of acidification that occurred in the Adirondacks. Soil composition is probably the single most important determinant of the rate and effect of acidification. Soils in the southern half of the Appalachian Mountains were not scraped away by glaciers and are deep and well developed. The more dirt there is, the more sulfates and nitrates it can soak up, keeping acid from passing into streams. Bedrock in the southern half of the Appalachians also generally contains more calcium carbonate, a base that neutralizes acids.

These characteristics, it was assumed, would protect prized trout streams, those headwater creeks with rushing water so white and innocent it makes your heart ache. One hundred fifty volunteers refuted that assumption in Virginia in 1987. Trained in stream sampling protocol by University of Virginia researchers and equipped with topographic maps, water bottles, gloves, tags, coolers, and data sheets, the volunteers collected samples from 350 native trout streams in thirty-one counties. Academic analysts found "greater than expected sensitivity" and concluded that "given the level of acid deposition in the region, it is probable that alkalinity and pH have been reduced in many of these streams." They predicted that at 1990 levels of pollution, one-third to nearly all of Virginia's native trout streams would become acidified over the next thirty to fifty years.

It had already happened in St. Mary's River. Just a few miles south of Shenandoah National Park, in the George Washington National Forest, the St. Mary's Wilderness Area has been famous for many years for its trout and its waterfalls. It also provides one of the longest records of change in an Appalachian aquatic community. It was nearly the shortest day of the year when I hiked up St. Mary's with Larry Mohn, and even at noon the sun hung low over Big Spy Mountain. We passed in and out of shadows that changed the complexion of the forest from bright and glittery to dim and solemn. As we followed the stream up its canyon of fractured cliffs and talus slopes, Larry pointed out his sampling sites. Larry was a fisheries biologist for the Virginia Department of Game. His surveys of the aquatic life of St. Mary's River can be compared with work by biologist Eugene Surber in 1936.

"The wild, reproducing population of rainbow trout that Surber observed disappeared by 1994," Larry said. We were standing beside a deep pool where cold, thin sunlight turned the water glassy-eyed, as in death. The loss of rainbows brought the number of extirpated fish species in St. Mary's to six, half of the original total of twelve. "Then last year's unusually wet winter badly hurt the native brook trout that moved downstream to reclaim their old range from the rainbows, which had been introduced long ago," Larry continued. "I wouldn't be surprised if the heavy rainstorm at the end of last January took the water pH down to 4.0." Brook trout eggs hatch around mid-January. Acidity is especially lethal to young trout, and reproduction generally fails below a pH of 4.7.

That one rainstorm reduced the brook trout population in St. Mary's by more than seventy percent, with almost no reproduction.

Meteorological events that send water rushing into streams without first seeping through the soil, where it may be buffered, are causing fish kills across the Appalachians. Beginning in 1981, the Cherokee Trout Hatchery on the Cherokee Reservation in North Carolina, located on Raven Fork downstream from the boundary with Great Smoky Mountains National Park, lost tens of thousands of pounds of fish whenever the watershed was flooded by heavy rains. Pulses of water with a pH of 4.0 still occur when big rain fronts come out of the west, but the owner installed an artificial buffering system with sodium hydroxide to protect his fish. In Pennsylvania, nearly two dozen streams and lakes have been removed from fish stocking programs because so few fish survive. Larry estimated that Virginia's stocking program experienced at least three fish kills from acidification in the 1990s.

I followed behind Larry as he passed a small pool. "I pulled a twelve-and-a-half-inch brook trout out of there eighteen years ago," he said. The last autumn leaves eddied in slow circles. Leaves are the first link in the food chain for mountain streams. Bacteria and fungi break down the cellulose and lignin, which few aquatic animals can digest. Researchers at the U.S. Forest Service's Fernow Experimental Forest in West Virginia recently identified 156 kinds of fungi on oak, maple, and beech leaves in mountain streams. The more acidic the stream, they found, the fewer the fungi. Invertebrates graze on the fungi, other invertebrates prey on the grazers, and fish eat them all.

In 1936, St. Mary's had thirty-one taxa of invertebrates—crayfish, mayflies, stoneflies, blackflies. In the 1990s, Larry was finding an average of fifteen taxa, some of them represented by only a single individual. During that time span, the pH fell from 7.0 to an average of around 5.0. St. Mary's had been protected for decades from human developments, and the possibility of lingering influences from earlier land uses had been investigated and discounted. Air pollution is the sole remaining culprit.

There were occasional sandy beaches along the St. Mary's that would have made for good tracking, but the stream was high and had washed away any scratchings of small feet. Whoever depends on the river for food is surely hurting. Mammals that eat fish, like the mahogany curve of a mink I once glimpsed from my downstairs window, are locally at risk of starvation. So is an uncommon species of water shrew *(Sorex palustris punctulatus)* in the Smokies and Alleghenies. Fish-eating birds have been forced to abandon waters where acidification has killed off their prey. Swallows and flycatchers, which feed on emerging aquatic insects, must feel the pinch too. My heart sank to think of the Louisiana waterthrush that returns each year to nest beside one of my creeks, and whose cascading call ushers in spring.

It was still winter when I visited Grandfather Mountain, the better to see green needles against bare mountains. The decline of red spruces in Appalachian spruce-fir forests has become a major focus of much of the controversy about acid rain. These forests are the last exhalations of the glaciers' icy breath. Native to cold northern regions, spruce and fir trees retreated far southward in response to the movement of glaciers tens of thousands of years ago. Conifers pushed out deciduous trees and covered much of the Southeast. As the climate warmed over the last fifteen thousand years, deciduous trees began reclaiming their former terrain. Spruces and firs found favorable conditions only on the highest, coldest mountains. There they formed a distinct ecosystem, with species of plants and animals that live nowhere else. At 5,964 feet, Grandfather has a mantle of spruce-fir forest.

Over the past decade, these dense woods, so dark that the Black Mountains of North Carolina were named for them, have been punched with holes. Dead trunks stand like stick figures amidst the full-fleshed green of still living trees. That's how it looked to me on MacRae Peak, one of Grandfather Mountain's series of promontories. There was snow on the ground. Against it, the blue-green stippling of fir and yellow-green of spruce were easy to trace as they sprinkled ever more sparsely down the slopes. The shriveled red of mountain ash berries gave a rosy glow to the brown screen of branches below.

In the crispness of morning, the view of mountains in all directions was piercingly clear, with every rock and ski slope sharply defined. As the day passed, mountains in the distance turned a nostalgic blue, tinged with melancholy purple. Mount Mitchell, at 6,684 feet the highest peak east of the Mississippi, lost its distinct contours against the horizon as haze thickened through the afternoon.

The trail was rooty and rocky. Some rock faces, glazed with ice, had knotted cables. Others had ladders. These were surprising and welcome amenities. On the whole, Hugh Morton, the owner of Grandfather Mountain, did not believe in coddling his customers. "You don't need to tell the public the obvious," he said. Signage and restraints at Grandfather, which is visited by some 250,000 people a year, are kept to a minimum. The mile-high swinging bridge, which Mr. Morton built in 1952 as one of the first steps in his tourism development plan, is perched on top of boulders. The bridge itself has guard rails, and a walkway rail guides people away from the largest concentration in the world of the endangered plant known as Heller's blazing star, but otherwise, there is no barring against precipices.

Up along the ridgeline of MacRae Peak, leaves on rhododendrons were laid flat back with frost, like the ears of a frightened animal. Today it was warm, and sun gleamed on the dead white trunks of spruce and fir snags, their branches broken off to stubs. I passed a tag on a tree. Grandfather Mountain is one of the Tennessee Valley Authority's forest monitoring sites, but the high-elevation plot was inaugurated too recently to come up yet for remeasuring, which would show changes.

Thirty years ago, Mr. Morton began worrying about the number of trees dying. He learned then about the balsam woolly adelgid, a European insect that has since killed many, perhaps most, of the mature Fraser firs in the southern Appalachians. Fifteen years ago, he saw that the red spruce was not affected by the adelgid but was also dying. Nearly half of all red spruce trees at high elevations, from the Green and White Mountains of New England, through the Adirondacks of New York, to the Blue Ridge, Balsams, and Smokies of the South, have died in the last fifteen years.

Surveys in the southern Appalachians show that growth rates of both spruce and fir trees began to slow markedly in the 1960s. West-facing slopes appear to have a higher rate of decline. Public relations officers for the Tennessee Valley Authority, the entity that Mr. Morton blames for most of Grandfather's air pollution, have published scientific papers identifying drought, ice storms, windthrows, and insects as causes of the spruce-fir decline. All unquestionably play a part in the intricate life of the spruce-fir community. Forest ecosystems are so complex that individual causes and effects are hard to tease out, but the correlation of spruce decline with air pollutants is overwhelming.

The greatest amounts of sulfur and nitrogen received in the Appalachians are concentrated at high elevations, where highly acidic fog hangs day after day, gathering and dripping from branches. Grandfather Mountain's backcountry manager recently measured the pH of ice rime there at 4.0. Soils at these high elevations tend to be poorly buffered. In Great Smoky Mountains National Park, which has the largest remaining chunk of spruce-fir forest, most of the park's high-elevation catchments are saturated with nitrogen. Unused nitrogen runs off downslope, acidifying lower reaches. The soils have reached toxic levels of aluminum.

European scientists established years ago that the chemical wash of airborne pollutants leaches out plant nutrients such as calcium and magnesium from the soil and activates formerly dormant toxins, especially aluminum. Aluminum and some trace metals are naturally present in soil, but they generally remain inert until activated by the chemistry of acid rain. Soils are the foundation of the forest's architecture of living forms. As a forest stand matures, its soil tends to become naturally more acidic, because older trees take up less of the available nitrogen. For a while, this fact added to the confusion over the effects of acid deposition, but there is now widespread acknowledgment that the rate of soil acidification is far greater than any normal process could produce.

As soil pH is driven down, the decomposition of leaves and woody debris from which humus is made slows down. The community of soil microbes that breaks down forest floor litter shifts from bacteria to fungi, some of which are more tolerant of acid conditions. But one of the most influential groups of fungi, the mycorrhizae, whose symbiotic relationship with root tips makes essential nutrients available to trees, declines with acidification.

Bacteria and fungi form the diet of most worms, and those that feed mainly on bacteria decline. Wood lice can shrug off fairly heavy doses of a single pollutant but succumb to the synergistic interaction of several. Populations of other soil invertebrates—mites, springtails, tardigrades, rotifers—shift toward species already adapted to acidic soils. In some studies, the total number of individual soil organisms remained roughly the same, as members of a few acid-tolerant species increased to fill the vacancies left by more sensitive species. In every study, the total number of species always declined.

In addition to the heavy metals naturally present in soil, others are deposited from the air. Metal accumulation through the food chain has been extensively documented. Arsenic emissions in a German forest in 1936 killed red and roe deer and rabbits. Cadmium has been found in tissues of sparrow hawks and song thrushes near a smelter in England, in wild rabbits near a smelter in Montana, and in moose in Canada and Maine along a gradient associated with industrial air pollution. Moose and deer have been found with enough cadmium in their livers and kidneys to threaten any humans that eat them.

Mercury is well known to accumulate at the top of aquatic food chains. The first documented case of mercury poisoning in a wild mammal was a female mink found near the South Saskatchewan River in 1975. Researchers in the northeastern United States found mercury-caused lesions on the central nervous systems of forty-four percent of the wild mink studied. Otters in a Wisconsin river watershed had the highest tissue levels of mercury of any of the furbearers analyzed, followed by mink, raccoons, foxes, muskrats, and beavers. The fur of mink and otters from the industrialized part of the watershed was higher in mercury.

Chronic mercury poisoning results in gradual incapacitation. Endangered Florida panthers, their total population hovering around fifty, have died from mercury poisoning after eating raccoons whose diet was largely aquatic. Other panthers are suspected of being prone to getting hit by cars because mercury has dulled their coordination and hearing. Mercury poisoning may be a widely unrecognized wildlife phenomenon, because the evidence—animals with poor judgment—is not easily detected.

Unrecorded chronic, sublethal impacts from air pollution may be insidiously affecting many members of the forest community. In Canada, studies suggest that sulfates in forest forage disturb enzymatic and other metabolic functions in herbivores. The depletion of soil nutrients has particular consequences for birds—in effect, a reprise of the DDT phenomenon, in which eggshells became too weak to function. A study in Sweden found that aluminum mobilized in soil contaminated the insects eaten by flycatchers, which caused a calcium deficiency in the birds' eggs. In the Netherlands, the reduction of soil calcium resulted in lower amounts of calcium in tree leaves, then in the caterpillars that ate the leaves, and then in the birds that ate the caterpillars, again resulting in thin-shelled eggs.

Grandfather Mountain hosts many rare species that are of concern to owner Hugh Morton. A tiny tarantula known as the spruce-fir moss spider, discovered on Mount Mitchell in 1923, lives only in moist mats of moss growing on rocks and boulders in the shade of conifers. By 1995, when the spider was officially added to the federal Endangered Species List, the largest and apparently the only reproducing population lived on Grandfather Mountain.

Mr. Morton was well versed in the spider's status. He is the only private owner among 311 global participants in the United Nations' Biosphere Reserve Program. He has white eyebrows that brim over his glasses and a heavy fringe of white hair around a bald pate. He speaks not so much slowly as with a quiet carefulness. When we met in his office complex near Grandfather's entrance gates, he was informally dressed in a yellow V-necked sweater over a white shirt. He was of comfortable girth and kindly mien. He looked . . . well, grandfatherly.

He was, in fact, a grandfather, and to continue the theme, it was his own grandfather who had had the greatest influence on him. But none of them were the inspiration for the name of Grandfather Mountain. Settlers thought that the silhouette of the rock cliffs looked like a bearded man lying faceup to the sky. The stone profile is so unusual and compelling that everyone assumes that Daniel Boone must have climbed it. He hunted in the area in the 1760s, and though there is no documentation, it's hard to imagine that the mountain didn't attract his keen attention.

In 1885, Mr. Morton's grandfather, Hugh MacRae, was twenty years old and a recent graduate of the Massachusetts Institute of Technology. His family was from Wilmington, North Carolina, where his father was involved in the railroad business. MacRae traveled to the western part of the state to prospect for mica. He got his father's backing to form the Linville Land, Manufacturing, and Mining Company, but early on, his father said, "I question the feasibility or the benefits of any efforts to organize a manufacturing or mining place, except to a limited degree. On the contrary, I think our way to success lies in making Linville a place of beauty and a popular resort for health and pleasure for the best class of cultivated people possessed of means to aid in adorning and beautifying the valley."

MacRae agreed. He changed the firm's name to Linville Improvement Company. He purchased sixteen thousand acres of land, including five thousand on Grandfather Mountain. He met a family from St. Louis,

Missouri, that was summering in the mountains; he married the daughter and established a seasonal family seat at the newly bustling town of Linville. Part of the area where Linville was built was called Stump Town, because local people said that the stumps were so dense you could walk the length of the cut area without touching ground.

The MacRae family had a lumber company from the beginning of their venture, and much of Grandfather Mountain was logged at least once, in some places several times. "But not since I've been in charge," Hugh Morton said. That happened in 1952, when he inherited the four thousand acres that remained of the family holdings on Grandfather Mountain. There had been interest in the 1920s in placing an Appalachian national park on Grandfather Mountain, but the Smoky Mountains were selected. Hugh MacRae had, however, succeeded in getting the North Carolina legislature to prohibit hunting on Grandfather Mountain above Route 221. "But it's hard to enforce," Hugh Morton said. "Bear hunters turn their dogs loose beside the road, and the dogs run uphill."

When he took over Grandfather Mountain, Hugh Morton was living in Wilmington but had spent his childhood summers hiking the mountains. He decided to make Grandfather a paying proposition and moved there full-time in 1974. "My family has been here a hundred years," he said, "but we're still considered summer people by the locals." During peak season, he employed seventy people, most of them from the immediate area. He grappled constantly with the demands of tourism versus conservation. Because of him, completion of the Blue Ridge Parkway was held up for nearly a decade, as he steadfastly refused to allow dynamiting at a high elevation on the rocky side of the mountain. But that was not what he referred to when he spoke of being engaged in "a great struggle."

He was talking about his battle against air pollution. Over the past fifteen years, he had become convinced of its effects. "I've noticed that the number of trees toppling over from the roots is far greater than when I was a boy," he said. "In pictures taken decades ago, you can see how many more spruce there were then." He had recently made a video, narrated by Walter Cronkite, entitled *The Search for Clean Air.* In it, scientists across the country discussed the impacts of air pollution not only on forests but also on human health. "People think that what's happening up here doesn't affect them down below," he said, "but they're wrong."

Air pollution blows into Appalachia out of factories and power plants from the Gulf of Mexico to the Great Lakes, but for Grandfather Mountain, the prevailing winds come out of the Tennessee Valley. "The Tennessee Valley Authority is our principal polluter in this part of the world," Mr. Morton said. "I don't think they're in cleanup mode. For some reason, they think they're immune to regulation."

The attitude that Mr. Morton perceived, when he met recently with TVA managers, may have grown out of the unusual political independence built into the agency's structure. President Franklin Roosevelt established the TVA during the depression of the 1930s as "a corporation clothed with the power of government but possessed of the flexibility and initiative of a private enterprise . . . for the proper use, conservation, and development of the natural resources of the Tennessee River drainage basin and its adjoining territory." It was responsible only to the president and Congress.

By the time the depression hit, the nearly forty-one thousand square miles of the drainage basin were already in sad shape. On many of the 350,000 farms, the rains that came heavily every winter fell on bare plowed land and carried off the topsoil. There were floods in winter and droughts in autumn. Malaria was endemic. The income of the nearly three million people within the watershed was less than half the national average.

Roosevelt's vision for the TVA was to use electricity as a tool to improve people's lives. Legislation specified that the TVA would provide power at the lowest possible rates to domestic and rural consumers, who would be encouraged to increase their use of power in every possible application. Many thousands of families were speedily bought out and removed through the TVA's no-negotiation process of land acquisition, and dams were built for hydroelectricity. Access to power and minerals also enabled the TVA to produce cheap fertilizer for farmers. The agency was hailed internationally as a massive experiment in democracy, a way to utilize the efficiency of large-scale planning without totalitarian regimentation. Life did improve for people in eastern Tennessee, although mountaineers, at the fringes of the TVA's impact, knew it mainly as a land grabber.

Rising demand for power prompted the TVA to start building coal-burning plants in the 1940s. Congress authorized the TVA to sell revenue bonds for new construction in 1959, and the agency's power sales became financially self-supporting. It has since become the largest single utility buyer of coal in the United States, purchasing forty million tons a year. Although it also operates twenty-nine dams and three nuclear power plants, its eleven coal-fired utilities produce most of the electricity used by 7.3 million people. It is difficult to find much mention of air pollution in TVA publications, but environmental protection is always listed as an agency goal. By putting scrubbers on emissions stacks, as well as shifting to coal with lower sulfur content, it has reduced the amount of sulfur it discharges by fifty percent since 1977. It has also made promises to install innovative equipment for further reductions.

In the meantime, quite a few scientists began to refer to ground-level ozone as even more detrimental to plants than acid deposition. Formed from reactions of nitrogen oxides and hydrocarbons in the presence of sunlight, ozone is a gas taken in by plant leaves. Damage is often clearly visible—red, brown, or purple stippling between veins on upper leaf surfaces, and leaves dropped too early in the fall. The result is reduced photosynthesis and plant growth, especially of seedlings. Ozone can also reduce pollen germination and flower and cone production in trees.

At higher elevations, ozone concentrations don't decrease at night as they do in the lowlands. Many early successional trees such as big-toothed aspen and white ash open their leaf stomata around dawn—earlier than late successional trees—and are more vulnerable to ozone. Trees that show ozone injury are attacked more often by destructive insects. The danger is not only that individual trees will produce less food but also that plants sensitive to ozone will gradually be outcompeted by those that are resistant. Creatures that rely on those plants for food or habitat will be diminished.

Researchers in Great Smoky Mountains and Shenandoah National Parks have found ninety-five plant species affected by ozone, among them some of the most important to wildlife and human beings: blackberry, sassafras, yellow poplar, yellow birch, red maple, sugar maple, sweetgum. By far the most sensitive plants are black cherry trees and several species of milkweed. From the goings-on in my butterfly meadow, I can testify to the nursery role of milkweed for monarchs. What really dominates the meadow, though, is a lone black cherry tree. Every August the pileated woodpeckers shriek with laughter like crazy women to find it laden with fruit. Chipmunks slide down drooping branches, stuffing their cheeks. Raccoons climb up at night. Most cherries are gone by heavy frost, to be finished off by late flocks of cedar waxwings.

Willing Our Wildernesses

Heartbreak and hope, that is the story of Appalachia. To know the place is to live with beauty tinged by bitterness, and with the paradox of an unredeemable promise. Yet it is a place so lovely that it lulls me into believing that anything is possible. The forest is all around, with no other house in sight. Cross Mountain is a constant presence. Every autumn, as leaves fall, I trace the outline of its body through a skeletal fringe of trees on top of the ridge.

Of course, we do have neighbors along our dirt road. They are decent people who will help you if you need it and otherwise leave you alone. There are two broad streams of Appalachian culture, at least in my community—the traditional and the alternative. Scattered through the hills are hippies who moved in years ago and raised families. They live in hand-built houses of pallet wood and recycled windows. They earn their living by making oak baskets or driftwood furniture or by holding down blue- or white-collar jobs. We socialize at potluck suppers, which, down to the details of screaming kids and rambunctious dogs, are probably quite similar to the family picnics of mountain people. But we don't mix much. It will be the young ones, mingling in school, who will accomplish whatever amalgamation is going to happen.

Having decided early and often not to have children, Ralph and I have a different entanglement with eternity. Public lands may be the ecological heart of Appalachia, but private owners are the body politic.

Surveys show that forest owners have a growing environmental consciousness and rank recreation and wildlife more highly than making a profit from their land. It's the on-the-ground choices that will count in the long run.

We don't harvest anything from our West Virginia property, though we did once find some ginseng and were tempted. It seems best to leave that land to recover itself. Because of the many large chestnut tree stumps there, Ralph would like it to become a chestnut nursery, from which the trees could move out and reclaim what's rightly theirs. Maybe we'll figure out a way to do that.

On the hundred acres in Virginia where we live, we cut two or three cords of firewood every year to heat the house. We sold a small amount of pulpwood when we first bought the place, and we once sold oak logs to a grower of shiitake mushrooms. He thinned out the medium-sized trees that this Japanese fungus likes to grow on, and after he left, it was difficult to tell where he'd been. I wouldn't mind if shiitake became trendy and the market for it grew.

Years ago, we did an inventory of our biggest white pines, forty-odd of them along a curving bank above North Creek, where I sometimes find spotted salamanders. I hope we never need money badly enough to log. So far, I haven't been able to talk Ralph into putting a conservation easement on our deed. This is a legal device that would prohibit anyone who bought or inherited our land from developing the property or otherwise changing its natural character. We might need all our options after he retires, Ralph says, if illness or bad fortune should strike. There must be some other way to protect the land. It will be something to ponder, as I rock on the deck through the turning autumn leaves, on the way to winter.

BIBLIOGRAPHY

ROOTS

Arnow, Harriette Simpson. *Seedtime on the Cumberland.* New York: Macmillan, 1960.

Batteau, Allen W. *The invention of Appalachia.* Tucson: University of Arizona Press, 1990.

Blake, J. W., ed. *The Ulster American connection, a series of lectures delivered in the autumn of 1976.* Ulster: New University of Ulster, 1981.

Campbell, John C. *The southern highlander and his homeland.* Lexington: University Press of Kentucky, 1921, 1969.

Caudill, Harry M. *Night comes to the Cumberlands: A biography of a depressed area.* Boston: Little, Brown, 1962.

Dickson, R. J. *Ulster emigration to colonial America, 1718–1775.* London: Routledge and Kegan Paul, 1966.

Dunaway, Wilma A. "Speculators and settler capitalists: Unthinking the mythology about Appalachian landholding, 1790–1860." In *Appalachia in the making: The mountain south in the nineteenth century.* Edited by Mary Beth Pudup, et al. Chapel Hill: University of North Carolina Press, 1995.

Fischer, David Hackett. *Albion's seed, four British folkways in America.* New York: Oxford University Press, 1989.

Fitzpatrick, Rory. *God's frontiersman: The Scots-Irish epic.* London: Weidenfeld and Nicolson, 1989.

Hall, Valerie. "The vegetational landscape of Mid Co. Down over the last half millennium: The documentary evidence." *Ulster Folklife* 35 (1989): 72–85.

Hsiung, David C. "Geographic determinism and possibilism: Interpretations of the Appalachian environment and culture in the last century." *Journal of the Appalachian Studies Association* 4 (1992): 14–23.

Jordan, Terry G., and Matti Kaups. *The American backwoods frontier.* Baltimore: Johns Hopkins University Press, 1989.

Leyburn, James G. *The Scotch-Irish, a social history.* Chapel Hill: University of North Carolina Press, 1962.

Martin, William H., et al., eds. *Biodiversity of the southeastern United States.* New York: John Wiley, 1993.

Maxwell, Hu. *The history of Randolph County, West Virginia, from its earliest settlement to the present.* Morgantown: Acme, 1898; Parsons: McClain, 1961.

Miles, Emma Bell. *The spirit of the mountains.* 1905. Reprint, Knoxville: University of Tennessee, 1975.

Ogburn, Charlton. *The southern Appalachians, a wilderness quest.* New York: William Morrow, 1975.

Ordnance survey memoirs of Ireland. Vol. 15. *Parishes of County Londonderry IV, 1824, 1833–5.* Edited by Angelique Day and Patrick McWilliams. Belfast: Queen's University in association with Royal Irish Academy, 1992.

Raitz, Karl B., and Richard Ulack. *Appalachia, a regional geography.* Boulder, CO: Westview Press, 1984.

Shackelford, Laurel, and Bill Weinberg, eds. *Our Appalachia, an oral history.* Lexington: University Press of Kentucky, 1977, 1988.

Shapiro, Henry D. *Appalachia on our mind.* Chapel Hill: University of North Carolina Press, 1978.

Solnit, Rebecca. "The lost woods of Killarney." *Sierra* (March–April 1997).

Turner, Frederick. "In the highlands." *Wilderness* (Fall 1990).

Weller, Jack E. *Yesterday's people, life in contemporary Appalachia.* Lexington: University of Kentucky Press, 1965.

White, Peter S. "Our eastern highlands." *Nature Conservancy Magazine* 38, no. 2 (March–April 1988): 5–11.

Williamson, J. W., ed. *An Appalachian symposium: Essays written in honor of Cratis D. Williams.* Boone, NC: Appalachian State University Press, 1977.

Young, Arthur. *A tour in Ireland, with general observations . . . 1776, 1777, and 1778.* Cambridge: Cambridge University Press, 1925.

OLD OLD GROWTH

Booth, Douglas E. "The economics and ethics of old-growth forests." *Environmental Ethics* 14 (Spring 1992): 43–62.

Bratton, Susan P., et al. "Disturbance and recovery of plant communities in Great Smoky Mountains National Park: Successional dynamics and concepts of naturalness." In *Proceedings Second U.S.-U.S.S.R Symposium on Biosphere Reserves, March 10–15, 1980, Everglades National Park, FL.* Edited by Miles A. Hemstron and Jerry F. Franklin. U.S. National Committee for Man and the Biosphere in cooperation with USDA and USDI, 1981.

Braun, E. Lucy. *Deciduous forests of eastern North America.* Philadelphia: Blakiston, 1950.

Busing, R. T. "Three decades of change at Albright Grove, Tennessee." *Castanea* 58, no. 4 (1993): 231–40.

Clinton, Barton D., et al. "Regeneration patterns in canopy gaps of mixed-oak forests of the southern Appalachians: Influences of topographic position and evergreen understory." *American Midland Naturalist* 132, no. 2 (1994): 308–19.

Davis, Mary Byrd, ed. *Eastern old growth forests: Prospects for rediscovery and recovery.* Washington, DC: Island Press, 1996.

Dickson, James G. "Birds and mammals of pre-colonial southern old-growth forests." *Natural Areas Journal* 11, no. 1 (January 1991): 26–33.

Durrell, Lucile. "Memories of E. Lucy Braun." Ohio Biological Survey Biological Notes 15 (1981).

Earley, Lawrence S. "Where the old trees grow." *Wildlife in North Carolina* 56, no. 4 (April 1992): 4–11.

Flebbe, Patricia A., and C. Andrew Dolloff. "Habitat structure and woody debris in southern Appalachian wilderness streams." *Proceedings of the Annual Conference of the Southeastern Association of Fish and Wildlife Agencies* 45 (1991): 444–50.

———. "Trout use of woody debris and habitat in Appalachian wilderness streams of North Carolina." *North American Journal of Fisheries Management* 15 (1995): 579–90.

Franklin, Jerry F., et al. "Tree death as an ecological process." *BioScience* 37, no. 8 (September 1987): 550–56.

Harmon, Mark E. "Decomposition of standing dead trees in the southern Appalachian mountains." *Oecologia* 52 (1982): 214–15.

Harmon, Mark E., et al. "Disturbance and vegetation response in relation to environmental gradients in the Great Smoky Mountains." *Vegetatio* 55 (1983): 129–39.

Hunter, Malcolm L., Jr. "What constitutes an old-growth stand?" *Journal of Forestry* (August 1989).

Klubnikin, Kheryn. "Species research at the Forest Service." *Endangered Species Bulletin* 21, no. 5 (September–October 1996): 12–15.

Leverett, Robert. "Big tree updates." *Wild Earth* (fall 1996).

———. "Identifying old-growth forest in the East." *Wild Earth* (fall 1991).

Lorimer, Craig. "Age structure and disturbance history of a southern Appalachian virgin forest." *Ecology* 61, no. 5 (1980): 1169–84.

Lutz, H. J. "Original forest composition in northwestern Pennsylvania as indicated by early land survey notes." *Journal of Forestry* 28 (December 1930): 1098–1103.

Martin, William H. "Characteristics of old-growth mixed mesophytic forests." *Natural Areas Journal* 12, no. 3 (1992): 127–35.

Maser, Chris, and James M. Trappe. *The seen and unseen world of the fallen tree.* Pacific Northwest Forest and Range Experiment Station, USDA, General Technical Report PNW-164. March 1984.

McCarthy, Brian C. "The ecology of old-growth forests." Paper delivered at the Faculty Development Lecture Series, Frostburg State University, Frostburg, MD, April 1991.

McGee, Charles E. "Loss of *Quercus* spp. dominance in an undisturbed old-growth forest." *Journal of the Elisha Mitchell Scientific Society* 102, no. 1 (1986): 10–15.

Meehan, William R., et al., eds. *Fish and wildlife relationships in old-growth forests: Proceedings of a symposium, Juneau, AK, April 12–15, 1982.* American Institute of Fishery Research Biologists, 1984.

Meslow, E. Charles, et al. "Old-growth forests as wildlife habitat." In *Transactions of the North American Wildlife and Natural Resources Conference,* vol. 46. 1981.

Meyer, H. Arthur. "The structure and growth of virgin beech-birch-maple-hemlock forests in northern Pennsylvania." *Journal of Agricultural Research* 67, no. 12 (December 1943): 465–84.

New forests for a changing world: Proceedings of the 1983 convention of the Society of American Foresters, Portland OR, Oct. 16–20. Society of American Foresters, 1984.

Parker, George R. "Old-growth forests of the central hardwood region." *Natural Areas Journal* 9, no. 1 (1989): 5–11.

Platt, Rutherford. *The great American forest.* Englewood Cliffs, NJ: Prentice-Hall, 1965.

Pyne, Stephen J. *Fire in America, a cultural history of wildland and rural fire.* Princeton, NJ: Princeton University Press, 1982.

Runkle, James R. "Gap dynamics of old-growth eastern forests: Management implications." *Natural Areas Journal* 11, no. 1 (January 1991): p. 19–24.

———. "Gap regeneration in some old-growth forests of the eastern United States." *Ecology* 62, no. 4 (1981): 1041–51.

Schafale, Michael, and Alan Weakley. *Classification of the natural communities of North Carolina: 3rd approximation.* North Carolina Natural Heritage Program, 1990.

Schoen, John W., et al. "Wildlife-forest relationships: Is a reevaluation of old-growth necessary?" In *Transactions of the North American Wildlife and Natural Resources Conference,* vol. 46. 1981.

Silsbee, David G., and Gary L. Larson. "A comparison of streams in logged and unlogged areas of Great Smoky Mountains National Park." *Hydrobiologia* 102 (1983): 99–111.

Smith, Ralph H. "This was the forest primeval, as revealed by pollen analyses and writings of early travelers and surveyors." *New York University Bulletin to the Schools* 40, no. 2 (1954): 138–43.

Smith, Winston Paul. "Old-growth temperate deciduous forests: Legacy or legend." *Natural Areas Journal* 11, no. 1 (January 1991): 4–6.

Spencer, Jim. "Is there a virgin forest in your neighborhood?" *American Forests* (January–February 1993).

Stahle, David W., and Phillip L. Chaney. *A new look at old growth.* Fayetteville: University of Arkansas, 1993.

Stuckey, Ronald L. "Braun, Emma Lucy." In *Notable American women: The modern period, a biographical dictionary.* Belknap Press, 1980.

———. "E. Lucy Braun (1889–1971), outstanding botanist and conservationist: A biographical sketch, with bibliography." *Michigan Botanist* 12 (1973): 83–106.

Thomas, Jack Ward, et al. "Management and conservation of old-growth forests in the U.S." *Wildlife Society Bulletin* 16 (1988): 252–62.

White, Peter S. "Pattern, process, and natural disturbance in vegetation." *Botanical Review* 45, no. 3 (July–September 1979): 231–97.

Zahner, Robert. "Benign neglect management." *Wild Earth* (spring 1992).

———. *The mountain at the end of the trail.* Highlands, NC: 1994.

———. "Restoring the old-growth forest." *Kituah Journal* (fall 1989).

CHEROKEES

Alderman, Pat. *Nancy Ward: Cherokee chieftainess.* Johnson City, TN: Overmountain Press, 1978.

Bassett, John S. *The life of Andrew Jackson.* 2 vols. in one. 1911. Reprint, Archon Books, 1967.

Davis, Donald E. "Where there be mountains: Environmental and cultural change in the Appalachian South, 1500–1800." Ph.D. dissertation, University of Tennessee, 1993. UMI microform order 9421622.

Duncan, Barbara Reimensnyder. "Going to water: A Cherokee ritual in its contemporary context." *Journal of the Appalachian Studies Association* 5 (1993): 94–99.

Finger, John R. Cherokee Americans, the Eastern Band of Cherokees in the twentieth century. Lincoln: University of Nebraska Press, 1991.

———. The Eastern Band of Cherokees, 1819–1900. Knoxville: University of Tennessee, 1984.

Hamel, Paul B., and Mary U. Chiltoskey. *Cherokee plants and their uses: A 400 year history.* Cherokee, NC: 1975.

Hatley, Tom. *The dividing paths: Cherokees and South Carolinians through the era of revolution.* New York: Oxford University Press, 1995.

Hill, Sarah H. *Weaving new worlds: Southeastern Cherokee women and their basketry.* Chapel Hill: University of North Carolina Press, 1997.

Hudson, Charles M. *Black Drink, a Native American tea.* Athens: University of Georgia Press, 1979.

Kephart, Horace. *The Cherokees of the Smoky Mountains.* Copyright 1936.

Kidwell, Clara S. "Indian women as cultural mediators." *Ethnohistory* 39, no. 2 (spring 1992): 97–107.

Loftin, John D. "The 'harmony ethic' of the conservative Eastern Cherokees: a religious interpretation." *Journal of Cherokee Studies* (spring 1983): 40–43.

Mails, Thomas E. *The Cherokee people: The story of the Cherokee from earliest origins to contemporary times.* Tulsa, OK: Council Oak Books, 1992.

Marrant, John. *A narrative of the Lord's wonderful dealings with John Marrant, a Black . . . taken from his own relation, arranged and corrected by the Rev. Mr. Aldridge.* 3d ed. Yarmouth, England: J. Barnes, 1824. Library of American Civilization Ultrafiche no. 40142.

Mooney, James. *James Mooney's History, myths, and sacred formulas of the Cherokees.* Asheville, NC: Historical Images, 1992.

———. "The Cherokee river cult." *Journal of Cherokee Studies* (spring 1982).

Parker, Sara G. "The transformation of Cherokee Appalachia." Ph.D. dissertation. University of California, Berkeley, 1991.

Parton, James. *Life of Andrew Jackson.* Boston: Ticknor and Fields, 1866.

Reimensnyder, Barbara L. "Cherokee sacred sites in the Appalachians." In *Cultural heritage conservation in the American South.* Benita J. Howell, ed. Athens: University of Georgia Press, 1990.

Rogin, Michael P. *Fathers and children: Andrew Jackson and the subjugation of the American Indian.* New York: Knopf, 1975.

Timberlake, Henry. *Lieut. Henry Timberlake's memoirs, 1756–1765.* Edited by Samuel C. Williams. Marietta, GA: Continental Book Co., 1948.

Tucker, Norma. "Nancy Ward, Ghighau of the Cherokees." *Georgia Historical Quarterly* 53, no. 2 , (1969): 192–200.

Wallace, Anthony W. *The long bitter trail: Andrew Jackson and the Indians.* New York: Hill and Wang, 1993.

CUTTING THE TREES

"The Appalachians of North America: Marginal in the midst of plenty." In *The state of the world's mountains, a global report.* Edited by Peter B. Stone. London: Zed Books, Ltd., 1992.

Arcury, Thomas A. "Ecological dimensions of Appalachian agricultural diversity, 1880–1910." *Human Ecology* 18, no. 1 (1990): 105–29.

Ayres, H. B., and W. W. Ashe. *The southern Appalachians.* Professional paper no. 37. U.S. Geological Survey. Washington, DC: U.S. Government Printing Office, 1905.

Barb, Mia, comp. *Tanbark industry: Oral histories.* Special Collections Oral History Project, James Madison University, Harrisonburg, VA, 1990.

Blethen, H. Tyler, and Curtis W. Wood. "The antebellum iron industry in western North Carolina." *Journal of the Appalachian Studies Association* 4 (1992): 79–87.

Bratton, Susan P., et al. "Agricultural area impacts within a natural area: Cades Cove, a case history." *Environmental Management* 4, no. 5 (1980): 433–48.

Brown, A. E. "Appalachian forests, effects of inroads of lumbermen upon them." *Manufacturers' Record* 57 (January 1910): 52.

Buxton, Barry M., et al., eds. *The Great Forest, an Appalachian story.* N.p.: Appalachian Consortium Press, 1985.

Caudill, Harry M. *My land is dying.* New York: Dutton, 1971.

Clarkson, Roy B. *Tumult on the mountain: Lumbering in West Virginia, 1770–1920.* Parsons, WV: McClain, 1964.

Collins, Tim, et al. *Kentucky River area development district: Historic trends and geographic patterns.* Lexington: University of Kentucky Appalachian Center, 1996.

Connelly, Thomas L. *Discovering the Appalachians.* Harrisburg, PA: Stackpole Books, 1968.

Davis, Richard C., ed. "Lumber industry." In *Encyclopedia of American forest and conservation history.* New York: Macmillan, 1983.

Dolloff, C. Andrew. "Large woody debris—the common denominator for integrated environmental management of forest streams." In Cairns, John, Jr., et al., eds. *Implementing integrated environmental management.* Blacksburg, VA: Center for Environmental and Hazardous Materials, Virginia Polytechnic Institute and State University, 1994, 93–108.

"Early iron works of the Virginias." *The Virginias* 3 (1882): 41, 62, 87–88.

Economic and social problems and conditions of the southern Appalachians. USDA misc. pub. 205. Washington, DC: U.S. Government Printing Office, 1935.

Eller, Ronald D. *Miners, millhands, and mountaineers: Industrialization of the Appalachian South.* Knoxville: University of Tennessee Press, 1982.

"Forest disturbances, a special issue." *Natural Resources Newsletter* (Department of Forestry, University of Kentucky) 11, no. 2 (fall 1993).

Frothingham, E. H. *Timber growing and logging practice in the southern Appalachian region.* USDA Technical Bulletin no. 250. Washington, DC: USDA, 1931.

Harrisonburg-Rockingham Historical Society. Collection. SC#2095, box 2, folder 15: bark business, 1890–92. Special Collections, James Madison University, Harrisonburg, VA; on deposit by the Historical Society.

Hepting, George H. "Forest pathology in the southern Appalachians." *Forest History* 8 (fall 1964): 11–13.

Johnson, E. A. "Effect of farm woodland grazing on watershed values in the southern Appalachians." *Journal of Forestry* 50, no. 2 (February 1952): 109–13.

Kalisz, Paul J. "Soil properties of steep Appalachian old fields." *Ecology* 67, no. 4 (1986): 1011–23.

Kellogg, R. S. "Future of the Appalachian forests." *Southern Lumberman* 53 (1907): 54–55.

Lambert, Robert S. *Logging in the Great Smoky Mountains National Park: A report to the superindendent.* October 1, 1958.

———. "Logging the Great Smokies, 1880–1930." *Tennessee Historical Quarterly* 20 (1961): 350–63.

Lewis, Ronald L. "Cutting West Virginia's virgin forest." *West Virginia Alumni Magazine* 19, no. 2 (summer 1996): 10–12.

———. "Railroads, deforestation, and the transformation of agriculture in the West Virginia back counties, 1880–1920." In *Appalachia in the making: The mountain south in the nineteenth century.* Edited by Mary Beth Pudup, et al. Chapel Hill: University of North Carolina Press, 1995.

Lillard, Richard G. *The Great Forest.* New York: Knopf, 1947.

Lotti, Thomas. *The forest situation in the mountain region of Virginia.* Asheville, NC: USDA Appalachian Forest Experiment Station, 1943.

McMaster, Richard K. "The cattle trade in western Virginia, 1760–1830." In *Appalachian frontiers: Settlement, society and development in the pre-industrial era.* Edited by Robert D. Mitchell. Lexington: University of Kentucky Press, 1991.

"Men, mountains, and pigs of iron, the story of charcoal iron making in the Shenandoah Valley of Virginia." Prepared by the George Washington National Forest, n.d.

Message from the president of the United States, transmitting a report of the secretary of agriculture in relation to the forests, rivers, and mountains of the southern Appalachian region. Washington, DC: U.S. Government Printing Office, 1902.

Otto, John S. "The decline of forest farming in southern Appalachia." *Journal of Forest History* (January 1983): 18–27.

———. "Forest fallowing in the southern Appalachians." *Culture and Agriculture* 33 (Fall–winter 1987): 1–5.

Price, Overton W. "Lumbering in the southern Appalachians." *Forestry and Irrigation* 11 (1905): 469–76.

Pudup, Mary Beth. "The limits of subsistence: Agriculture and industry in central Appalachia." *Agricultural History* 64, no. 1 (Winter 1990): 61–89.

Ritter, W. M. Lumber Company. *The romance of Appalachian hardwood lumber.* Richmond: Garrett and Massie, 1940.

Schallenberg, Richard H. "Charcoal iron: The coal mines of the forest." In *Material culture of the wooden age.* Edited by Brooke Hindle. Tarrytown, NY: Sleepy Hollow Press, 1981.

Sorrells, Nancy, and Jennifer E. Kunkle. "Agricultural practices on an Ulster farm in the 1830s." Unpublished paper, Museum of American Frontier History, Staunton, VA, 1994.

Strickler, Robert H. Collection. SC#3025, Zigler pottery and tannery daybooks and ledgers, 1816–1903. Special Collections, James Madison University, Harrisonburg, VA.

Weigl, Peter D., and Travis W. Knowles. Megaherbivores and southern Appalachian grass balds. *Growth and Change* 26 (summer 1995): 365–82.

Wilson, James W. "The Mossy Creek area of Augusta County, VA, during the eighteenth century: The land and the people." Master's thesis, James Madison University, 1993.

Yarnell, Susan L. *The southern Appalachians: A history of the landscape.* Research Triangle Park, NC: Southeastern Center for Forest Economics Research, 1995.

OUT OF THE CRADLE OF FORESTRY AND PROFILES IN CONTROVERSY

Adams, Sherman. *The Weeks Act: A 75th anniversary appraisal.* New York: Newcomen Society, 1986.

Barber, Michael B. "Industry as rural landscape: The Fenwick iron mining complex, Craig County, VA." Paper prepared for the Society for Historic Archaeology annual meeting, Cincinnati, OH, 1996.

Bartram, William. *The travels of William Bartram.* Edited by Francis Harper. New Haven, CT: Yale University Press, 1958.

Berman, Gillian Mace, Melissa Conley-Spencer, and Barbara J. Howe. "The Monongahela National Forest, 1915–1990." Unpublished paper, Monongahela National Forest, Elkins, WV, 1992.

Clark, L. D., and A. C. Volkmar. "Report on the technical examination of the lands of the Allegheny Ore and Iron Co., Rockingham and Page Counties, VA. May 1912." Special Collections #2086, James Madison University, Harrisonburg, VA.

Clayton, Richard R. *Marijuana in the Third World: Appalachia, U.S.A.* Prepared for the United Nations Research Institute for Social Development, Geneva, Switzerland, and the United Nations University, Tokyo. Boulder, CO: Lynne Rienner, 1995.

Collins, Robert F. *A history of the Daniel Boone National Forest, 1770–1970.* Edited by Betty B. Ellison. Lexington, KY: n.p., n.d.

Conners, John A. *Shenandoah National Park, an interpretative guide.* Blacksburg, VA: McDonald and Woodward, 1988.

Devall, Bill, ed. *Clearcut: The tragedy of industrial forestry.* San Francisco: Sierra Club Books and Earth Island Press, 1993.

Duerr, William A. *The economic problems of forestry in the Appalachian region.* Cambridge, MA: Harvard University Press, 1949.

Duffy, David Cameron, and Albert J. Meier. "Do Appalachian herbaceous understories ever recover from clearcutting?" *Conservation Biology* 6, no. 2 (June 1992): 196–201.

Elliott, Charles N. "The lure of the Chattahooche [*sic*]." *American Forests* 45 (May 1939): 247–52, 270.

Frome, Michael. *Whose woods these are: The story of the national forests.* Garden City, NY: Doubleday, 1962.

Garvey, Edward B. "Corbin describes life in Nicholson Hollow." *Potomac Appalachian Trail Club Bulletin* 38, no. 2 (April–June 1969): 31–33, 41–47.

George Washington National Forest. *Final revised land and resource management plan.* U.S. Forest Service, 1993.

Harmon, Michael A., and Rodney J. Snedeker. "Cultural resources of the Pisgah National Forest: Exploitation of the forest environment." Paper delivered at the Southeastern Archeological Conference, Charleston, SC, 1987.

Highlights in the history of forest conservation. USDA Forest Service AIB-83. Washington, DC: U.S. Government Printing Office, 1976.

Hirt, Paul W. *A conspiracy of optimism: Management of the national forests since World War II.* Lincoln: University of Nebraska Press, 1994.

Horning, Audrey. "Material culture and the mountain folk image: Archaeological investigations in Virginia's Blue Ridge." Paper presented at the Shenandoah Valley Regional Studies Seminar, James Madison University, Harrisonburg, VA, 1996.

Jefferson National Forest. *Incomplete working paper of the analysis of the management situation.* 1996.

Jolley, Harley E. "The Cradle of Forestry, where tree power started. Part 1." *American Forests* (October 1970): 16–21.

———. "The Cradle of Forestry. Part 2." *American Forests* (November 1970): 36–39.

———. "The Cradle of Forestry. Part 3." *American Forests* (December 1970): 36–51.

———. "Southern Appalachian forests: The last fifty years." In *The Great Forest, an Appalachian story.* Edited by Barry M. Buxton and Malinda L. Crutchfield. Appalachian Consortium Press, 1985.

Kalisz, Paul J. "Cromer Ridge, Kentucky, obituary for a landscape." *Wild Earth* 6, no. 2 (summer 1996): 17–19.

Kalisz, Paul J., and Susan E. Boettcher. "Active and abandoned red-cockaded woodpecker habitat in Kentucky." *Journal of Wildlife Management* 55, no. 1 (1991): 146–54.

Kalisz, Paul J., and Martina Hines. "Foraging of red-cockaded woodpeckers *(Picoides borealis)* in Kentucky." *Transactions of the Kentucky Academy of Science* 56, nos. 3–4 (1995): 109–13.

LaFollette, Julie Devereux. "Some aspects of the history of the black bear *(Ursus americanus)* in the Great Smoky Mountains. *Master's thesis, University of Tennessee, 1974.*

Lambert, Darwin. *The undying past of Shenandoah National Park.* Boulder, CO: Robert Rinehart, in cooperation with Shenandoah Natural History Association, 1989.

Martin, William H. The role and history of fire in the Daniel Boone National Forest. Winchester, KY: Daniel Boone National Forest, n.d.

Mastran, Shelley Smith, and Nan Lowerre. *Mountaineers and rangers: A history of federal forest management in the southern Appalachians 1900–81.* FS-380. Washington, DC: USDA, 1983.

Nantahala and Pisgah National Forests. *Final supplement to the final environmental impact statement, land and resource management plan.* Atlanta, GA: U.S. Forest Service, 1994.

National Forests in North Carolina: 1995 general report to the public.

Perdue, Charles L., and Nancy J. Martin-Perdue. "Appalachian fables and facts: A case study of the Shenandoah National Park removals." *Appalachian Journal* 7, nos. 1–2 (autumn–winter 1979–80): 84–104.

Rice, Richard E. "Old-growth logging myths: The ecological impact of the U.S. Forest Service's management." *The Ecologist* 20, no. 4 (July 1990): 141–46.

Riddel file correspondence, 1929–1949, in the land acquisitions files of the Dry River Ranger District of the George Washington National Forest, Bridgewater, VA.

Robinson, Glen O. *The Forest Service, a study in public land management.* Baltimore: Johns Hopkins University Press, 1975.

Robinson, Gordon. *The forest and the trees: A guide to excellent forestry.* Washington, DC: Island Press, 1988.

Sarvis, Will. "History of the Jefferson National Forest." Unpublished paper, Jefferson National Forest, Roanoke, VA.

Satterthwaite, Jean L. "George Washington National Forest, a history." George Washington National Forest, Roanoke, VA, 1991.

Schenck, Carl Alwin. *The birth of forestry in America: Biltmore Forest School 1898–1913.* 1955 Reprint, Santa Cruz, CA: Forest History Society and the Appalachian Consortium, 1974.

Shands, William E., and Robert G. Healy. *The lands nobody wanted.* Washington, DC: Conservation Foundation, 1977.

Shenandoah National Park, official pictorial book. Published under the approval of Southern Appalachian National Park Commission [et al.]. Compiled and published by the National Survey Institute, 1929.

Sherman, Mandel, and Thomas R. Henry. *Hollow folk.* 1933. Reprint, Berryville, VA: Virginia Book Co., 1973.

Snedeker, Rodney J. *Who passed this way? Heritage resources management, National Forests in North Carolina.* N.d.

Speer, Jean Haskell. "The hegemony of landscape in Appalachian culture." *Journal of the Appalachian Studies Association* 4 (1992): 24–33.

Steen, Harold K. *The U.S. Forest Service, a history.* Seattle: University of Washington Press, 1976.

Steen, Harold K., ed. *Origins of the national forests: A centennial symposium.* Durham, NC: Forest History Society, 1992.

Turbak, Gary. "National forests gone to pot." *VFW* (March 1997).

Wear, David N. and Richard Flamm. "Public and private forest disturbance regimes in the southern Appalachians." *Natural Resource Modeling* 7, no. 4 (fall 1993): 379–97.

Wood, Nancy. *Clearcut: The deforestation of America.* San Francisco: Sierra Club, 1971.

NEW OLD GROWTH

Burgess, Robert L., and David M. Sharpe. *Forest island dynamics in man-dominated landscapes.* New York: Springer-Verlag, 1981.

Clark, Thomas D. *The greening of the South: The recovery of land and forest.* Lexington: University Press of Kentucky, 1984.

Harris, Larry D. *The fragmented forest: Island biogeography and the preservtion of biotic diversity.* Chicago: University of Chicago Press, 1984.

Holt, Jane P. "The Montreat wilderness, a mountain treasure at risk: Conservation strategy for preserving biodiversity in a private wilderness area." Ph.D. dissertation, Union Institute, 1990.

Johnston, David. Personal communication concerning cowbirds at University of Virginia Mountain Lake Biological Station, July 23, 1997.

Laitin, Jon. "Corridors for wildlife." *American Forests* (September–October 1987).

Line, Les. "Silence of the songbirds." *National Geographic* (June 1993).

———. "Tale of two warblers." *National Wildlife* (October–November 1994).

Luman, Ira D., and William A. Neitro. "Preservation of mature forest seral stages to provide wildlife habitat diversity." *North American Wildlife and Natural Resources Conference Transactions* 45 (1980): 271–77.

Lynch, James F., and Robert F. Whitcomb. "Effects of the insularization of the eastern deciduous forest on avifaunal diversity and turnover." In *Classification, inventory and analysis of fish and wildlife habitat: The proceedings of a national symposium, Phoenix, AZ, Jan. 1977.* U.S. Fish and Wildlife Service, FWS/OBS-78-76.

MacClintock, Lucy, et al. "Evidence for the value of corridors and minimization of isolation in preservation of biotic diversity." *American Birds* 31, no. 1 (January 1977).

Newman, Brownie, Hugh Irwin, et al. "Southern Appalachian wildlands proposal." *Wild Earth,* Special Issue, The Wildlands Project (1992).

Nolt, John, et al. *What have we done?* Washburn, TN: Earth Knows Publications, 1997.

Petranka, James W., et al. "Effects of timber harvesting on southern Appalachian salamanders." *Conservation Biology* 7, no. 2 (June 1993): 363–70.

Robbins, C. S., et al. "Habitat area requirements of breeding forest birds of the middle Atlantic states." *Wildlife Monographs* 103 (1989): 1–34.

Southern Appalachian Man and the Biosphere. *The southern Appalachian assessment report.* 5 vols. Atlanta: U.S. Forest Service, Southern Region, 1996.

Wilcove, David. "Empty skies." *Nature Conservancy Magazine* 40, no. 1 (January–February 1990): 4–13.

Wilcove, David S. "From fragmentation to extinction." *Natural Areas Journal* 7, no. 1 (1987).

Zahner, Robert. "Restoring forest diversity in the southern Appalachian mountains." *Tipularia: A Botanical Magazine* 5, no. 1 (spring 1990): 2–8.

PLAYGROUND OF THE EAST

Ahrens, Frank. "A walk in the woods." [Appalachian Trail] *Washington Post* sec. C, August 16, 1995.

Baldwin, Fred D. "Appalachian highways: Almost home but a long way to go." *Appalachia* 29, no. 2 (May–August 1996): 4–13.

Cohen, Stan. *Historic springs of the Virginias.* Charleston, WV: Pictorial Histories, 1981.

Hare, James R., ed. *Hiking the Appalachian Trail.* Emmaus, PA: Rodale Press, 1975.

Kephart, Horace. *Our southern highlanders.* 1913. Reprint, Knoxville: University of Tennessee Press, 1984.

McDade, Arthur, ed. *Old Smoky Mountain days, selected writings of Horace Kephart, Joseph S. Hall and Harvey Broome.* Seymour, TN: Panther Press, 1996.

Roth, Dennis M. *The wilderness movement and the national forests: 1980–1984.* Forest Service History Series F-410, 1988.

Wetzler, Brad. "I hear America slogging." [Appalachian Trail] *Outside,* May 1996.

GRASS ROOTS

Boettcher, S. E., and P. J. Kalisz. "Single-tree influence on earthworms in forest soils in eastern Kentucky." *Soil Science Society of America Journal* 55, no. 3 (May–June 1991): 862–65.

Clay, William. "The Chattooga River sourcebook, an interpretive guide." Unpublished report. A cooperative project between the Chattooga River Outfitters, Clemson University, and the U.S. Forest Service, 1993.

Cooter, Ellen J., et al. "Climate change: Models and forest research." *Journal of Forestry* 91, no. 9 (September 1993): 38–43.

Dotson, D. B., and P. J. Kalisz. "Characteristics and ecological relationships of earthworm assemblages in undisturbed forest soils in the southern Appalachians of Kentucky, USA." *Pedobiologia* 33, no. 4 (1989): 211–20.

Fisher, Stephen L. *Fighting back in Appalachia: Traditions of resistance and change.* Philadelphia: Temple University Press, 1993.

Gates, David M. "Climate change and forests." *Tree Physiology* 7 (1990): 1–5.

Innes, J. L. "Climatic sensitivity of temperate forests." *Environmental Pollution* 83, nos. 1–2 (1994): 237–43.

Kalisz, Paul J. "Sustainable silviculture in eastern hardwood forests." *Wild Earth* (fall 1995), 48–51.

Kalisz, Paul J., and D. B. Dotson. "Land-use history and the occurrence of exotic earthworms in the mountains of eastern Kentucky." *American Midland Naturalist* 122 (1989): 288–97.

"Over the river, perhaps, but not through the woods." *Atlanta Journal,* November 28, 1995, A22.

Pelton, Christopher Muir. "Corporate power and community toxics struggles: The case of Yellow Creek." Master's thesis, University of Tennessee, Knoxville, 1995.

Rundle, Trevor. "Annotated bibliography of research in the Chattooga River and adjacent watersheds." Unpublished final report. Biology Department of Western Carolina University and U.S. Forest Service Challenge Cost-Share Agreement #94-03-28, 1995.

Van Lear, D. H., et al. "Sedimentation in the Chattooga River watershed." Unpublished report. Clemson University Department of Forest Resources Technical Paper no. 19, 1995.

CHESTNUTS AND THE PLANT KINGDOM

Britton, K. O., et al. "Effects of pretreatment with simulated acid rain on the severity of dogwood anthracnose." *Plant Disease* 80, no. 6 (June 1996): 646–49.

Brown, Margaret L., and Donald E. Davis. "'I thought the whole world was going to die: The story of the American chestnut.'" *Now and Then* 12, no. 1 (spring 1995): 30–31.

Burnham, Charles R. "A Minnesota story: Restoration of the American chestnut." *Journal of the American Chestnut Foundation* 5, no. 2 (summer–fall 1992); 82–90.

Carlson, Alvar W. "Ginseng: America's botanical drug connection to the Orient." *Economic Botany* 40, no. 2 (1986): 233–49.

Cochran, M. Ford. "Back from the brink." *National Geographic* 177 (February 1990): 128–40.

Davids, Richard C. *The man who moved a mountain.* Philadelphia: Fortress Press, 1970.

Duncan, Barbara R. "American ginseng in western North Carolina: A cross-cultural examination." *May We All Remember Well, a Journal of the History and Cultures of Western North Carolina* 1 (1997): 201–13.

Ferguson, Carol, ed. *Threats to forest health in the southern Appalachians: Workshops.*, 1994. Asheville, NC: U.S. Forest Service, 1994.

Fogelson, Matthew A. "Exotic pests of American forests." Unpublished paper, Natural Resources Defense Council, 1992.

Ganser, David A., et al. "After two decades of gypsy moth, is there any oak left?" *Northern Journal of Applied Forestry* 10, no. 4 (1993): 184–86.

Gottschalk, Kurt W., and Mark Twery. "Gypsy moth impacts in pine-hardwood mixtures." In *Proceedings, pine-hardwood mixtures: A symposium on management and ecology of the type, April 18–19, 1989.* Forest Service Gen. Tech. Rep. SE-58.

Kains, M. G. *Ginseng, its cultivation, harvesting, marketing and market value, with a short account of its history and botany.* Rev. ed. New York: Orange Judd, 1914.

Newhouse, Joseph. "Chestnut blight." *Scientific American* (July 1990).

Persons, W. Scott. *American ginseng, green gold.* Rev. ed. Asheville, NC: Bright Mountain Books, 1994.

Roberts, Paul. "The federal chain-saw massacre." *Harper's* (June 1997): 37–51.

Schneeberger, Noel F. "Gypsy moth populations plummet in 1996 while 'the fungus' skyrockets." *Gypsy Moth News* 42 (December 1996): 1–2.

Smith, Richard. "Biodiversity research in forest insect and disease research." Unpublished paper, U.S. Forest Service, Forest Insect and Disease Research Branch, Washington, DC, 1992.

———. "Introduced forest pests: The hidden hand of man." Unpublished paper, U.S. Forest Service, Forest Insect and Disease Research Branch, Washington, DC, 1992.

BLACK BEARS AND THE ANIMAL KINGDOM

Bait station surveys to monitor relative density, distribution, and activities of black bears in the southern Appalachian region. Annual progress report, 1993. Department of Tennessee Wildlife Resources.

Biggins, Richard G., et al. "The return of the riversnails." *Endangered Species Bulletin* 22, no. 3 (May–June 1997): 8–9.

Clark, Joseph D., and Michael R. Pelton. "Management of a large carnivore: Black bear." In *Ecosystem management for sustainability.* In press.

Kasbohm, John W. et al. "Black bear denning during a gypsy moth infestation." *Wildlife Society Bulletin* 24, no. 1 (1996): 62–70.

Martinka, Clifford J., and Katherine L. McArthur, eds. *Bears: Their biology and management, a selection of papers from the Fourth International Conference on Bear Research and Management, Kalispell, MT, 1977.* Bear Biology Association, 1980.

Pelton, Michael R., and Frank T. van Manen. "Benefits and pitfalls of long-term research: A case study of black bears in Great Smoky Mountains National Park." *Wildlife Society Bulletin* 24, no. 3 (1996).

Raybourne, Jack W. "The black bear: Home in the highlands." In *Restoring America's wildlife, 1937–1987, the first 50 years of the Federal Aid in Wildlife Restoration (Pittman-Robertson) Act.* Edited by Harmon Kallman. Washington, DC: U.S. Fish and Wildlife Service, 1987.

Wapner, Kenneth. "Appalachian trailblazing: A town of 5,000 adopts a forest." *The Amicus Journal* 26–30 (winter 1995).

Wigginton, Eliot, ed. *Foxfire 5, ironmaking, blacksmithing, flintlock rifles, bear hunting, and other affairs of plain living.* Garden City, NY: Anchor Press, 1979.

DROPPING ACID IN THE APPALACHIANS

Adriano, D. C., and A. H. Johnson, eds. *Acid precipitation.* Vol. 2. *Biological and ecological effects.* Advances in Environmental Science series. New York: Springer-Verlag, 1989.

Air pollutants effects on forest ecosystems, May 8–9, 1985, St. Paul, MN. Sponsored by National Acid Precipitation Assessment Program, USDA Forest Service, et al. Acid Rain Foundation, 1985.

Baker, Joan P., et al. "Biological effects of changes in surface water acid-base chemistry." NAPAP Report 13. In National Acid Precipitation Assessment Program, *Acidic Deposition: State of Science and Technology,* vol. 2, 1990.

Barker, Jerry R., and David T. Tingey, eds. *Air pollution effects on biodiversity.* New York: Van Nostrand Reinhold, 1992.

Bartuska, Ann M., and Susan A. Medlarz, "Spruce-fir decline—air pollution related?" In *Atmospheric deposition and forest productivity: Proceedings of the 4th regional technical conference at the 65th annual meeting of the Appalachian Society of American Foresters, Raleigh, NC, Jan. 29–31, 1986.* Blacksburg, VA: Society of American Foresters, 1986.

Bruck, R. I., et al. "Forest decline in the boreal montane ecosystems of the southern Appalachian mountains." *Water, Air and Soil Pollution* 48 (1989): 161–80.

Bulger, A. J., et al. "Shenandoah National Park: Fish in sensitive habitats." Second annual report, unpublished, October 1994.

———. "The Shenandoah National Park: Fish in sensitive habitats (SNP: FISH) project, an integrated assessment of fish community responses to stream acidification" *Water, Air and Soil Pollution* 85 (1995): 309–14.

Camuto, Chris. "Dropping acid in the southern Appalachians." *Trout* (winter 1991): 18–39.

Chappelka, Arthur, et al. "Effects of ambient ozone concentrations on mature eastern hardwood trees growing in Great Smoky Mountains National Park and Shenandoah National Park." Prepared for presentation at the 85th annual meeting of the Air and Waste Management Association, Kansas City, MO, June 21–26, 1992.

———. "Evaluation of ozone injury on foliage of black cherry *(Prunus serotina)* and tall milkweed *(Asclepias exaltata)* in Great Smoky Mountains National Park." Unpublished.

Charles, Donald F., ed. *Acidic deposition and aquatic ecosystems: Regional case studies.* New York: Springer-Verlag, 1991.

Cook, R. B., et al. "Acid-base chemistry of high-elevation streams in the Great Smoky Mountains." *Water, Air and Soil Pollution* 72 (1994): 331–56.

Davis, Donald D., and John M. Skelly. "Growth response of four species of eastern hardwood seedlings exposed to ozone, acidic precipitation, and sulfur dioxide." *Journal of the Air and Waste Management Association* 42, no. 3 (1992): 309–11.

Dennis, T. E., et al. "The association of water chemistry variables and fish condition in streams of Shenandoah National Park (USA)." *Water, Air and Soil Pollution* 85 (1996): 365–70.

Deviney, Frank A., and James R. Webb. "St. Mary's River watershed database reference." Unpublished, 1993.

Dubey, Tara, et al. "Effect of pH on the distribution and occurrence of aquatic fungi in six West Virginia mountain streams." *Journal of Environmental Quality* 23 (1994): 1271–79.

Eshleman, K. N., et al. "Long-term changes in episodic acidification of streams in Shenandoah National Park, Virginia, USA." *Water, Air and Soil Pollution* 85 (1995): 517–22.

Flum, T., and S. C. Nodvin. "Factors affecting streamwater chemistry in the Great Smoky Mountains, USA." *Water, Air and Soil Pollution* 85 (1995): 1707–12.

Fredericksen, T. S., et al. "Diel and seasonal patterns of leaf gas exchange and xylem water potentials of different-sized *Prunus serotina* Ehrh. trees." *Forest Science* 42, no. 3 (1996): 1–7.

———. "Predicting ozone uptake from meteorological and environmental variables." *Journal of the Air and Waste Management Association* 46 (1996): 464–69.

Gill, John D., ed. *Acidic depositions: Effects on wildlife and habitats.* Technical Review 93-1. Bethesda, MD: Wildlife Society, 1993.

Gilliam, Frank S., et al. "Ecosystem nutrient responses to chronic nitrogen inputs at Fernow Experimental Forest, West Virginia." *Canadian Journal of Forestry Research* 26, no. 2 (February 1996): 196–205.

Godbold, Douglas L., and Aloys Huettermann, eds. *Effects of acid rain on forest processes.* New York: Wiley-Liss, 1994.

Hildebrand, Elisabeth, et al. "Foliar response of ozone-sensitive hardwood tree species from 1991 to 1993 in the Shenandoah National Park, Virginia." *Canadian Journal of Forestry Research* 26 (1996): 658–69.

Huxley, Julian. *TVA: An adventure in planning.* London: Architectural Press, 1943.

Hyer, K. E., et al. "Episodic acidification of three streams in Shenandoah National Park, Virginia, USA." *Water, Air and Soil Pollution* 85 (1995): 523–28.

Jensen, Keith F., and Leon S. Dochinger. "Response of eastern hardwood species to ozone, sulfur dioxide and acid precipitation." *Journal of the Air Pollution Control Association* 39 (1989): 852–55.

Johnson, D. W., et al. "Simulated effects of atmospheric sulfur deposition on nutrient cycling in a mixed deciduous forest." *Biogeochemistry* 23 (1993): 169–96.

Johnson, Dale W., and Steven E. Lindberg, eds. *Atmospheric deposition and forest nutrient cycling: A synthesis of the Integrated Forest Study.* New York: Springer-Verlag, 1992.

Leetham, J. W., et al. "Response of soil nematodes, rotifers and tardigrades to three levels of season-long sulfur dioxide exposures." *Water, Air and Soil Pollution* 17 (1982): 343–56.

Likens, G. E., et al. "Long-term effects of acid rain: Response and recovery of a forest ecosystem." *Science* 272 (1996): 244–46.

Little, Charles. *The dying of the trees.* New York: Viking, 1995.

MacAvoy, S. E., and A. J. Bulger. "Survival of brook trout *(Salvelinus fontinalis)* embryos and fry in streams of different acid sensitivity in Shenandoah National Park, USA." *Water, Air and Soil Pollution* 85 (1995): 445–50.

Neufeld, Howard S., et al. "Ozone in Great Smoky Mountains National Park: Dynamics and effects on plants." In *Tropospheric ozone and the environment II: Effects, modeling and control.* Edited by Ronald L. Berglund. Pittsburgh, PA: Air and Waste Management Association, 1992.

Newman, K., and A. Dolloff. "Responses of blacknose dace *(Rhinichthys atratulus)* and brook char *(Salvelinus fontinalis)* to acidified water in a laboratory stream." *Water, Air and Soil Pollution* 85 (1995): 371–76.

Nodvin, S. C., et al. "Acidic deposition, ecosystem processes, and nitrogen saturation in a high elevation southern Appalachian watershed." *Water, Air and Soil Pollution* 85 (1995): 1647–52.

Owen, Marguerite. *The Tennessee Valley Authority.* New York: Praeger, 1973.

Parsons, John L., et al. "Final report: The diversity of mammals found in declining spruce-fir populations of the southern Appalachian mountains, to the Nature Conservancy." Unpublished.

Ruess, Liliane, et al. "Acid deposition in a spruce forest soil: Effects on nematodes, mycorrhizas and fungal biomass." *Pedobiologia* 40 (1996): 51–66.

Samuelson, L. J. "Ozone-exposure responses of black cherry and red maple seedlings." *Environmental and Experimental Botany* 34, no. 4 (1994): 355–62.

Shaver, Christine L., et al. "Clearing the air at Great Smoky Mountains National Park." *Ecological Applications* 4, no. 4 (1994): 690–701.

Shubzda, J., et al. "Elevational trends in the fluxes of sulphur and nitrogen in throughfall in the southern Appalachian Mountains: Some surprising results." *Water, Air and Soil Pollution* 85 (1995): 2265–70.

Smith, William H. *Air pollution and forests: Interactions between air contaminants and forest ecosystems.* 2d ed. Springer Series on Environmental Management. New York: Springer-Verlag, 1990.

Stanosz, G. R., et al. "Effect of ozone on growth of mosses on disturbed forest soil." *Environmental Pollution* 63 (1990): 319–27.

U.S. Fish and Wildlife Service. "Endangered and threatened wildlife and plants: Spruce-fir moss spider determined to be endangered." *Federal Register* 60, no. 24 (February 6, 1995): 6968–74.

Webb, J. R., et al. "Acidification of native brook trout streams in Virginia." *Water Resources Research* 25, no. 6 (June 1989): 1367–77.

———. "Change in the acid-base status of an Appalachian mountain catchment following forest defoliation by the gypsy moth." *Water, Air and Soil Pollution* 85 (1995): 535–40.

Wheeler, Q. D., and J. V. McHugh. "A new southern Appalachian species, *Dasycerus bicolor* (Coleoptera: Staphylinidae: Dasycerinae), from declining endemic fir forests." *Coleopterists Bulletin* 48, no. 3 (1994): 265–71.

White, Joseph J. "Woodlice exposed to pollutant gases." *Bulletin of Environmental Contamination and Toxicology* 30 (1983): 245–51.

INDEX

PAGES IN ITALICS INDICATE ILLUSTRATIONS

OHIO
Ohio River
VI
Charleston
Winchester
KENTUCKY
Pikeville
DANIEL BOONE
NATIONAL FOREST
JEFFERSON
NATIONAL FOREST
London
Meadowview
CUMBERLAND GAP
NATIONAL HISTORICAL PARK
Big Stone Gap
Johnson City
BIG SOUTH FORK NATIONAL
RIVER & RECREATION AREA
ROAN MOUNTAIN
(6285')
TENNESSEE
Knoxville
French Broad River
PISGAH
NATIONAL FOREST
GREAT SMOKEY MTS
NATIONAL PARK
Little Tennessee River
Asheville
(6684')
Cherokee Reservation
CLINGMANS
DOME (6643')
CRADLE OF FORESTRY
HISTORIC SITE
CHEROKEE
NATIONAL FOREST
Fontana Lake
Tennessee River
NANTAHALA NATIONAL FOREST
Hiwassee River
WHITESIDE MOUNTAIN
Hiwassee
Lake
Highlands
Copperhill
RABUN BALD (4696')
Ocoee River
Clayton
COHUTTA
MOUNTAINS
BRASSTOWN
BALD
SUMTER
NATIONAL FOREST
(Andrew Pickens District)
Chattooga River
Conasauga River
SPRINGER
MOUNTAIN
CHATTAHOOCHEE
NATIONAL FOREST
Dahlonega
GEORGIA